Bio   Wayne, Jane Ellen.
Cra
       Crawford's men

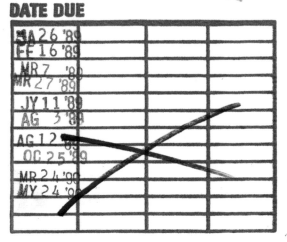

DATE DUE

JA 26 '89			
FE 16 '89			
MR 7 '89			
MR 27 '89			
JY 11 '89			
AG 3 '89			
AG 12			
OC 25 '89			
MR 24 '90			
MY 24 '90			

CRAWFORD'S MEN

JANE ELLEN WAYNE

CRAWFORD'S MEN

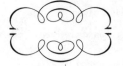

PRENTICE HALL PRESS
New York   London   Toronto   Sydney   Tokyo

For Everyone from the Wrong
Side of the Tracks . . .

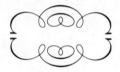

All insert photos courtesy of the Kobal Collection.

Prentice Hall Press
Gulf + Western Building
One Gulf + Western Plaza
New York, New York   10023

Published by the Prentice Hall Trade Division

PRENTICE HALL PRESS and colophon are registered trademarks of Simon & Schuster Inc.

Library of Congress Cataloging-in-Publication Data

Wayne, Jane Ellen.
  Crawford's men.

  Includes index.
    1. Crawford, Joan, 1908–1977.   2. Motion picture
actors and actresses—United States—Biography.
I. Title.
PN2287.C67W38   1988   791.43'028'0924 [B]   87–35718
ISBN 0-13-188665-7

Manufactured in the United States of America

10 9 8 7 6 5 4 3 2 1

First Edition

AUTHOR'S NOTE

Joan Crawford talked to me at length about her life, the Golden Era, and Metro-Goldwyn-Mayer. Although she had agreed to discuss my biography of a male star, Miss Crawford charmed, shocked, and delighted me during my three lengthy visits with stories and gossip about the frustrations, indiscrétions, and romances involving her and others in the limelight.

She also gave me stern advice on how to research a good book. "Impressive names mean nothing," Miss Crawford said, "because the bigger they are, the less they tell. Talk to the technicians, writers, security guards, and photographers. I leaned on them. From the very start they knew more about me than I did."

By being a good listener and with no ulterior motive, I entered into the glittering world she helped create. If the glamour of Miss Crawford and Hollywood had remained a little longer, the chiffon and tinsel might still be there.

CONTENTS

PREFACE

Joan Crawford was shorter than I had expected. Her hair was carrot orange, and a layer of pancake makeup covered a multitude of freckles. She wore an expression of superiority that was her trademark, but she smiled when her dog ran over to greet me. "I have a Shetland sheep dog," I said. We agreed that no matter who you were or how many friends you had, you could always depend on your dog. Then she glanced at her notes and asked, "You're writing Robert Taylor's biography?"

"Yes," I replied.

"Bob was a beautiful person. We made two films together. There are more dogs in Hollywood than anywhere else in the world, but Bob wasn't one of them. How's your research coming . . . interviews and so forth?"

I gave her an impressive list of names . . . at least I thought so. She looked at me as if to say, "Well, you have to begin somewhere . . ."

"What about Stanwyck?" she asked.

"She canceled two appointments. Her secretary said it was very difficult for her to talk about Robert Taylor."

"Is Jane Ellen Wayne your real name?"

"Yes . . ."

"J. Wayne," she smirked, ". . . like John. Christ, without a horse he's lost. What do you want to know about Bob Taylor? Anything in particular?"

"Did you enjoy working with him? Your opinion of Taylor as an actor . . . amusing stories . . . anything that comes to mind, I guess."

"You haven't a list of specific questions?" she asked.

"In Hollywood my discussions were informal."

"That's the trouble with Hollywood," she exclaimed. "Formal out there means tuxedo and floor-length dress. My dog eats with more dignity. So, where do we begin, Wayne?"

"What did you think of Taylor's acting ability?"

"Bob had a complex because he was so damn handsome. He knew the public didn't give a damn if he had talent or not. They came to see his face. Would you like a drink?"

"Thank you."

As I was taking my first sip of Scotch she glared at me and said, "You'll gain more respect by not drinking even if you're invited for cocktails during interviews. I barely touched a drop until I was over thirty."

She lit a cigarette with so much finesse that I almost decided never to smoke again. "As I was saying, Wayne, it's your business if you drink during an interview, but why not let *them* get high? You'll have the upper hand. You'll be in control. Even if they agree to talk to you, this doesn't mean they have any intention of telling you a damn thing. Also, pretend you know more than you do, but be subtle. If they think you know, they'll tell you more about whatever it is they *weren't* going to volunteer. No one wants to be the first to let the cat out of the bag."

I nodded with a smile and put down my drink.

"You don't have to go through that phony crap with me," she said, "because I didn't know Bob intimately. He was such a dear, in fact, that the two dreadful movies we made together were almost bearable because he was such a sweetheart . . . refreshing and innocent and eager. He stuck it out at M-G-M for twenty-five years—the longest contract in movie history. He went from 'Pretty Boy' to 'Our Knight in Shining Armor' and was one of the few who survived after L. B. Mayer was ousted."

For more than an hour she discussed M-G-M and Mayer. "I was terrified in the beginning," she continued. "I didn't have any friends I could trust except Clark."

"Clark Gable?"

"Not Clark Kent for Christ's sake!" she snapped. "I'm surprised you weren't torn to pieces when you put on that dumb act in Hollywood."

"I had no idea you and Gable were so close," I managed.

"We almost got married."

"That isn't common knowledge."

She made another drink for herself, leaned back on the yellow and green pillows, and smiled. "It was hushed up and I don't talk about it much. Clark never did . . ."

"Did Robert Taylor have anything like that to hide?" I asked. "Was he . . . ?"

But she interrupted. "You see, Clark and I . . ." A few hours of "Clark and I" passed with no mention of Taylor. Her stories were fascinating—revealing and funny and rather sad. Meanwhile she was drinking and doing precisely what she had warned me *not* to do—talk impulsively while someone (me) nursed her cocktail. I wasn't interested in Clark Gable at the time. My heart sank because I was sure Crawford would not see me again. I'd never have another chance to discuss Taylor with her.

Despite the liquor, she managed to light her cigarette with great elegance. I was hypnotized. The Alpine cigarette, lighter, and smoke blended smoothly and gracefully. I managed to grasp the technique if nothing else.

Eventually it was time for me to leave. She smiled and said, "I hope you have a better insight as to what we went through in those days. I'm sorry we only touched on Bob. Did you go to bed with him?"

"No."

"I might not admit to it, either. Have I been of any help at all?"

"Immensely."

"I'm a very busy woman, but perhaps next week we might get together again. I promise to talk about Bob."

"Thank you, but . . ."

"Are you going out of town or something?"

"No."

"Then why the fuck can't you make it? I'm rearranging my entire schedule to be of some help to you!"

"I don't want to impose."

"You didn't finish your drink," she scowled. "Scotch isn't cheap."

I shook her hand and left, but before hailing a taxi, I went to the nearest bar and had a double.

I didn't expect Crawford to remember our next appointment. I was not about to show up at her door and I didn't have her telephone number. To my amazement, she called me to confirm. "And you might jot down a list of questions," she said before hanging up. "If you don't, how the hell do you expect to get any answers?"

She was already having a drink when I arrived. Before I had a chance to reach for my notes, she began telling me about Robert Taylor. He had a perfect face and he was dedicated to Barbara Stanwyck even after their divorce. "Once he made up his mind to marry again, he devoted himself to his second wife and children. I think he resented paying alimony to Barbara. No comment . . . but she didn't need the money, I guess, and he did. She started out as a chorus girl in New York, too. I like Barbara, but I won't discuss her. Did you have an affair with Bob?"

"I didn't meet him until he was married to Ursula [Thiess]."

"What difference did that make?" she laughed.

"He did a talk show at NBC, where I worked. We had a lengthy conversation before airtime. I recall he and Ursula held hands under the table when they were on camera."

"How sweet . . ."

"I thought so. Taylor was everything I expected and more."

Crawford smirked. I knew she didn't believe a word I said. She made herself another drink. "Would you like one?" she asked.

"Maybe later, thanks."

"I don't like to drink alone."

"In that case, I'll have a Scotch."

"I'll give you some more advice. Learn to drink vodka. You won't reek of booze."

I looked at my notes and asked her about *The Gorgeous Hussy.*

"Christ!" she laughed. "Horrible choice on my part, but Bob was very good. Franchot [Tone] was in it, too. We had a good time. That's about all I can say about that movie. Bob was being groomed at the time. He was an all-American boy who came from a refined family in Nebraska."

"But when Taylor came to Hollywood he didn't have a rich wife to support him like Gable did," I said. "Even in those days thirty-five dollars a week didn't go very far, and he had to support his mother."

"My, my. We're on the defensive, aren't we?"

"It's not so bad if one has never known security, but to have it and lose it . . ."

"Gable had balls!" she exclaimed.

"I read somewhere that he said you had them, too."

I regretted those words when they rolled off my tongue, but Crawford laughed. "Bob wasn't a saint, you know."

"He played around? Is that what you mean?"

"How the hell do I know?"

"But you said . . ."

"Probably Ava [Gardner]," she interrupted. "And he wanted to marry Lana [Turner]. Thank God he didn't. And then there was Eleanor . . ."

"Parker?"

"Fine actress. She co-starred with Bob in several movies. As I said, I don't know about his affairs. Readers love that stuff, but you're approaching Taylor the wrong way. It bothers me."

"Doing him justice and satisfying my readers might conflict."

"And selling the idea to a publisher is another aspect, but you can do anything if you put your mind to it. You're new at this. When you return to Hollywood for more interviews, lead with strength. Otherwise they'll bury you out there."

"So far I haven't had a problem," I said.

"In that case you're doing something wrong," she said, lifting up her chin and, in essence, looking down at me. "You're putting Bob on a pedestal because you were in love with him or . . . or you're a damn fool."

"Most likely the latter," I said politely.

"You don't know?"

"What I *do* know is that Taylor did not give in to temptation."

"Bullshit!"

"Meaning booze, dope, and scandal."

"He was a royal cocksman like all men, but I admit he was discreet about it. Can't say the same for Clark. He was always screwing and he wasn't that great. I loved him but tried to stay out of the bedroom occasionally. With Clark this was routine."

"Is that why you didn't marry him?" I asked.

"Hell, no. We were too much alike to make a go of it. Bless L. B. for stopping us. We would have destroyed a wonderful relationship that lasted until he died. Part of me went with him. He knew more about me than anyone else." And she went on to tell me about her tough life "from the day I was born."

"Were you ever happy, Miss Crawford?"

"I was the most frightened when I was happy. When I won the Oscar I knew it was the beginning of the end. So, I played it to the hilt, took every damn advantage, but from then on it was just a matter of survival. With Clark it was in reverse. *It Happened One Night* was supposed to fizzle in 1934, but the fuckin' movie won every major award. Then he played Rhett Butler and was on top of the world, but he didn't win an Oscar. He was very bitter. He was heartbroken and stunned. It wasn't the prestige. He disliked Vivien [Leigh] and fought like hell to get rid of the director, George Cukor. Did I tell you about that?"

"Referring to Billy Haines?"

She laughed. "Clark was upset with everyone because he was forced to play Rhett. Everything went wrong. What saved him was taking a few days off to marry Carole [Lombard]. She wanted kids so much. She said they would fuck in a pile of manure if it did the trick. They were so right for each other, but if you find real love just once in your life, you're a winner. Mine was Alfred [Steele]."

"You waited a long time for him, didn't you?" I asked.

She shrugged. "I don't wait for anything, Wayne. I make things happen. That's what you have to do with this book you're trying to write. Nobody's going to give you a damn thing. Nothing. Jesus, I have a date for dinner, but we can talk while I freshen up."

She startled me by not using a lip brush. Joan Crawford actually used her finger to put on lipstick. I asked her about it.

"It's the only way," she said. "Didn't you read my book?"

"But it stains the fingers."

"Ever hear of soap and water?"

"Have you tried a brush?" I asked.

"Why the fuck do you think I use my finger?"

What else could I say? "I'm fascinated . . ."

"I'm a little bit older than you, my dear. I didn't get where I am following the mundane habits of the masses. You didn't tell me if you read my book."

"*A Portrait of Joan?*"

"No, *My Way of Life*. Buy it," she said, primping her hair. "I see you like basic black with pearls. But you wore the same thing last time. Since you made a good first impression, it's perfectly all right to wear a cheerful color the next time. Tell me, Wayne, do you have the heart and soul of the Golden Era now? The family ties at M-G-M? . . . how hard we worked, our sacrifices, our vulnerability, our confusion, and our living death when Hollywood sold out to television?"

"I think so."

"I wonder if you have the guts and patience to get the damn book published."

"If I give it all I have and fail, it wasn't meant to be," I said.

"Bullshit!"

I left so she could finish dressing. When I got home I wrote a warm thank-you note and extended a luncheon invitation to express my gratitude. A few months later she called. She said nothing about lunch but wanted to know how my book was progressing. I told her it would be on the stands in six months.

"Really?" she asked as if I were not telling the truth. "Have you signed the contract?"

"Of course."

"I'm delighted, but did your lawyer go over the fine print?"

"Yes."

"Is the book finished?"

"Almost."

I got the feeling she couldn't have cared less about Taylor's biography. This was her way of finding out if I still needed her. It was so obvious to me that she loved to talk about her past in an era that belonged to her and very few other legends. I knew Alfred Steele had left her in debt, and she was forced to give up their magnificent duplex apartment on Fifth Avenue in New York City. She told me it was too big now that she was alone. And every columnist told a different story about her financial situation.

I wasn't a friend of hers, but I feigned that I needed her help to put the finishing touches on my book. As usual, she pretended to be very, very busy, but gave me a date and time. I mentioned lunch.

"That's a pain in the ass," she said. "Besides, I only dine at '21'."

Our last session was depressing for me. Crawford talked about herself and her hardships. Was it worth it? Her friends were dying off. Her children had lives of their own. (This was the first time she had mentioned them.) When there was a lull in the conversation, I told her how much I valued her encouragement and advice. I had taken Taylor off that pedestal and given him the human element.

Joan talked about her childhood, dramatizing the pain and disappointments. In the middle of her heartbreaking memories she asked me where I was born. "You haven't got an accent, Wayne."

Finally I felt we had something in common. I also came from a small town where the railroad tracks divided the affluent from the factory workers. I made the mistake of mentioning the American Academy of Dramatic Arts. "The fact that you chose not to marry the boy back home because you wanted to make something of yourself takes guts," she exclaimed, "but I doubt you had to wait on tables or scrub floors to pay your tuition at that fancy acting school. I didn't have the time or assurance to think about the theater. I had to work damn hard for food and clothes."

"I had to hock a few things so I could eat," I mumbled.

"I had nothing to hock!" she retorted.

She had been drinking; her words were slurred. I spent the entire afternoon with Crawford while she reminisced. At one point she asked me if I had a tape recorder. I told her I never carried one. "Not that I care," she said, pouring her first "official" drink. "Here, try vodka."

"Straight?" I winced.

She didn't answer. "I've been thinking, Wayne. You won't like what I have to say, but the hell with it! Taylor was one of the very few who had it made when the rest of us were groveling. He left M-G-M with a million bucks! I had to mortgage my fuckin' home, Gable had to live in Europe for tax purposes, and God knows how many careers were ruined. Then what did Bob do? He did a television series! He gave in to that boob tube!"

Crawford had turned on me for no reason. It had to be the liquor. She roasted Norma Shearer, Bette Davis, and Judy Garland. She cursed L. B. Mayer one minute and lauded him the next. She qulped down a whole glass of vodka after a brief denunciation of Spencer Tracy. But through it all, there was only love and admiration for Clark Gable.

As I was about to leave, she said, "I'm proud of you, Wayne, and do you know why? Because you set out to write about a gentleman when the whole world wants to read about murder and sex. You'll send me a copy, of course." As I was putting on my coat, she asked me, "Did you go to bed with Taylor?"

I smiled. "You asked me that before."

"Take my advice and let people think you did, honey."

On May 10, 1977, Joan Crawford died. She had adopted three rules for living:

1. Never quit a job until you finish it.
2. The world isn't interested in your problems. When your problems are the greatest, let your laughter be the merriest.
3. If you find you can do a job, let it alone, because you're already bigger than the job and that means you will shrink down to its size. If the job is impossible, you may never get it accomplished, but you'll grow by trying.

PART ONE

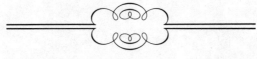

1

SHOPGIRL'S DREAM

A security guard recognized the way the woman walked through the door. He knew right away it was Joan Crawford. No one made an entrance like she did. She had a mellow voice that carried across the empty set, and he didn't have to get closer to see that every inch of her was flawless. She was wearing a white felt hat, a navy blue crepe suit with a peplum jacket, and white gloves. He couldn't see her shoes but was sure they blended elegantly.

She was talking to the stagehands eating box lunches. They were friends of hers, and they talked about their families. She seemed genuinely interested in whose wife was having a baby, how to take off five pounds, and who was having a birthday. If there was a hush, someone was telling a dirty joke.

The guard felt a hand on his shoulder. "Hey, Joel, is that dame still in Tone's dressing room?"

"How do I know?"

"That's what you're gettin' paid for around here."

"Frank, I haven't seen Mr. Tone."

"Then he's in deep trouble."

"Is that why Miss Crawford's here?"

"Yep."

"I'll get him on the phone right away . . ."

"Too late," Frank cringed. "Here she comes."

She smiled. "Hello, boys. It's such a beautiful day I thought it might be nice to have lunch with my husband. You look well, Joel. How's your mother?"

"Fine. Just fine. Thank you for asking, Miss Crawford. I . . . well, I think Mr. Tone is on another set."

"That's all right. I'll wait in his dressing room," she said with a wave.

The guard followed her casually, watched her open the door, and heard her scream, "You son of a bitch."

A shaky voice mumbled, "Joan, please close the . . ."

"I suppose you've been sneaking off with this tramp every day!"

"I suppose so . . ."

"If you don't know, who does?"

"To tell you the truth, Joan, I haven't kept a ledger."

"Get that harlot dressed and out of here!"

The guard saw a cute young movie extra scurrying out of the room, trying to tie the sash of her robe. The door was still ajar, and he felt slightly embarrassed listening in on the conversation, but if there was trouble, it was his job to notify the front office.

"Won't you sit down, darling?" Tone asked, mixing a drink and dropping ice cubes on the floor.

"You bastard!"

"You caught me in the act. How careless of me. I'll never forgive myself, of course."

"Don't you get enough at home?" she asked sarcastically.

"I know you did your best, but facing the camera every day and romancing Spencer Tracy every night left very little for me."

"I have only deep admiration for the man."

"What a coincidence. That little girl and I feel the same way about each other. Mutual respect."

"Cut the crap!" she hissed. "What were you doing with that . . . thing?"

"Do I have to go into detail?"

"Shut up! How long has this been going on?"

Silence.

"I asked you how long . . ."

"You told me to shut up," he chuckled.

"How long?"

"Every day or so . . ."

"Why?"

"I have to prove to myself I'm a man."

"It will take more than a little whore to accomplish that, you fool!"

"Joan, it was an honor for her to be seduced by talent."

"Holy shit."

"She idolizes me. Please, Joan, have a glass of champagne."

"Warmed by the heat of passion? Shove it."

"Chilled to your liking," he said, opening another bottle.

She took a sip. "Our marriage is over."

". . . has been for a while."

"I knew about the others."

"It never occurred to me you were faithful."

"I'm fighting like hell to survive at this fucking studio! My mind is not consumed with sex."

"Neither was our marriage, my dear."

"Maybe that's why I'm making three hundred thousand dollars a year and you make only fifty thousand dollars. Everything, sex included, should be kept in proper perspective. I might add that your excessive drinking hasn't helped."

"How else can I face you at the front door each night?"

"Perhaps you blame my ambition, but I put the blame on your lack of it!"

There was a loud noise like a table or chair falling to the floor. The guard moved closer to the door. "Go ahead," she said to Tone. "I've become quite adept at covering black eyes and bruises with clever makeup."

"You make all the arrangements, Joan."

She laughed. "It's a divorce, not a funeral."

"Our life might have continued just the way it was . . . such as it was . . . if you hadn't walked in here today. Am I right?"

"Probably . . ."

"From the first moment I saw you, I fell in love, and my feelings haven't changed."

"Just your bed partners. We adjust to life, not love."

"I'll be home early."

"You're goddamn right, because I want you packed and out of my house tonight!"

"After all we've been through?"

"The last straw, Franchot. I will not tolerate indiscretion. Isn't it enough that the whole town knows I support you? That you've lost all ambition? That you're turning into an alcoholic if you aren't one already?"

"I miss my friends in the theater, darling."

"Strange," she smirked. "Seems to me they're lounging around my pool most of the time. They enjoy my food and wine. If they're so goddamn talented, why are they always out of work?"

"The money's in films. Why do you think I'm here?"

"I've been trying to figure that out."

"We planned to team up on the stage, remember? You were so enthused and so exhilarated. Maybe you were playacting, Joan, but our readings were good. The stage was your greatest challenge, and I blame myself for not taking advantage of your drive and determination in the beginning."

"That was almost five years ago . . ."

"The theater might have saved my pride, and our marriage."

"Beautiful speech. Good try." She applauded.

"Let's get out of Hollywood while we still have our sanity and what's left of our love."

"Sure! The rotten bastards here would like that. Well, I'm not finished with them yet! I don't give a damn what you do, but I'm not giving up. I'll never give up."

"Stay with me, Joan."

"Shouldn't you be concerned about getting on the set? Waiting to be called is damn unprofessional."

"Why don't you stay, darling, and watch us shoot. Then we'll drive home together."

"I have a better idea. I'll go home and pack your belongings. That way you'll be out of my house . . . tonight!"

"Yes, darling."

The door was wide open now. The security guard could see Joan powdering her face, freshening her lipstick, pinching her curved eyebrows, and straightening her peplum. Pulling white gloves firmly over her fingers, she looked in the three-way mirror, stood absolutely still, and made sure she was perfection before leaving. Her head high, she strolled on the set and greeted the cast as if nothing had happened.

Observing "the Queen of M-G-M," who was about to lose her throne, brought tears to Franchot's eyes. They needed each other now more than ever, but she'd punish him anyway. Pride alone would force her to go through with a divorce. Joan was thirty-five and resented every new starlet. To find one in the arms of her husband was hell.

He wasn't seeking youth or revenge for his wife's dalliances. Bed-hopping was one of Hollywood's sophisticated hobbies, but the rule was not to fall in love with your co-star until you had made two films together. Franchot and Joan shared the screen in four movies before getting married. He proposed many times before she accepted. What is not commonly known is that Franchot fell in love with the woman, not the star. He gave more of himself to Joan than her other husbands did and remained a faithful friend until his death in 1968.

A notable stage actor who'd performed with Katharine Cornell, Franchot remained in Hollywood to be with Joan. His peers considered him one of the most underrated movie actors. He didn't have the magnetism required to compete for leading roles, although M-G-M gave him several opportunities. He was in seven of Joan's films; unfortunately, this labeled him. "The theater was in my blood," he once said.

The consensus was that his failure to match Joan's star stature caused the breakup of their marriage, but this was not the case; rather, it was his failure to cope with a life so far beneath his capabilities and expectations. Boredom led to endless hours of drinking, resentment toward his M-G-M contract, and disdain for Hollywood's phony society. Joan had no sympathy for weakness. She overcame far more serious difficulties and got stronger with every battle won.

"When Barbara Stanwyck was married to Frank Fay, she went through the same thing," Joan said. "They lived next door to me. One night she climbed over the wall and said she was leaving Frank. Could she spend the night? He was 'Mr. Broadway' back in New York and she was nothing. They came to Hollywood, he failed in movies, and Barbara became a star. Frank turned to the bottle. Their fights were dreadful. He hit her often. Franchot hit me, too. When it goes that far, the time has come to call it quits. Barbara and Frank might have made a success of their marriage if they'd gone back to New York. She had experience in theater and was making a name for herself on the stage. Franchot had me convinced I could do it, too.

"Like Barbara, I was challenged by Hollywood. We fought and starved and begged. How could we give it up even for a good marriage? We couldn't.

Barbara and I had a lot in common. We were ex–chorus girls who never had a normal childhood. We were hoofers who were snubbed by Hollywood producers. But we were driven. I know how deeply hurt Barbara was when her marriage to Frank ended. They had adopted a child just as I was planning to do, hoping it would mend my life with Franchot. The rest is history. Frank Fay went on the wagon and returned to the Broadway stage in *Harvey*. He was a smash. They fought bitterly over custody of their son and were not friendly after that. Fortunately, Franchot and I got closer after our divorce."

But the day Joan found her husband with another woman, she was shattered despite her cool at the studio. Always the star, she composed herself magnificently. If Franchot was having an affair, every member of the crew knew about it, and Joan would never allow anyone to feel sorry for her. After she was beyond the studio gates, tears of hate burned her face; she drove to the beach. "I didn't love him anymore," she said. "It was as simple as that. The minute I saw him with another woman, whatever I felt for him was gone."

Franchot hated himself for being careless. He was used to pleading with Joan, getting on his knees to ask for forgiveness, cajoling her into reconciliations, but this time he did not want another confrontation. He had known her for a long time, but he never knew which personality would greet him at the door. She might be waiting for him with a vengeance tonight, or she might help him pack, or she might not come home until he had gone. The arguments, physical abuse, and accusations were over, however.

Franchot hit the bottle until his five-year contract with M-G-M expired. That event coincided with his divorce, which had been postponed because he and Joan were seen nightclubbing in New York the night before the divorce was to be granted. The judge had refused to grant a decree. A month later he listened to Joan's testimony and reluctantly allowed the divorce, although he expressed his dismay because she and Franchot were seen dancing cheek-to-cheek in public. Glaring at the judge, Joan exclaimed, "I hope I am intelligent enough to be friendly with my husband!"

Although her marriage to Douglas Fairbanks, Jr., provided an introduction to the Hollywood upper crust, it was Franchot who gave Joan an appreciation of elegance and finesse. Much like Marian in *Possessed*, this "little nobody from nowhere" became a connoisseur of fine wines and cuisine. Although she would always read the funnies first, Joan learned to share Franchot's love for Shakespeare and Keats and classical music. Despite his stuffy, intellectual air, Franchot was a rebel at heart who had a rare sense of humor and enjoyed a good time. Joan saw only good in him, and she was right. But if the best of Franchot rubbed off on Joan, the worst of Joan rubbed off on Franchot. He would never be the same after their divorce. He would go on and off the wagon, waver between New York and Hollywood, and jump in and out of disastrous marriages. Joan and M-G-M drained Franchot of his pride, despite their faith in him.

In 1935 Bette Davis co-starred with Franchot in *Dangerous,* for which she received an Oscar for Best Actress, and fell deeply in love with him. She kept these feelings to herself because his obsession with Joan was obvious to everyone long before there was a hint of marriage. Davis said she would wait eagerly for him to come back to the set after lunch only to find Joan's lipstick smeared all over his face. Davis considered Franchot to be the ideal man— suave, considerate, debonair, handsome, and charming. To her knowledge, Joan never knew about the attraction, and, in later years, when the two women were at odds, probably would have gotten a great deal of satisfaction out of the fact that she, not Bette, had married Franchot.

During her marriage to Franchot, Joan rarely drank anything more than a glass or two of champagne. Although he built her a well-stocked wine cellar, she only sipped to test the grape and to appreciate the aroma of the proper wine served with each dinner course. She put Franchot's family heirloom silverware to good use at her popular dinner parties and treasured the antique furniture that he chose. In her Bristol Avenue home in Beverly Hills, the library contained classic leatherbound books selected by Franchot, who had read them all at least once. Joan managed a few, but only she knew the truth about her lack of interest. Her guests were impressed. Her old friends were amused. But all agreed Crawford emerged the wiser and victorious.

The fact that her second marriage to a son of society had failed was apparently to her advantage. Articles emphasized it was Joan who had wanted to be free. There was no hint that either Fairbanks or Tone had wanted or asked for a divorce or had fallen out of love with her. She had made the long journey from the third row of a sleazy chorus line to the prestigious receiving line at Pickfair and found the pace too slow. With no education, she could discuss the arts with a Phi Beta Kappa and keep him vitally interested in her. She had lived a life that playwrights attempted to emulate.

Regardless of her roots, Joan was admired for the progress she had made in a town of failures. And not only her peers were in awe. American women could identify with Joan—the poor girl who made good. She was a woman's woman. Possibly men feared what Joan represented; they felt inferior to her drive and ambition. With few exceptions, her male co-stars fell by the wayside. Whatever role she played, her character kept pace with any masculine rivals on the screen. Gable complemented her best because his role was to dodge or dominate dames. Moviegoers' subconscious identification with this image is one reason why Crawford's fans did not abandon her. Letters with the same theme poured in to M-G-M: "Dear Joan, if you can do it, so can I."

This admiration had to do not only with the roles she played but also with the men she dated and married. Movie magazines sold out if they featured Joan either on the cover or in a revealing article. She never turned down an interview or photo session, but the public did not tire of reading about her or finding out more about her wardrobe and makeup. She openly apologized for her mistakes and divorces, forged ahead with faith and determination, and never complained. She alone was responsible.

Her dedication to being an actress did not end when the camera stopped rolling. She urged American women to be themselves, to have pride in neatness regardless of social or financial status, to be feminine and gay. Even at her glamorous pinnacle, Joan never talked down to her fans. She was one of them despite the furs and diamonds and famous husbands.

"Perhaps if I learn to believe in myself I shall lose my fear of the future," she said in a 1932 interview. The title of the article is "The Girl with the Haunted Face"—the girl searching for happiness but believing down deep in her heart that she would never find it. "I was born with such an inferiority complex that I must keep doing things to retain self-respect. Now I'm a star and yet that mysterious force keeps urging me on." The reader is asked to look closely at the picture of a radiant and happy Joan Crawford to spot the intense sorrow in her eyes. She fears the dark. She lies in bed alone, contemplating the future. "Perhaps there is a new experience which, when I find and conquer it, will satisfy this longing of mine. In the meantime I must try to develop."

She describes her wild night drives along the ocean. "I feel that I'm Lord of All. Watching the white foam lash the rocks, I order my car to move faster and faster as though to rush away from the terror of the night even as it hems me in." Joan's fretful thoughts are those of a frightened child trying desperately to find out who she is regardless of the consequences. She searches for peace but gives the impression she would be bored if she found it. Her restlessness is infinite. "To stand still is to exist and to go backwards is death," she says.

In a typical Crawford interview she bares her soul. "If only I had the ability to laugh at myself . . . to accept my mistakes. But I'll learn and face life bravely." Corny, trite, and trashy? Not sixty years ago, when Americans were reeling from the stock market crash and standing in breadlines. Not when people were committing suicide, losing their homes, and begging for money on the streets. Not when the proud and the rich found themselves with nothing but their strength and prayers. Joan Crawford was molding a "touchable" star status. She was not embarrassed to be earthy and human. There was no mystery of a Greta Garbo, no aloofness of a Norma Shearer, no endless humor of a Carole Lombard.

Joan's love affair with her fans was more important to her than anything or anyone else: It was the longest and truest relationship of her life. In her quest to be somebody, she feared she would not be accepted, admired, and loved. During the dark days when she had no one to lean on, she could rely on flattering fan mail. From the very start Joan believed her public was just as vital to her future as the brass at M-G-M, for they could not save her if moviegoers lost interest.

* * *

Joan was twenty-one when she arrived in Hollywood in 1925—an unwanted, overworked, lonely girl. Her M-G-M personnel card described her as being plain, with light brown hair, and weighing 145 pounds. She gave her age as seventeen and never admitted the truth. Was she clever enough even then to know that birth certificates were not issued in Texas until 1908, making it impossible for anyone to prove otherwise? Although she fluctuated when recounting other details of her life, Joan was steadfast about her "teenage" years in Hollywood. In her book *My Way of Life,* she wrote, "I married Douglas Fairbanks, Jr., when we were both teenagers. Fun was the word for that one." But she was actually twenty-five and he was approaching twenty. Theirs was a storybook marriage, a true-to-life version of Cinderella swept off her feet by the Prince of Pickfair. Her stepmother did not accept the daughter of a laundress. Joan's fans rallied with sympathy and encouragement. The official picture of the newlyweds is a masterpiece: Doug standing with one hand in his pocket and Joan sitting by his side, her head resting on his arm, their fingers entwined. Doug was a fair-haired, tall, thin gentleman. Joan was frilly, sweet, and yielding in a demure frock.

Even if Doug Jr. was not well known, he carried his famous father's name, and the marriage attracted another generation of moviegoers. Mary Pickford's stepson had not been successful in films until his relationship with Joan the starlet. It is not generally known that Doug couldn't get a good part in a movie. He had given up by the time Joan entered his life. She gave him encouragement. M-G-M cashed in on the publicity ignited by fan magazines that couldn't get enough of the most attractive couple in Hollywood. Joan stole the limelight without trying, however. F. Scott Fitzgerald spotted her a few years earlier and said, "Joan Crawford is doubtless the best example of the flapper, the girl you see in smart nightclubs, gowned to the apex of sophistication, toying with iced glasses with a remote, faintly bitter expression, dancing deliciously, laughing a great deal with wide, hurt eyes—a young thing with a talent for living."

Now Joan closed the door on that part of her past. Her manner of dress changed. She toned down her laughter and threw away her beloved chewing gum. Joan was clever enough not to lose her identity, but she was a married woman now and determined to behave like a lady. The timing was right because M-G-M wanted her to concentrate on acting. Her personal and professional image were blending together nicely. She was suspected of planning it this way, of marrying Fairbanks to boost her popularity at the box office and to gain access to Hollywood's crème de la crème. "What did they expect?" she commented to a friend. "I'd marry some truck driver I didn't love?"

Fairbanks had Joan to thank for another chance to make movies, and he proved his talent admirably. His good reviews had a positive effect on Joan's career, but she was doing nicely on her own. When dress designer Gilbert Adrian came to M-G-M, he was assigned to the most glamorous leading ladies and was responsible for Joan's new look and ultimate trademark. He accentuated her broad shoulders with pads, ruffles, and wide collars. By putting the emphasis above the waist, Adrian made Joan's full hips appear slimmer. The "padded look" had one of the greatest effects on fashion history. Women demanded the Crawford style, and although Joan and Doug would part company, she and Adrian would be a stylish team for a long time.

Joan's full and heavily painted lips replaced the perky, rosebud ones featured in silent films. Writers would refer to her mouth as "the slash." Joan had her own ideas, and regardless of the trend, Crawford featured Crawford. "That's what the public expects and that's what they're going to get," she said.

During the Depression, Hollywood celebrities lived and partied outlandishly. Letters from the struggling public complaining of the shame and vulgarity poured into the studios. Joan came forth boldly in defense of her peers, but most likely she had her own motives. She said owning a Beverly Hills house befitting a star was her duty to her fans; her public was inspired when she was photographed in diamonds and furs and expensive clothes. "I believe in the dollar," Joan stated. "Everything I have, I spend." She was proud to help the economy by putting money in circulation!

Joan had the ability to communicate with her fans, to speak the truth and remind them she came from nothing and deserved every cent she earned. Was there any woman who wouldn't do the same if she were in Joan's rhinestone-studded brocade slippers?

Inspiration. Obligation. Appreciation.

Sincere words from a star to her adoring fans. Did she ever forget to mention them in her interviews?

Hollywood insiders found it hard to believe that Joan volunteered to tell the American public she had every intention of living glamorously because she owed it to them. But why did M-G-M give Joan more leeway than their other contract players? A veteran studio publicist explained, "Joan was our first attempt at actually creating a screen personality from scratch. She was more ambitious and was, above all else, true to herself. Most stars were glorious puppets who did and said what was dictated to them. Joan had a mind of her own, but she was not excluded from the usual editing or criticism. She was watched very carefully, but her public relations proved to be a Hollywood dream and the fan magazines' delight."

Billy Haines, one of her oldest and dearest friends, said, "Joan is not a phony, but I have to defend her on many occasions. She lives up to her name and imagery. She has respect for what it represents. I remember when she came to Hollywood, and the transformation was and is remarkable. This is a town of miracle workers, but no one could accomplish what she did on her own. She dramatizes life. Always onstage because of her natural ability as an actress. I told her that Pickfair was better than any finishing school, and Joan emerged as a lady with polish. The difficulty with her in-laws was exaggerated. Problems existed, but Joan couldn't breath without a challenge. If something came easy, she wasn't interested. When people talked behind her back, I suggested that they meet Joan before criticizing her so unmercifully."

For five years Joan Crawford was among the top ten most popular stars in Hollywood. *Life* magazine gave her the title of "First Queen of the Movies" in 1937: "It is an axiom in Hollywood that movie favorites are usually created by women. Joan Crawford's public is predominantly female, predominantly low-brow. A former shopgirl herself, she has risen to stardom as the Shopgirl's Dream."

Twice a year she went to New York City, where her fan clubs greeted Joan at all her scheduled appearances. The M-G-M publicist commented, "Miss Crawford demanded that her fans know where she was staying and what her plans were. The crowds were well mannered because she had police protection. Joan never rushed past them, though. She let them get a good look and signed autographs. For most stars, these trips to New York are frightening and exhausting, but Miss Crawford thrived on it. She believed the public had every right to know her whereabouts and that she was everything they imagined her to be. Only once she was mobbed and that was somewhere in Europe. They almost tore her clothes off. She was in heaven."

When a friend asked her why she exposed herself (and her husbands) to so much publicity, Joan snapped, "If it wasn't for my fans, baby, I'd still be in Kansas City!"

L. B. Mayer, head of M-G-M, would try to talk to Joan out of a role she was fighting for by suggesting that her fans would be offended. Occasionally she retorted. "Disappointed, maybe, but never offended!"

Joan kept an accurate count of her mail, and in 1937 she was close to her millionth letter. It didn't matter if another star received more letters. Who cared, as long as they continued coming? But the "First Queen of the Movies" had the proof, and the studio took advantage of her undisputed popularity. As David Shipman wrote in his 1970 book *The Great Movie Stars: The Golden Years*:

> The length of Crawford's career is awesome, especially as she has never been considered much of an actress—nor has she made a habit of appearing in good films. Yet she remains the only major female player surviving from the Silent era. She must be, as she looks, tough as old boots. Her life, as with many others, might be fashioned after one of her scenarios: struggle, fight, get to the top, stay there. Some accounts reckon that she survived because she changed her style, adapted herself to new fashions; but only in the physical sense did she adapt— new hairstyles, modes. The essential Crawford didn't change whether as dancing daughter, sophisticated heroine or tragic lady. She has played one sort of American woman all these years. She admits that she has worked hard at the acting game—but she has achieved little beyond the projection of that woman.

Bosley Crowther, film critic for the *New York Times,* agreed, but he impugned her womanliness on the screen. Joan claimed she paid little attention to reviews, but she cried over lunch with Ed Sullivan because he criticized her for not granting interviews during her marriage to Fairbanks.

Dabbing a white lace hankie under her mascara-laden lashes, Joan said she had been fair with the press, but they wrote what they damn pleased! "My problem is," she sniffled, "I can't ignore reporters even though I have a scrapbook of clippings, and most of them are raps and digs." Joan said letters from fans kept her going. "They are intelligent, hardworking people. If they don't like my hair or wardrobe, they tell me what they prefer. And do you want to know something? They are usually right. I have an obligation to them, not to the goddamn press!"

In 1928, when her determination and guts made her a star in *Our Dancing Daughters,* Joan answered each fan letter personally, stamped the envelopes, and took them to the post office herself. "This was the turning point in my life," she said. "The fact that anybody would write me a letter was a thrill. They deserved to be acknowledged. They believed in me."

Thus began Joan Crawford's longest and greatest love affair, which was just as strange and twisted as her role as mother to four adopted children. She allowed her fans (she called them "friends") to gather near her Bristol Avenue home. She put them to work doing odd jobs around the yard and house or helping with the mail. They scrubbed floors and cleaned out the garage and basement. Joan did not believe in wasted time. If her loyal subjects had nothing better to do than to wait for a glimpse of her, she'd give them something constructive to do, and they were honored to get down on their knees. Depending on her mood, she would pay them, but most often she would not. Being able to serve their idol was payment enough.

Between husbands, Joan allowed these girls to be a part of her household, and those who qualified were hired as secretary or baby-sitter. The "First Queen of the Movies" made no exceptions if her instructions were not carried out precisely as dictated. Her abusive tongue and obsession with cleanliness stung her faithful fans whether they were on the payroll or not. The girls worked harder to please her; they would do anything for a compliment. Joan's friends wondered about the odd arrangement. "I've always had a servant problem," Joan explained. "During the war I saw no reason not to use these healthy young girls, some of whom had skills. Not that anyone cares, but there's a right and wrong way to clean a house. If they think life's easy, they'll find out soon enough that it isn't. Men appreciate an immaculate house, but I haven't seen many in my travels. By God, if anyone looks under one of my chairs he won't find a speck of dust!"

Joan began this strange habit of allowing fans into her home as she embarked on twenty-five years of alcoholism. She wasn't a drinker until her third marriage, so, gradually at first, the cocktail hour became an appointment with herself that wasn't logged on her daily schedule. When her guests had gone home and the children and servants were in bed, she took her drinking seriously.

In the lonely hours of the night, Joan was too intoxicated for pretense. Friends got accustomed to being awakened by her weird telephone calls, but the household staff were appalled and frightened by her nocturnal demands. Joan's attempts at being seductive were obvious. "I hate to drink alone" or I hate to sleep alone" meant trouble. These hints became requests and finally advances. In her drunken rages she cried out for intimate adoration from subservient females. There are many accounts of Joan's close relationship with her fans. Indeed, on the morning she died, Joan made breakfast for a young girl who had spent the night.

"Tomorrow morning we'll be divorced, darling."

    "You've learned to dance so divinely, I almost hate to give you up."

    "Suppose we forget the whole thing," Franchot smiled down at her.

    She laughed. "No way!"

    "If it's your pride, Joan . . ."

    "Why are you trying so hard to ruin a perfectly delightful evening?"

    "How many people celebrate a divorce?" he asked, looking around the nightclub.

    "We're sophisticated. Have you no courage, Franchot?"

    "I married you, didn't I?"

    "Must we quarrel on our last night as man and wife? We haven't had this much fun in years."

    "You'll need someone, Joan. I'd like to think that someone is me."

    "How very different you are here in New York."

    "The theater is my life," he said, taking her hand and walking back to the table. "It could have been *our* life," he whispered, helping Joan with her chair. "You'd love living in the city, performing on the stage, bowing to the applause . . . the late suppers . . ." He paused to light her cigarette and place the napkin on her lap. ". . . and the people, Joan, the museums, concerts, opening night, the orchestra tuning up for the overture, the . . ."

    "I'd like more champagne," she interrupted.

    He waved to the waiter, leaned across the table, took her hand, and said earnestly, "Think about it, Joan. Save yourself while there's still time."

    "Is that what you're doing?" she said with a livid glare.

    "I'm trying to keep my sanity and hang on to whatever dignity I have left."

    She looked around the room. "Where the hell is my drink? I want another glass and a clean napkin, too."

    Franchot motioned to the waiter again. "Look, darling," he continued, "I don't want to interfere with your life, but . . ."

    "The waiter's over there."

    "Waiter! Waiter! Darling, if I find a good script, will you read it?"

    "If I have the time," she said, taking a deep breath. "Waiter, this glass hasn't been washed properly. Disgusting! And there are spots on the utensils. Franchot, tell him how bad the service is here. Tell him how long we've been waiting for a drink. Tell him this dump hasn't got class anymore."

"Would you like to dance, darling?"

"No."

The maitre d' recognized her and within a few seconds several waiters were changing the tablecloth, ashtrays, glasses, plates, utensils, and fresh flowers. Impressed, Franchot smiled through the efficient production.

"Please accept a bottle of our best champagne," the maitre d' said.

Joan ignored him. "I want to go home, Franchot! How can you allow people to take your money after they've treated you like shit? This wouldn't happen in Hollywood. This place is a dump! You're just a number in this city, honey."

"Unless you're Joan Crawford," Franchot smiled, helping her with her coat.

"You're goddamn right!"

As they walked out to the street he was not surprised to see the same familiar faces. "Your loyal fans, darling."

Joan was radiant and called them by name. "I want you all to go home now." She waved from the limousine. "Promise you will?"

They nodded and blew kisses.

Franchot turned to Joan, who was still looking out of the window and smiling. "Will there ever be anyone else in your life so important?" he asked.

"Maybe, but whoever he is, those girls will be around a lot longer. I can assure you of that."

Lucille Fay LeSueur was born on March 23, 1904, in San Antonio, Texas. Her father, Thomas, was a French-Canadian laborer who married Anna Bell Johnson around the turn of the century. They had three children. Their firstborn was a girl, Daisy, who died as an infant. A boy, Hal, was born in 1902. Thomas deserted his family before the birth of Lucille.

"My mother was a nagging bitch," Joan said. "Maybe she wasn't legally married, or, if she was, she never got a divorce before taking another husband. Sometimes I got the feeling I was illegitimate because she never got over Daisy's death and loved Hal so much. To her I was a tomboy who never did anything right and never told the truth."

Anna, broke and desolate, took her children to Lawton, Oklahoma, where she married Henry Cassin, owner and operator of the Opera House and an open-air theater on C Street. Henry was a small man who wore flashy gold rings on his stubby fingers. Lawton's nine thousand people envied him because he was in show business, but they had no real respect for him. He drank too much and was too friendly with the transient, frivolous, gay, and indiscreet performers. Joan remembered him with great warmth and gratitude.

Hal nicknamed his sister "Billie" because she followed him everywhere. He was never the protective older brother and took advantage of his mother's fawning. To protect this favoritism, he blamed Billie for his pranks, and she suffered the switches across her legs. Henry, who was rarely at home, was her only salvation, and she took for granted that he was her real father. It was odd that she took Cassin as her name, but Hal did not. "There were rumors that I was illegitimate," Joan confessed. "I suppose the town had a lot of reasons for talking about us."

Many of her neighbors were interviewed when Billie became a Hollywood star. They said she and Hal were nothing alike. He was tall, thin, and blond. She was short, chunky, and brunette. He was easygoing and well behaved. She was restless and defiant.

In 1916 Henry booked a second-rate ballet company featuring "The Pavlova of America" at the Opera House. Billie was spellbound by the beautiful ballerina. Although she preferred the wild kicking and shaking of the usual chorus girls, she saw the graceful lady who balanced on her toes as a fairy godmother who should have arrived at the theater in a golden coach instead of a broken-down old car. Billie managed to watch every performance and became friends with the ballerina, who showed the little girl how to apply makeup. "I can remember vividly the cherry lipstick and purple eye shadow," Joan said, "but I never expected the lady to give me an old pair of her toe shoes. She told me it would take time to learn how to use them properly. From that moment on I wanted to be a dancer. I treasured those shoes."

The ballerina would always be a symbol to Joan Crawford. She was apart from the other performers. She was a lady. But twelve-year-old Billie Cassin had no illusions about dancing on her toes. She was too energetic to go through extensive training even though Henry allowed her to take lessons. He encouraged Billie to put on her own shows in a barn behind the house where he stored old scenery. Hal and some of his friends put on a trapeze act that seemed appropriate with a backdrop from Robin Hood. Billie wore her gypsy dress and toe shoes for the first and last acts. One Lawton old-timer said, "The kids put on two performances. They put a lot of effort into the show. Billie was very proud, I recall. She stood erect and wasn't nervous. At the end she tried to stand on her toes."

Billie's enthusiasm kept all eyes on her as she danced frantically to the harmonica beat while the patched gypsy dress whirled around her thighs. "She had the devil in her," the neighbor said, "but she tried to look like a saint in that ballerina pose."

Knowing what she wanted to do for the rest of her life gave Billie confidence. It didn't matter any longer that she had no girlfriends or that Hal teased and ignored her. It wasn't important that her mother wasn't more attentive and encouraging. She could overlook the snide remarks about her father's off-color shows. Dancing was in her blood. Her heart beat to the rhythm of music, real or make-believe. Billie watched her father's minstrel shows, chorus lines, and stage plays come and go. She listened to performers' tales of the Yukon and New York and Chicago. They were happy-go-lucky. Sometimes they changed costumes backstage "as if they were family." It was exciting and fast. Did a secretary or a housewife get applause?

Anna allowed Billie to put on her little backyard shows but had no idea what her daughter had in mind for the future. Henry understood it might be a childhood fantasy that was so important to a youngster. He would never try to erase Billie's dreams.

She was allowed to continue her dancing lessons only if she also practiced the piano. Anna made this very clear. One hot summer day, when Billie was playing the scale over and over again, she heard Hal and his friends gathering on the lawn.

"Are you going to meet the train?" she yelled from the window.

Hal laughed. "Yeah. The show train and it's a long one!"

"Wait for me!"

Anna pulled her daughter from the window. "You'll finish practicing," she said sternly. "Now sit down and begin again. I can hear you from the kitchen."

Billie began the scales again, but Hal taunted her. "Too bad. Everyone's goin'. Clowns and Indians arrivin' on this one. They're puttin' on a show at the station."

Billie pounded on the piano to drown out his voice, but she could see her brother and his friends disappearing up the block. She heard Anna scrubbing vigorously in the other room. Maybe she wouldn't be missed and even if she was, she was used to having her legs switched and being sent to her room without dinner. Billie dashed for the screen door and flung it open with a bang. Trying to catch up with Hal, she jumped off the porch over a bush and fell on a broken milk bottle. The pain was so excruciating she lost consciousness. Don Blanding, the boy across the street, was just leaving his house when he noticed her lying on the front lawn. He thought she was playing a joke on him until he saw the blood. Don carried her into the house. Anna, who had just discovered an empty piano seat, was furious until she realized the seriousness of Billie's injury.

The artery and tendon in her right foot were severed. She was rushed to the hospital and only remembered coming out of the ether and hearing the doctor say, "Billie will have to stay off her feet for a month or so. I've stitched the arch that needs pliability. She must be very, very careful."

"She'll miss not being able to dance," Henry sighed, squeezing his daughter's hand.

"Dance!" the doctor exclaimed. "She may never walk again, and if she does, Billie will have a limp the rest of her life."

Anna was too upset for tears. "I'll take care of Lucille," she said lovingly.

Henry smiled. "Maybe you'll get to know each other."

The doctor took the Cassins aside. "Your little girl is going to be in a great deal of pain. I can't guarantee those stitches will hold. Someone should be with her all the time."

"You weren't serious about a limp, were you, Doc?" Henry asked.

"That's the best you can hope for right now."

"She wants to be a dancer. This will break her heart."

"The only thing Billie has goin' for her is youth, Mr. Cassin, but if she tries to stand on that foot, the arch will split open again."

"What about school next month?" Anna asked.

The doctor scowled. "From what I hear she was absent most of the time, anyway."

"Her marks are satisfactory," Henry spoke up. "If necessary, I'll hire a tutor."

"I've never seen Lucille so pale and weak," Anna sighed.

For the next few days mother and daughter were inseparable. Billie stayed in bed and tried to sleep until Henry came home with gifts and candy. He told her funny stories about what went on at the theater. She always laughed and forgot about the throbbing pain when her father was in the room. "Only one good thing came out of my accident," Joan said. "I realized that my mother loved me very much. She carried me from room to room, spooned chicken broth into my mouth, brushed my hair until it shone, told me about her childhood and my grandmother, read my favorite stories to me over and over again, bathed me every day, and never complained until I decided I could walk. The stitches broke and I had to have a second operation. There would be a third one because I tried to hop on one foot to the theater, but my mother never scolded me. What I remember most vividly was her hearty laughter when we hobbled around the house together. It occurred to me that I had never heard her laugh before. Unfortunately, those were the only happy months we spent together in her lifetime. I never heard her laugh again."

Billie showed her courage and determination by not sitting still after regaining her strength. She refused to believe what the doctor had said after the third operation. "Looks like you're gonna be a pathetic cripple," he warned. She managed to hop a little farther each day and stayed close to home in case blood soaked through the bandages. She sat on the porch swing, hobbled to the barn, and stared at the Sherwood Forest scenery. There was no doubt in her mind that she would put on those ballerina slippers again for another show. It was, however, a lonely time for her. Henry arranged for a tutor, who said, "Billie is bright, but she has no interest in learning. She can't concentrate. Her mind is always somewhere else. She's capable of passing the tests, but doesn't want to. I don't know what grade to put her in."

Henry thought it best to wait until the January semester. "I'm more concerned about her foot. When we know that she can walk again we'll concern ourselves with school."

"I became an explorer," Joan said, "spying underneath the porch, looking for four-leaf clovers, going through old boxes in the barn, and snooping in the cellar. I hadn't been down there since the night of a terrifying cyclone. I knew my mother's preserves were in the basement, but I thought it would be fun to look around. I had all the time in the world. I don't know why, but I poked behind a jar of cherries, and there was a canvas bag that didn't look familiar.

I pulled it out and found hundreds of gold coins. Naturally, I started to count them and just then my mother came looking for me."

Anna was stunned and trembling. "Where did you find that?"

"Behind the cherries . . ."

"Put them back and don't tell anyone—not even your father—about this. Do you hear me, Lucille? Never tell anyone!"

Billie had never seen her mother in a panic and very seldom saw her cry. They had an early dinner. Anna helped her daughter into bed. "Are you still in pain?"

"A little. That's why I keep busy. That's why I went down to . . ."

"Never mind."

"The stitches haven't come out in almost two months. It's healing. And I'm not going to limp."

"Be glad you can walk, Billie. Don't look for miracles. Good night."

Billie was awakened by her parents fighting bitterly in their bedroom. It had something to do with the gold. Anna wanted Henry to give the money back and he refused. "I'll go to jail!" he shouted.

Anna was hysterical. She demanded an explanation. Henry repeated over and over again, "If I give the money back we'll be ruined!" They fought most of the night. Billie didn't understand. She loved her father because he was an honorable man. Why would he steal? And if he did take the gold, why didn't he spend it? Why didn't Anna rejoice at their good fortune?

Nothing was the same after that night filled with bitter words. Billie looked for a sign of reconciliation, but her parents barely spoke to each other. Within a week, there were hushed phone calls and rumors that the Cassins' house was up for sale. Henry was seen at the sheriff's office. Someone overheard the deputy mention a trial. Hal told Billie, "If we move, I'll die."

"Who said we're leaving Lawton?"

"The whole town. Dad's in some kinda trouble. I sure would hate to leave my friends."

"Is that all you care about? Your friends?"

"Yeah, but how would you know. You ain't got any."

"That's because my daddy owns the theater. They're afraid to play with me. He's very special in this town."

"Well he's sure gettin' a lotta attention now!"

Within a week or so it would be Christmas, but Billie did not feel very festive when Anna announced, "You and Hal are going to Arizona for the holidays. My family has a nice farm outside Phoenix."

"Why?"

"I would think you'd like a vacation, Lucille, after being cooped up in this house for six months."

Henry joked about the trip. "You kids will be fit and tanned when you get back. And Billie's foot will be all healed. You'll see."

The family put on a joyful act at the railroad station. Anna was worried about her children traveling alone, but Henry said it was a wonderful adventure and they would be home soon, anyway.

Billie did not tell Hal about the canvas bag of gold, but they discussed the mysterious circumstances. Was their house up for sale? Maybe Anna was leaving Henry. All they did was fight in a whisper these days. Hal defended his mother. "She works hard and what does she have to show for it?"

"Daddy treats her very well," Billie fought back. "He's a busy man. A successful one, too. Aren't you proud to have a father who owns two theaters?"

"Our real father doesn't own two theaters, stupid."

"What are you talking about? Of course he . . ."

"Henry isn't our real father."

"What do you mean?"

Hal reached into his suitcase and handed his sister a picture of Thomas LeSueur. "He's our real father. We were born in San Antonio."

"I don't believe you!"

"I remember him vaguely," Hal said. "He's still alive, I think."

"Why did Mother lie?"

"She just never told you the truth. I got it out of her when I found this picture and then it all came back to me."

"He didn't love us," Billie sobbed.

"How do you know so much?"

"Why isn't he part of the family? Why isn't he taking care of us like Daddy Cassin?"

"Mother said he left us."

"Then maybe that man isn't my father."

"All I know is that our real name is LeSueur."

"My name is Cassin!" she shouted.

"Shut up and forget about it. Do you want to get me in trouble?"

"I won't say anything."

Hal smirked. "As if everyone doesn't already know."

Billie didn't sleep that night. She stared into the darkness, searching for lights in the distance. Hal regretted telling her if for no other reason than that it was the wrong time. He didn't try to comfort his sister but told her, "Your eyes were open all night. Weird."

"Maybe I'm weird, but you're cruel, Hal. You're very, very cruel."

When the children returned to Lawton they found a house almost devoid of furniture. "We're selling everything and moving to Kansas City," Anna said sternly.

Hal ran off to find his friends, who told him, "Your father's a crook, but he beat the rap."

Billie was anxious to see Henry, who was busy trying to sell his theaters. She overheard him tell a prospective buyer, "I'm taking a loss on the house, but I need the money. I've terminated the leases on the Opera House and will leave the Air Dome on the market." The unidentified man patted Henry on the back. "I hope you make a new start in Kansas City," he said sadly. "All this could have been avoided."

Although Joan maintained her father was covering up for a "crooked partner," everyone in Lawton knew Cassin was in business alone. She claimed it was a complicated matter because she didn't know her father was involved in the insurance business. "His partner was the real thief and Daddy hid the money," she said. "A woman who was in jail claimed she gave him the bond money. He denied it. I don't think there was a trial. My mother demanded he return the coins and that was the end of it. Daddy was vindicated before we left town."

There was little mention of the episode in the local newspaper, but Henry was well known on the show-business circuit and was blackballed in the Midwest. He was not aware of the consequences when his family boarded the Rock Island express for Kansas City. Hal resented the move and said very little. Anna was sarcastic and bitter. Billie sat with Daddy Cassin, who shared the sights along the way. Tulsa and Wichita were exciting stops. They were enthusiastic about beginning a new life, but Henry explained it might take a while for him to find a job. They would have to make sacrifices, but she could take ballet lessons when her foot was completely healed.

The Cassins were overwhelmed by Union Station in Kansas City, which was then the second-largest railroad terminal in the United States. They took a taxi downtown to the New Midland Hotel. Anna was appalled. They were on a very limited budget, Henry reminded her. "Besides," he said cheerfully, "you haven't been inside yet."

"I don't have to," she sneered, standing on the sidewalk. "I can smell it from here."

"It's only temporary," he said, taking Billie's hand.

The fighting and complaining began all over again. Anna was distraught—only one room for a family of four. How could she cook on a hot plate? How could she sit in a lobby filled with bums and drunks? When was Henry going to demand the money for their Lawton house to buy another in Kansas City? She continued to nag while he helped the children unpack. The following morning Cassin had an appointment with a friend who operated a theater. "Henry, I suggest you forget about show business," he said. "That embezzlement charge in Lawton damaged your reputation. I don't think anyone on the circuit will hire you."

"You can't be serious! I was proved innocent but gave the money back anyway."

"I made some calls. No one will take a chance on you, Henry."

The grave situation went from bad to worse. Billie had to walk more than thirty blocks to school because there was no money for a streetcar. Her right foot ached every night but the pain was nothing compared to Anna's tongue-lashing. She refused to work until Henry could find a job.

Joan remembered her mother's constant nagging. "I felt very sorry for Daddy. He wasn't strong or big enough to do physical labor. Every day he went out and came home so worn out and tired but not discouraged. We were alike that way because no matter how bad things were, there was hope around the corner."

Out of desperation, Henry worked the hotel desk at night. The owner needed help during the day, but Anna refused. She could not stand the clientele. The fact that her husband stayed up all night, dozed for a few hours, and went out to look for a decent job didn't impress her. What did was the few thousand dollars they received for the Lawton house. The very day it arrived she insisted that Henry look at a lovely home not far from the school. The price was outrageous. "This money is all we have," he said. "It isn't enough for a down payment on a shack."

It was sufficient, however, to lease the New Midland Hotel. The owners wanted to move on and asked the Cassins if they'd like to take over. Without consulting his bitter wife, Henry signed the papers. It was the only solution. "You can take the streetcar to school," he told Billie. Hal assumed he could ride, too, until Henry explained, "Your sister's foot is not healing. The doctor said it would take a year. Sixty blocks every day is too much for Billie."

Hal couldn't have cared less about Billie's health. It infuriated him that Anna had nothing to say in the matter. He was used to getting his own way with her, but Henry had taken over not only the hotel but also family matters. The only thing Hal could hold over Billie was school. He was being advanced to the next grade, and she was three grades behind. She didn't make friends because her classmates were much younger. There was nowhere to hide on the back streets of Kansas City, no theater to run to after school, no candy store, no front and back yards, no barn, no young man across the street, no trees or porch swings. And where were the ballerinas?

It was just a matter of time before the lobby of the New Midland Hotel became her playground. Someone was usually playing the piano and Billie began to dance again. She endured pain and fell down, but each day her foot was getting stronger despite a slight limp. She believed if she could dance again, the limp would disappear. Billie had no one to confide in during these days. Henry was busy at the desk or drunk. Anna hated the hotel, her husband, and the burden of her children, who had no supervision. The Cassin reputation became worse in downtown Kansas City than it had been in Lawton. They were no longer a family; they were four strangers. Before Henry fell apart from the strain, he sobered up long enough to take care of his little girl.

"You know Daddy is a Catholic," he said to her.

"Yes."

"You kids had no religious training because Mother is a Protestant. We made the mistake of not taking you and Hal to church in Lawton, Lucille.

Folks didn't accept us for that reason. They were God-fearing people and the church was the hub of the community."

"What will I be?" she asked.

"You'll decide for yourself, but in the meantime I've made arrangements for you to study and live at St. Agnes Catholic School. The hotel is no place for a child. You're going on twelve, and in no time, my pretty little girl will be a young lady. I want you to make nice friends and learn and have fun, too."

"Do we have to pay?"

"Yes, but you'll be expected to work, Lucille. I've arranged to give them what I can. Do you understand?"

"I'd rather stay with you, Daddy."

Henry tried to be humorous. "I'm so darn busy we never see each other. It's best this way, honey."

Although Billie hated the public school she was attending, she was becoming accustomed to it. The teachers were understanding, and her classmates were friendlier. But she didn't want to hurt Henry's feelings.

At first she resented the dormitory, the uniform, and the strictness of the nuns, but as the weeks passed, Billie appreciated the cleanliness and routine. She volunteered for extra kitchen duties partly because she enjoyed it, partly to avoid studying. It was her first experience at working as part of a team. She would always be a loner, but the feeling of belonging was secure and warm. She dreaded going hone on weekends and found excuses to avoid the dirt, the quarreling, and the depressing transients at the New Midland. Only her desire to see Daddy Cassin made her go back to the hotel for a visit.

"Your father's gone," Anna said without looking up from the desk.

"Where?"

"I don't know."

"When's he coming back?"

"He's gone for good."

"You're not married anymore?"

"Lucille, we're on our own. I'm broke. The trash that comes here runs out without paying."

"What are we going to do?"

"I got a job managing the City Gate Laundry but that won't be enough. Hal will have to quit school and go to work. You'll have to leave St. Agnes."

"No!"

"Lucille, don't always be so stubborn and selfish! You'd better get used to not having your father around to spoil and pamper you."

Billie wanted to fight back with the name LeSueur, but she was too shocked, confused, and depressed over Daddy Cassin's leaving. For a few moments she sat in the shabby, unkempt room with its smell of disinfectant and greasy food. "If I work at St. Agnes," she told her mother, "maybe the nuns will let me stay. Some girls pay their tuition that way."

Anna was relieved at the prospect of not having her daughter around. "I'll go to the school and explain our situation."

Joan was not consistent when talking about her three years at St. Agnes. She overemphasized the amount of work she was required to do. Except for the students from wealthy families, all the girls washed dishes, served meals, scrubbed floors, waxed furniture, and cleaned windows. Maybe she was snubbed, but in later years she admitted, "I waited on tables and made beds. I enjoyed it. I still enjoy housework. Scrubbing and cooking were better for me than algebra, I'm sure."

Her foot healed. She walked without a limp and performed in ten musical recitals at St. Agnes. Billie had friends, too, although shyness kept her from the great popularity she might have attained. Her world had collapsed so often it was difficult for her to trust or get close to anyone. She felt safe within the walls of St. Agnes, and those who remembered her there would see Billie in Joan Crawford's face . . . the big, frightened eyes that stared right through you . . . the serious expression that became her trademark . . . the determined but sad mouth . . . the sturdy hands and body . . . the forced smile that lacked sincerity.

St. Agnes was the first phase of Billie's transformation. She was aware of this on visits to Anna's stale and musty apartment over the laundry. Hal expected his sister to help out, and she did, but it was disgusting to see her mother with drifters, bums, and drunkards. Henry was an Adonis compared with them. It was obvious these men were only after a good time, and Anna encouraged them.

Billie was determined to find Daddy Cassin. She roamed the downtown streets until her wish came true. It was a tearful and happy reunion. She hugged him tight. "I've missed you so much!"

"How about an ice cream soda?"

He was interested in how she was doing at school. Billie did not mention the hard work. "I'm doing very well. I'm dancing, too."

"Any pain in that foot?" he asked.

"A little, but I'm used to it."

"You're a brave girl, Billie."

"When can I see you again?"

"I don't know."

"Where do you live? I'll visit you."

"Here's money for the streetcar. It's getting late."

He kissed her and waved good-bye. Billie was so happy she walked home, but she never saw Henry Cassin again.

"I envisioned his coming back to us," Joan said. "We'd all go to a small town where life was not so hectic and complicated. I'd light his cigars and get his slippers when he came home. But then I thought about my mother and how she made life miserable for him. All he was to her was a meal ticket, and maybe that's how he got into trouble. I don't know, but I convinced myself he was better off without her."

Although Billie was able to dance again, she could not dance on point. She was as good as the other girls in the corps de ballet at St. Agnes but was unable to balance on her toes. Her dream of becoming a ballerina was fading, but the colorful gypsy dancers whirled around in her head. When she felt sorry for herself, Billie remembered the doctor's prediction that she would be a miserable cripple even if she walked again. It had taken her almost five years of constant pain to get this far. Being onstage was a thrill except when friends and family were invited. When Anna brought her cheap boyfriends to the school Billie suddenly went into a shell. The nuns noticed her withdrawals and knew that Anna was a bad influence. They didn't encourage a close relationship or force Billie to go home on weekends.

The rich girls referred to Billie as "that thing" because she didn't like to take a bath or brush her teeth. "She was more concerned about makeup," a former student said. "And it's a fact she snuck out to the park to meet boys. The nuns gave her extra work as a punishment. They probably thought Lucille didn't know any better because her mother ran around."

Billie enjoyed watching the Northeast High School football team practicing in Budd Park. Her classmates couldn't figure out why she got more attention than they did. "She wasn't that attractive," one student remembered, "but there was something daring and mysterious about her. She had a crooked smile . . . a smirk that was a come-on. She used it in her films, but when Joan Crawford was a plump, dirty kid at St. Agnes, we figured she got the boys because they knew she was easy. Billie had a wild reputation. She always looked as if she had a secret, and I'm sure she had many."

A player on the Northeast team remembered Billie sat alone even if some of her classmates were there. "She never talked to them," he said. "We all knew her. Some of the guys laughed about the good times they had with Billie. She was a tomboy and liked to play tag. We'd tackle each other and roll around in the grass. She was a big flirt—always daring one of the guys to chase her. We tried to fix her up with Ray Sterling, who never went out with girls. He was a real square. Ray just looked at her, nodded, and ran away. Billie thought that was very funny."

"Lucille, I want you to meet Harry Hough," Anna said. "He's our chief delivery man at City Gate Laundry and the man responsible for getting me the job."

Billie looked up at the tall, ugly man in a worn, baggy suit. "Hello," she mumbled. He glared back at her. Anna babbled on about how kind Mr. Hough had been and how appreciative she was. "He's helping us with the apartment, too." This meant only one thing to Billie. Her mother was living with this dreadful man and would probably marry him. The very thought made her sick.

It also meant Daddy Cassin was never coming back, but Anna gave her little time to fret. "When you come home, Lucille, you'll be expected to do your share of the work, so don't just stand there!"

Immaculate housekeeping was Billie's way of life these days. She couldn't bear the disgustingly dirty apartment behind the laundry. If she had to visit, it was worth the effort to clean it thoroughly. More than once she missed the strict curfew at St. Agnes and was given extra work for tardiness.

Joan Crawford claimed her mother took her out of school to help in the laundry, but the reality is that Billie Cassin was told to leave St. Agnes. "You have been warned about your bad conduct," the nuns said. "We've given you many chances to abide by our rules. Pack your things."

According to her classmates, she was sneaking out to the park at night to meet boys. The nuns were aware of the situation for a long time, but couldn't catch Billie. Exactly what convinced them to expel her isn't known, but twenty years later St. Agnes sent a letter to Joan Crawford, asking for a contribution. Instead, they received a scathing reply.

Anna assumed her daughter had decided it was time to come home. "I'm glad you've finally gotten some sense in your head," she shouted. "Why the hell do you need an education? I didn't have none. Or did you realize it was time to show some gratitude by doing your share of the work? Hal and Harry are exhausted and my good health won't last long if I have to do your share and mine, too. I took this job to keep our family together, but how would you know about such things? You've had your fun, but it's over."

Joan said she learned how to iron shirts and pleated skirts expertly. This period in her life was a quiet nightmare. There was a world war going on overseas and at the City Gate Laundry. Anna told the children, "After my marriage to Harry, we're moving to his house."

Hal rebelled. "We're doing all right without him!"

For a change, Billie agreed with her brother.

Anna was furious. "I'm tired of raising two kids by myself," she yelled. "I have a son who thinks he can afford to take out rich girls and a slut for a daughter. Harry gets around. He hears what people say, and he wants to get a few things straight. We're living in his house by his rules."

Hal said he had saved some money and was going to live with his grandparents in Arizona. Desperate, Billie tried to convince him to share the laundry apartment with her, but he left without further discussion. Anna refused to allow her fourteen-year-old daughter to live alone, so Billie reluctantly moved into Hough's home. Supposedly he was her legal stepfather, but she had her doubts. Each morning before dawn they went to work, making deliveries along the way. "The only thing my mother and I had in common was the laundry," Joan said. "We knew our business."

Stories about why Billie was sent to nearby Rockingham Academy in 1919 vary, but Harry Hough had something to do with it. Joan claimed he tried to seduce her. In one version she claimed she didn't tell her mother, but in another explanation she hinted that Anna was no fool. Another version stressed Billie's desire for a high-school education, but this is unlikely even though St. Agnes gave her the incentive to improve her manners and speech. She wanted to become a dancer, but in the meantime getting a better job was the only way to escape Harry and her mother's laundry.

Another possibility is that Hough didn't want Billie around. In one version, he noticed a "help wanted" sign at Rockingham and made inquiries. In exchange for hard work, he discovered, his stepdaughter could live there and get a high-school education. Billie took more of an interest in classes but had little time to study. Work came first.

Rockingham was a stone and wood-frame three-story house, a detention school for homeless, unwanted, and unruly children, many of whom came from wealthy homes. The headmistress demanded hard work, and Billie was singled out because she rebelled. A policeman found her in a park late one night and brought her back to Rockingham. She was dragged to the kitchen, pushed onto the floor, and kicked repeatedly. From then on, Billie was hit across the back with a broomstick whenever the headmistress wasn't satisfied. According to Joan, the beatings occurred daily. It was inhuman and cruel but apparently better than toiling at the laundry and living with Anna and Harry. How severe the beatings were isn't known. Joan's hunger for sympathy and publicity is common knowledge. Her stories changed from year to year. Her book *Portrait of Joan,* published long before tell-all biographies, differs from well-researched biographies and her daughter's *Mommie Dearest.*

Supposedly Billie was caught talking to another girl one day while they were cleaning. The principal dragged her by the hair to an office, closed the door, and threatened, "I'll teach you to work if I have to kill you!" Billie was beaten with a cane until she was barely conscious, but she had the strength to sneak away from Rockingham to Hough's house. Without opening the door, he grumbled, "Who is it?"

"Billie! I want to see my mother."

"Go away. She doesn't live here anymore."

It had been a two-mile walk, but she continued on to the laundry, where she found Anna and, to her surprise, Hal, who had returned. Billie realized she had hit bottom by going back to a hell worse than Rockingham. She returned to school ostensibly because there was nowhere else to go, but there were two other reasons.

The headmistress needed someone to care for the younger children and suggested Billie for the job, which was a form of punishment because Billie would also be responsible for her regular duties and schoolwork. "The kiddies were my only comfort," Joan said. "They were unwanted and neglected, too. I understood those children. I read them bedtime stories and tried to make each one feel loved."

Joan did not mention her other reason for going back to working long hours and occasional beatings. The principal was amazed and disappointed to

find out that one of the wealthiest boys in school wanted a date with Lucille
Cassin. He had his choice of girls but requested permission to take Cinderella
to the dance. Billie was summoned to the main office. The principal gave her
permission, "providing you can find a suitable dress." In a romantic spin,
Billie called Anna.

"Please, Mother, I have to wear something nice. Tommy's very rich."

"We have some unclaimed dresses at the laundry. There's a taffeta one."

"I'll come over and try it on."

"The boy's rich?"

"Very."

"We'll work something out."

Needless to say, Joan Crawford's first date was an important event. It was
glamorized, dramatized, romanticized, and memorized. "I wandered with my
youthful sweetheart through a beautiful yard in which we came upon a
gardenia tree," she said. "The fragrance of the blossoms combined with the
beauty of the occasion and the happiness of love to give me a heart-stirring
thrill."

Joan apparently forgot that gardenias are subtropical flowers and do not
grow in Kansas.

Most likely, it was a neighborhood dance in a gymnasium, but it was the
ballroom of the Waldorf-Astoria to Lucille Cassin, who wore the most beautiful dress in the world. She would always remember her first dance. It had
been a long time since Billie had felt so free and gay, but she kept in perfect
step to the rhythm and felt her energy surge. The boys lined up for a dance
while their girlfriends eyed the good-looking Tommy. No matter how many
different descriptions Joan provided of her first date, one thought remained
true. She was dancing and nothing else mattered. She was alive again.

Billie obeyed her curfew, crawled into bed, and did not close her eyes,
but this night daze was different from the one she experienced on the train
to Arizona. She was sixteen and had only two wishes for her lifetime—to
live with Daddy Cassin and to become a ballerina. It was time to face the
truth. Henry had wanted the best for her and had disappeared because he
could offer nothing. The door to success belonged to the wealthy and what
was the key?

Men!

The blue taffeta frock might have been faded, but the feel of it was soft
and light. Billie was not the same girl in that dress. It wasn't the makeup that
gave her femininity. Tommy's image and his fine friends had a lot to do with
it. He accepted her and danced with her, and she knew he wanted her. Young
men, she concluded, were idiots. Sex was all they thought about, and Billie
oozed it. She thought about her mother, whose attempts at becoming a
well-to-do lady had failed because she was attracted to the wrong kind of men.
If Anna had not been so greedy with Henry, they might still be together and
prospering. Billie had a better understanding of her mother after that starry

night at Rockingham and called her the next day. They went to see Mary Pickford in *Little Lord Fauntleroy*. Over lunch they discussed the dance.

"There was a big band," Billie beamed, "and pretty decorations. It was great. Just great."

"And the boy?"

"He's a lotta fun."

"Are you seeing him again?"

"I suppose so, but he isn't the only guy who wants to take me out."

"You'll need dresses, Lucille. Nice dresses, and I can't afford them."

"Some of the girls at school have stuff they don't wear anymore. They promised I could have them. I don't mind the mending."

Anna took her daughter shopping that afternoon and bought her a dress for $4.95.

Billie's last year at Rockingham was the best. Her popularity with the smart crowd was condoned by the principal, who thought the school could only benefit from the shiny new cars pulling up to the entrance. Lucille was clever with a needle and thread. Although her clothes were hand-me-downs, they were bright and crisp. She was still plump but wore everything with confidence and flair. Spunk and a devil-may-care attitude transformed her plain face. Several boys described "falling under her spell." Billie was ready for anything. Unlike the other girls, she was a good sport and kicked up her heels on the dance floor. Cheek-to-cheek wasn't her style. Neither was going steady or finding a boy to marry, and she was honest about that. This attitude was unusual in 1920, but growing up with Anna and the fighting, scandals, failures, and hardships had a profound effect on Billie. It was a delightful surprise when Billie found out that her mother had moved into a spacious apartment in a nice neighborhood. "Why didn't you tell me?" she asked. "I coulda helped."

"I asked a guy who . . ."

"Not another one!"

"He moved all the heavy stuff."

Billie looked around the apartment for another bum with dirty fingernails.

"I couldn't be bothered with him," Anna said. "He was around at the right time, that's all."

"What about Harry?"

"We're havin' problems."

"Are you getting a divorce?"

"Lucille, that's none of your business."

"If you want me here on weekends, it's my business."

"Harry and I still have to work together at the laundry."

"But you're dating other men?"

"Yeah."

"Why don't you . . ."

"Lucille, you're welcome to come home anytime, but don't tell me how to live my life."

"You married Harry and took on a lot of his debts. That's not fair."

"Look who's talkin'! You're goin' to that fancy school as if I were made of money."

"Doesn't cost you anything," Billie snapped.

Anna glowered at her daughter. "I thought by movin' to a decent neighborhood I might change my luck. Nobody knows us here. I told our next-door neighbor I was a widow and that you were going to Rockingham, but I said nothin' about workin' there, so keep your mouth shut."

Billie enjoyed the spring of 1920. She tolerated the hard work by looking forward to dating and dancing with men who picked up her in their Packards and Pierce Arrows. To impress Anna's neighbors, she always had them park in front of the apartment house while she went to say hello to her mother. Although Billie did not have a typical teenage life, there was a "boy next door" whose only chance to be with her was when he walked her home from school. "I carried her books," he said, "but she didn't talk much. I wanted to ask her out but couldn't compete with the rich guys who drove expensive cars. I didn't even own an old heap, and even if I had, she wouldn't get into it. For a girl who was so popular with the boys, she was shy and never talked about herself. I had a real crush on Lucille Cassin, but I really didn't know her until the night I saw her dance. She was a wildcat. Every move she made was frenzied and provocative. She was a holy terror. At first I didn't know Billie, but she waved, and I stood there staring at her like a lump.

"All I really knew about Lucille Cassin was that she was around sixteen and looked older. Her family didn't have much money, but she was going to overcome that by meeting men who could introduce her to the right people. That was my impression. I began to realize her not talking very much was her lack of education. When the Cassins moved out of my neighborhood, I learned that Lucille had barely passed the sixth grade and would never get any further. She used a seductive smile, wore sheer dresses, and had boundless energy and an untamed nature.

"I didn't see much of her mother, but she had plenty of men, too. We didn't know she was married. Her son kept to himself. He was a good-looking guy who went out every night. I used to see him at the amusement park riding the roller coaster or going into the strip show. He was never with the same girl twice."

"You've completed all the courses, Lucille. I see no reason for you to remain at Rockingham."

"But I haven't learned anything."

The principal looked at Billie sternly. "You've finished the equivalent of a high-school education."

"I haven't had time for classes because of so much work."

"When you came here, it was understood you would have to manage a busy schedule."

"Couldn't I stay for another year and concentrate on . . ."

"I doubt very much that you have an interest in education, Lucille, but I'll arrange for your credits."

"What does that mean?"

"It means you've graduated."

"What will I do?"

"Get a job."

Joan said she was deliberately passed because she had served her purpose at Rockingham as a domestic. This sudden announcement was a shock. She wanted to take dancing lessons, but that wouldn't be possible now.

"What're you crabbin' about?" Hal asked. "You'll come back to the laundry where you belong."

"The hell I will!"

"Lazy bitch."

"Give my love to Harry," she laughed, running out the front door.

She wasted no time looking for a job but hated the idea of going back downtown, where her life in Kansas City started at the New Midland Hotel. Billie reminded herself that if she instinctively searched for Daddy Cassin on the crowded streets, she would be hurt again with another farewell. She took a job selling notions at Kline's Department Store, making $12 a week; she was able to buy her clothes at discount.

"I want you to be well dressed," Anna said, "but I expect you to pay your share of the rent."

"I want to take dancing lessons, too."

"Always thinking of yourself."

"I don't intend to sell notions all my life."

"Lucille, think about marriage. You'll get nowhere as a dancer."

"I don't ever want to get married. I want to be somebody."

"You've had more chances than most girls and failed. We've got a good thing goin' at City Gate."

"You call that a good thing, Mother? Washing and ironing? Having a chief delivery man for a husband? Big-time stuff."

"Nobody can handle you, Lucille. Nothing or nobody is good enough. You have no girlfriends. That doesn't say much for you."

"Girls don't like me. They're jealous and there's nothing I can do about that."

"Running with boys all night doesn't help your reputation."

"As long as I run with the right boys, I don't need girlfriends who talk behind my back."

"Then I repeat: You'll have to get married, Lucille."

"And turn out like you? I wouldn't have to give you so much money for rent if you weren't paying off Harry's debts."

"He's still my husband and his debts are my debts."

Billie went home only to sleep. She met her dates in front of Kline's Department Store after work so that they were obligated to buy her dinner. On weekends she went from one boy to another.

The boy next door never got a chance with Billie. As he sat on his front porch and watched the comings and goings, he wondered if she would ever meet her match. Was she immune to love? How would she handle rejection? Laugh it off? Ignore it?

Or fall apart?

2

FIRST LOVE

In 1921 Kansas City was the hub of bootleg booze, marijuana, sex, cocaine, opium, casinos, cabarets, and cheap stage shows. It had taken two years since Prohibition for bootleggers to thrive in speakeasies, but the "industry" that prospered in New York and Reno flourished out in the open in Kansas City. The meat-packing business brought more than three hundred trains into town every day. Business prospered from farming, automobile distribution, and other profitable industries. Kansas City was known as "the capital of sin."

The high-school kids took advantage of every temptation, but Ray Sterling wasn't one of them. He was well educated and religious, quiet about his achievements, and he rarely dated girls. His blond hair was slicked down and his lips were too thin. But his oval face and dreamy brown eyes gave him presence. Ray was kind and patient, but his classmates considered him a bore. Sometimes he'd attend the country club dances, where he would stand in a corner and observe.

One evening he watched Billie Cassin dance with a guy named Eddie, who loved girls and booze. Handsome, tall, and suave, Eddie could have his pick of young ladies, but he chose Billie because she was an uninhibited tiger. Holding the Cassin girl in your arms attracted everyone's attention, and Ray Sterling was no exception. She wasn't the prettiest or the best-dressed girl. In fact, Billie was overweight and wore too much makeup. Ray was, however, impressed by her boundless energy as she danced the black bottom and the cakewalk with a frenzy, not caring that her thighs were exposed. He knew all about her. He knew the gossip about Lucille Cassin was true, but underneath the heavy eye shadow, layers of rouge, and caked lipstick, he saw a frightened little girl.

Ray was staring without realizing it. She smiled at him and got no reaction. Billie caught his eye several times that evening, but he made no attempt to dance with her. When the ballroom got crowded, Ray walked out onto the terrace for some fresh air.

"You're Ray Sterling," she said.

He was startled. "Hello, Lucille."

"Remember me?"

"Budd Park, three years ago."

"You were on the Northeast football team, right?"

"Nice seeing you again," he said, walking down the steps.

"Don't you dance, Ray?"

"Occasionally."

"How about this one?"

"No, thanks. It's getting late."

"Why do you come to a dance and stand around?"

"To watch everyone having a good time and to listen to the music."

She laughed. "That never occurred to me."

"What?"

"To sit out a dance."

"I admire your energy."

"Once I get started, I can't stop."

"You're a very good dancer," he said, putting his hands in his pockets.

"That's what I want to do."

"Professionally?"

"Yes, if I can make a buck doing it."

"Don't you have any other interests?"

"Like what?"

"Reading, for example."

"I can't make money reading a book! I work all day and dance all night. Anything wrong with that?"

"Not if that's what you want to do for the rest of your life," he shrugged, strolling down the path behind the clubhouse.

She followed. "Why don't you like me, Ray?"

"I never said that."

"But you don't. You were scowling at me all night."

"I think you're unhappy."

"Don't feel sorry for me, Ray Sterling!"

"You feel sorry for yourself," he said, looking over at her.

"Do I look unhappy?" she asked, lifting her chin with a broad smile, hands on hips.

"That's what I mean. You're always laughing."

"And you never do!" she said sarcastically, walking away.

"I admire your dancing, Lucille. Have you taken lessons?" he asked, sitting down on a park bench.

"Whenever I can afford to . . ."

"You're a natural, but what happens when the music stops? Like now. We're arguing because you're on the defensive."

"So?"

"There's more to life than dancing, Lucille."

"I'm not happy doing anything else."

"How do you know?"

"What did you have in mind?" she asked, sitting next to him.

"Everyone should take time to read and talk."

"At the school I went to, they didn't give me time to read, and I was beaten if I talked."

"I'm sorry."

"Stop feeling sorry for me! I'm very happy!"

"I was reading just the other day that happiness is like a butterfly. The more you chase it, the more it will elude you. But if you turn your attention to other things, it comes and softly sits on your shoulder."

"Too bad I've never seen you dance or smile," she said, walking back to the ballroom. "Bye, Ray."

He sat alone for a while, thinking about Billie Cassin, the last girl in the world he'd pick for himself. She was everything he disliked. She was loud, cheap, gaudy, vulgar, brazen, loose, and uneducated. But she had the most beautiful and piercing eyes he had ever seen. They spoke to him of sadness, fright, and bitterness, but that didn't lessen their magic. She undressed him with those blue eyes and stabbed him in the soul.

Ray understood why Billie was so popular. Part of her hypnotic allure was an inborn, radiant quality that was never nurtured. Apparently, Billie wasn't aware of her worth. She covered up the cute freckles, pink lips, and tanned cheeks with cosmetics, drank whiskey to be accepted, and, he concluded, was running away instead of running around.

They often ran into each other at the country club dances. She always made a point of saying hello, and he would nod. Once or twice Billie sat out a dance with him, but the conversation was light—the weather, his courses at Northeast, her job at Kline's. Then came the night of reckoning at the Jack O'Lantern Club. Billie planned to enter the dance contest with a hundred other couples. Her date was in the car spiking their drinks when she noticed Ray standing with a lovely girl.

"Are you competing?" Billie asked.

"No. The fox-trot is my speed."

"See ya," she said, motioning to her date. "Give me a sip before we start." She took a big gulp and laughed. "Whew, that should do it!"

The music started, and the couples began hopping to "Running Wild," a new song by Harrington Gibbs. The boys in the combo knew Billie Cassin was going for this one. Her partner was good, but he had a hard time keeping up with her rollicking tempo. Never off the beat, she devoured her competition and clung to the grand-prize trophy. Billie looked to Ray for recognition but he had disappeared. She found him sitting alone near the door. "Where's your girlfriend?" she asked.

"I don't have a girlfriend, Lucille."

"Well, do you still think dancing doesn't pay off?"

"You can't buy food with that trophy."

"No, but it means I'm a damn good dancer."

"I've never seen a better one."

"Ha! So, you're finally admitting I have a chance."

"Lucille . . ."

"Billie, for Christ's sake. Do you want a sip of my drink?"

"I don't care for alcohol, thank you."

"Neither do I, but it's the thing to do."

"Look, Billie, I hope you make it as a dancer. If anyone can do it, you can."

She put the drink aside. "You really mean that, don't you?"

"Yes, I do. But don't you want to better yourself?"

"Sure!"

"I have to go, Billie. Congratulations."

"Wait a minute. I'd like to talk."

"I have a date, and so do you."

"So, take her home and pick me up in an hour."

Ray shook his head but said, "All right."

Billie's date was disappointed and aggravated that she wanted to go home so soon. "I don't get it!" he said, putting his arm around her.

"What's there to get?" She jumped out of his car. "Call me."

Ray showed up a few minutes later. "We're not fooling anybody," he told her. "The guy you were with is parked around the corner."

"So what?"

"It's not nice."

"I feel like talking, Ray, and you're the only one who's interested in me."

"You have more boys than any girl in town."

"I wasn't referring to that. I mean, you seem to care what happens to me . . . what's going to become of me."

They drove around for a while. He showed her where he lived and then parked on a hillside overlooking the Missouri River. "Something wrong with your car?" she asked.

"Would you rather go for a drive?"

"No, but it makes so much noise!"

"It's old, but runs good and I repair it myself. Otherwise, I wouldn't have a car."

"Can we be friends, Ray? Can we go out once in a while?"

"I'm not your type, Billie."

"You really mean I'm not *your* type. I took a good look at your date in that prissy dress with the high lacy neck and little rosebuds. She's probably on the honor roll and goes to Sunday school."

"What's wrong with that?"

"Are you going steady?"

"Billie, I don't have a girlfriend. I don't want one. She's a classmate and a nice girl."

"Do I have to look like her for you to take me out? What's wrong with me, Ray?"

"You're trying too hard, Billie. You're pushing."

"With you?" she asked, holding back tears.

"In general. You have a pretty face. Why cover it with all that makeup? And your dresses are too short."

"I have nice legs. Everyone says so!"

"You don't have to flaunt them, Billie. And the low necklines aren't necessary."

She began to cry, but Ray didn't try to comfort her or apologize. "I'm trying to tell you, Billie, there's no need for you to paint your face or show yourself off. Even if you want to be a dancer, don't you want to be admired for good taste and a fair amount of intellect? Don't you want to be a lady?"

"I suppose so," she sobbed.

"I know more about you than you think, Billie. It's been tough, hasn't it?"

"Yes . . ."

"I'll be your friend."

She wiped her nose on her jacket sleeve. "That would be swell, Ray. Do you really mean it?"

"I want you to have more confidence in yourself. Tone down the makeup and buy some plain dresses. If you'd like, I'll drop off a book. If you don't like it, we can discuss another."

Joan said she poured her heart out to Ray. It was the first time in her life she had opened up with anybody. "I told him about Daddy Cassin and the theater, the gash in my foot, the work at St. Agnes, and the beatings at Rockingham. I told him about my mother and Hal. We sat in his car and talked all night; he just listened. I wanted to be somebody. Even if I got an education, my heart would be in the theater—on the stage. I had to prove myself. I told him about the ballerina and the gypsy dancers. I expected him to laugh, but he took me seriously."

Billie got home around dawn. Ray didn't touch her. There was no good-night kiss. He hadn't held her hand or asked for a date. She was exhausted from dancing, talking, and sobbing. She slept soundly for a few hours and woke up to a room filled not only with sunshine but also with love for Ray Sterling. The trophy on her dresser had a different significance, too. It was a reward for a job well done, not something to be flaunted. There was no need to remind anyone she was a winner. If she were worthy, there would be other trophies.

A few days later she called Ray. "Are you still speaking to me?"

"Of course. How about a drive in my jalopy?"

Billie toned down her makeup and wore a fresh cotton dress. They went to the park and talked. "You'll have to be patient with me, Ray. I'm going to do my best to improve myself, but you know I can't change. Not really."

"I don't expect miracles."

"Did you just smile?"

"I think so."

"Maybe I can make you laugh someday."

"Which book do you want?"

"How do I know until I read them?"

"No novels, Billie. There's one on social graces, one on American history, and a good one on vocabulary. Take one at a time, and we'll talk about it."

"You'd make a great teacher, Ray."

"I hope so. I thought that's what I wanted. Now I'm not sure."

"I thought you had your life all planned."

Ray Sterling finally laughed. "I think you're way ahead of me. Dancing is your goal without question. My future is uncertain. So I envy you in that respect."

She wanted to reach out and hug Ray but asked instead to see the books. "These don't look so hard."

"Do you like music besides jazz?"

"Well, I only remember the ballet in Lawton. And band concerts."

"That's a start," he said. "You'll learn to relax with soothing music. It will stimulate your mind and give you a sense of serenity and confidence. Good music is tranquil."

"Tranquil?"

"Soothing . . . peaceful."

"Oh."

"As for the books, if you have any questions . . ."

"I'll have lots. Are you going to the country club dance tomorrow night?"

"I don't know."

"If you're there, I'll sit one out."

Billie continued to date other boys every night and wore out her dancing shoes in Kansas City's hot spots. She managed to set aside time for reading and for listening to phonograph records loaned to her by Ray. Classics and ballads depressed Billie, but Ray wanted her to be acquainted with them. "You don't have to like something to learn about it," he explained. "I sign up for subjects I hate, but without some knowledge, how would I know what people are talking about? I didn't like the sight of string beans, but I tried them. I don't eat them, but at least I know why and can turn them down for a good reason."

"I hate life."

"Why? Because you have to take the bad with the good?"

"Christ, that's all I've been doin', with not much good."

"I said you felt sorry for yourself, Billie, but try to look at it this way. Scrubbing and doing laundry is no fun, but you're an expert. I'm sure your house is cleaner than mine because you wouldn't have it any other way. And your dresses are pressed and neat. That's more than I can say for a lot of girls."

"I never thought of it that way."

"If you're going to be a dancer, be admired offstage as well as onstage. Be a good listener, because you'll learn and people will think they're interesting. There are many empty-headed dancers who assume their faces and bodies are more important than anything else. Don't be one of them. Show them you didn't neglect your education. Gentlemen will be proud to introduce you to people outside of the theater. That's important."

"You're a gentleman, Ray."

"We're just friends."

"I know you want a virgin!" she almost blurted out, but Billie couldn't discuss sex with him. It was an embarrassing subject because of her promiscuity. She wondered about Ray. He was one of the few boys who were not affected by the opposite sex. Always involved in homework or responsibilities as president of his class and school clubs, Ray was content. Aside from their drives in the country and chats at dances, he asked Billie on a formal date only once. He managed a fox-trot at the Kansas City College ball and then gave her freedom to dance with others. An hour or so later she'd reappear for a glass of soda with him. How difficult it was for Ray to take her home knowing another boy was waiting in a car with its headlights off can only be imagined. He probably felt disappointment rather than jealousy. The late nights, booze, and sex would show on her face and body. Ray knew little about the theater, but common sense dictated that only young and vivacious girls were picked to attract an audience. Billie was burning herself out.

Billie's "lessons" continued in 1922.

"Billie, don't gulp. It isn't polite."

"But I'm thirsty."

"Keep your lips together and sip."

"Maybe you're right, Ray. I won't get drunk so fast."

"Sit with your knees together, Billie."

"It's hot. I need some ven . . . venti . . ."

"Ventilation?"

"That's the word, Ray!"

"I could hear you laughing across the ballroom."

"So?"

"Billie, the people standing next to you weren't deaf."

"The music was loud."

"So were you."

"I'm not gettin' nowhere."

"Anywhere."

"What's the difference?"

"A double negative."

"A what?!"

"Not getting nowhere translated means you *are* getting somewhere."

"But I'm not, Ray! How can I, sellin' notions at Kline's Department Store? I'd leave, but jobs are hard to find and gettin' a discount means a lot."

"You'd get a good job if you went to college."

She laughed. "College?"

"You have the qualifications, Billie."

"That piece of paper from Rockingham means nothin'. It's a joke."

"Give it a try."

She laughed out loud again but covered her mouth when Ray glared at her. "Who's gonna pay the tuition, smarty-pants?"

"You'll have to work for it."

"Forget the whole thing. I'd flunk every course."

"You might be qualified for a working-girl scholarship."

"What's that?"

"We're in a postwar recession."

"Whatever what means . . ."

Ray suggested Stephens College for girls in Columbia, Missouri, 125 miles away. Billie's false credits were adequate, and Rockingham verified she was a reliable worker.

Anna was reluctant. "You're eighteen, Lucille. It's time to make up your mind what you want, and school is a waste of time. You're doin' well at Kline's, goin' out with rich guys, and livin' in a nice place."

"I want to get a good job."

"Plenty of those around."

"I want more."

Anna scowled. "You always do, but you don't care how it hurts us. How can Hal and I stay where we are without your share of the rent? Ever think of that?"

"Moving there was your idea."

"We're used to a better way of livin' now."

"If that's your idea of good living, I sure would hate to be poor," Billie smirked.

"What do you expect to do about clothes?"

"I got enough to get by for a while."

"What're you gonna study?"

"Secretary stuff . . . typing, shorthand . . ."

Anna stopped folding the laundry. "That's hell of a lot more respectable than dancin'!"

Billie ignored the sarcastic comment and began packing for college. She had doubts and sometimes wanted to back out, but her apprehension was assuaged by Ray's constant encouragement.

In September 1922, Ray drove her in his black jalopy to Union Station. "The last time I was here," she said, "Daddy Cassin and I were scared to death. Gosh, that seems so long ago."

"You'll be leaving that all behind."

"Do you think so, Ray?"

"If you apply yourself."

Ray didn't kiss her, but he smiled and waited for the St. Louis local to disappear. He saw her wave until the train was out of sight, and Ray Sterling felt an emptiness he hadn't expected. To be in love with someone who is wrong for you is painful and useless, but reality and common sense are no cure. Fortunately, Ray had made up his mind to be an attorney; he buried himself in preparing for law school. He missed seeing Billie dance at the country club and the Jack O'Lantern, as well as their drives along the muddy Missouri River, and he worried that her desire for men might destroy her last chance.

Columbia was buzzing with students from the prim Christian College and, to Billie's delight, the coeducational University of Missouri. She had expected nothing but a sedate and boring Stephens College for girls.

The counselor helped her select the proper course. "Lucille, we have you scheduled for bookkeeping, typing, shorthand, and English composition. Religion is required. May I suggest health and psychology?"

"Psychology? Okay," she replied, knowing Ray would be impressed.

"Home economics is useful."

"I guess so. Do you have a dancing class?"

"We call it 'rhythm.' "

"I don't care what it's called."

"You'll work in the dining room in Main Hall and live upstairs with the other girls on working scholarships."

Billie looked at her schedule, which was carefully planned to allow time for all activities. She tried to concentrate on her studies but found them difficult and boring. English composition was dull, and psychology baffled her. "I don't get it," she complained to a roommate. "My boss'll dictate and I'll type it. He knows what to say and how to say it. Why do I have to learn this crap?"

"Sometimes you'll have to revise and correct."

"And psychology?" Billie asked.

"That will help you understand people."

"What's the big deal?"

"Are you honestly interested in secretarial work, Lucille?"

"I'd rather be a dancer."

"So, go out and have some fun!"

"In this town?" Billie laughed.

"Some of the girls go to the College Inn."

"Sounds like Sunday school."

"They dance until two or three in the morning. Some of them even drink."

"No kidding? How do they get away with it?"

"I'm not sure, but the watchman at the back door lets them in and doesn't say anything."

"Sounds too easy. There has to be a catch."

Waiting tables in the dining room gave Billie a chance to listen in on the hush-hush talk while leaning over to serve the mashed potatoes. Within a few days she joined a small group of girls and went to the College Inn. Besides the cozy collegiate atmosphere, it was not much different from the country club in Kansas City. Boys with slicked-down hair and bow ties stood around in groups, holding glasses of spiked punch. Once on the dance floor, Billie Cassin was the only girl in the room. She had no inhibitions. She flew and bounced to the music, flirted outrageously, and ignored the girls who'd brought her to the College Inn. She didn't need them anymore.

With a new bobbed hairdo, rolled-down stockings, and a skirt that whirled to her waist, Billie left nothing to the imagination. There was no question who the boys wanted, and not just for her dancing. She said very little about herself, and the boys didn't care. For Billie, dancing and sex were fun without an afterthought. No obligations, no promises, and no complications.

Billie was a favorite with the Phi Delta Theta fraternity and was a regular at weekend parties. People who remembered from her college days said she loved to do the hot dances on the table in the hallway. Some of the parties were wild and continued upstairs until after dawn. Billie was described as a very ambitious girl who knew what she wanted and would do anything to get it. She preferred the company of boys and thought nothing of being the only girl who danced and drank with a fraternity in their living quarters. She appeared to have no moral standards at all.

Billie attempted to study and pass her tests but was totally unprepared. She did not have the patience or discipline for the drudgery of bookkeeping and shorthand. She was, however, an excellent worker who never complained. But in class sat a restless student with too much energy for desk work.

In late October Ray called to tell her he had gotten a scholarship. "I'm going to the University of Kansas."

"I wish I had your brains. When are you coming to see me?"

"Is this weekend convenient?"

"Swell, Ray. I have good news, too. The girls want me to join a sorority. I'll tell you all about it when you get here."

Ray hung up the telephone. He knew he had done the right thing by urging her to go to college. A sorority would give Billie a feeling of belonging and acceptance. If her classmates liked her, perhaps she was a different girl. He looked forward to seeing for himself and giving her inspiration.

It's doubtful that Lucille Cassin would have adapted to college even if she had tried. She was a loner, a nonconformist, but being a member of a sorority meant a great deal to her—then there would be very little distinction between her and the girls who could afford Stephens. *That* was an accomplishment. She had made it into their world. Was it possible to be so happy? Ray was coming to Columbia. They would celebrate their good fortunes. She might even be good enough now for Ray to kiss her, and if he did, they wouldn't stop there. Few boys did. All Ray needed was some stimulation. She hadn't thought much about it, but Ray was a *challenge*. Billie had never been with someone she loved. Was the thrill any different? Better? Did it last forever?

She had the urge to be more optimistic about studying. At mealtime, she was more outgoing and friendly, brisk and cheerful. She thought the students being served approved of her despite the uniform.

"I should have known better," Joan said. "A friend told me I had been blackballed by one member of the sorority, Josephine McCarthy, because I waited on tables. They had to be very, very particular."

It was a blow to Billie but not a surprise. Her friend said, "The rest of us wanted you. I'm sorry. She's my sorority sister, but Josephine's very stuck up."

"I know. I wait on her every day."

"I think she's jealous, Lucille, because you get all the boys."

"Does it matter?"

"I don't want you to feel bad about having to work your way through college, that's all. It can't be helped, and Josephine knows that."

Billie shrugged. "I don't care. I don't give a good goddamn."

"Maybe next time."

"I'll get over it."

Joan never did. "For a long time, when I'd be discouraged about some setback and ready to give up, I only had to think of Josephine McCarthy and I'd be inflated with ambition and determination again."

Ray made light of the sorority rejection. "I was happy for you, but social clubs aren't important."

"That's because you don't like them."

"The girls gossip and giggle at their meetings. The boys play cards and drink beer. They plan dances and parties and think as a group."

"But . . ."

"Are you going to allow one snob to get you down? What's important is getting an education."

"I suppose so."

"Have you met any nice boys here?"

"Yeah, a guy from Phi Delta Theta. Since I can't get into a sorority I thought I'd try a frat! We're going to a party there, and I have some swell friends at the College Inn, the Century Club, the Daniel Boone Tavern and . . ."

Ray forced a smile. "I don't have to be entertained, Lucille. It was a beautiful autumn drive from Kansas City. The leaves are changing color. How about a picnic in the country?"

"Sure, but at night the gang's lookin' forward to meetin' you!"

"How do you like shorthand and typing?"

"I'm not sure about being a secretary. Sittin' all day . . . and I can't spell or punctuate."

"English composition will help."

She had skipped that class so often she avoided discussing the course with him. Ray checked into the Columbia Hotel. As he was getting dressed for the evening, he decided that seeing Billie was a mistake. Helping her get over the disappointment of not being accepted into a sorority was important, but he wasn't looking forward to the nightlife. Sharing Billie again was a letdown. He was accustomed to watching her dance with other boys and waiting until she sat one out, but he wanted to have long talks with her, stroll around the campus, and discuss the future.

When he called for her that evening, Ray felt a sting of humiliation. She wore cheap bangles and beads on her neck, wrists, and ears. Her dress was ostentatious and vulgar. Lucille Cassin stood out, all right, with Stephens' simplicity and charm as the backdrop. Her school chums were curious to see what Billie's boyfriend looked like. They didn't expect the young gentleman who got out of the jalopy to open the door for her. There was no kiss or mad embrace, and he pulled slowly away from the curb. He was a square but a well-dressed one.

There are several accounts of what happened that night, but all agree that Billie lured Josephine McCarthy's boyfriend away from her by dancing with him until she was ready to return the reluctant young man to the girl who had blackballed her. No one doubted who won the final round.

Ray followed Billie from club to club, paid the cover charges and other expenses, sat alone while she bounced, swirled, and wiggled in her flashy dress, and worried that he wouldn't get her back to the Main Hall by midnight curfew.

Surprisingly, it was Billie who reminded him. "It's eleven-thirty." At the dormitory entrance, they talked in his parked car. "I have to work tomorrow, Ray, but drop by in the afternoon for a while and then we'll go out for some fun around seven." He waited until she was safely inside the Main Hall. Then Ray heard a car engine start and looked in his rearview mirror. Billie was doing the same thing to him that she had done to many poor saps in Kansas City! He drove back to the Columbia Hotel without waiting to see her sneaking out to meet another man. No wonder the curfew was so important. Was she going back to the dance or to a lovers' lane? Ray didn't want to know the truth. He had seen enough. Billie was the same girl. He didn't approve, but she was happy and doing what she wanted to do, which was more than he could say for himself. The world was made up of people who died without having lived. How many of us, he asked himself, aren't afraid to reach out for what we want—to make our own path and ignore the one beaten by the masses? Right or wrong, Billie wasn't standing still despite the detours, barriers, and ugly gossip.

The next day he walked around the campus, spent a few hours in the library, and peeked in to see a weary and hung-over Billie. "Maybe you'd like to relax tonight," he said politely. "We'll have a quiet dinner and take a drive."

"You gotta be kiddin', Ray!"

He pretended to enjoy himself. Billie was showing off more than usual but not to attract the college crowd, and he knew it. She was trying to impress him. Their eyes met often, and he danced the slow dances with her. He listened to the lies about her good grades and how she owed it all to him.

"You have the strength, Lucille, but not the courage."

"That doesn't make sense," she mumbled, resting her head on his chest. "Have you gotten taller? The last time we danced . . ."

"Last time we danced," he interrupted, "you fluttered around me like a firefly."

She laughed. "It's been swell, Ray. Your comin' here means a lot to me."

"I'm driving back to Kansas City tonight, Lucille."

"Why?"

"Homework and studying."

"What time are you leavin'?"

"After I've seen you home."

Good-bye was different this time. He kissed her, and they held hands for a moment. Feelings had deepened. Ray had mixed emotions. He waved and began the long drive back to Kansas City. His heart raced as he thought about holding Billie in his arms, despite the lingering scent of Billie's harsh perfume. He wasn't sure about what might have happened if circumstances had been different. Leaving a day early was the only way to avoid finding out. As for Billie, she wanted Ray more than ever. Her friends at Stephens liked Ray. He had class and wisdom. And he was loyal to the Cassin wildcat. They were like an old married couple who had gone their separate ways but would always be together. Josephine McCarthy told a friend in strict confidence that Ray was perfect, but he didn't talk to her when "the tramp" ran off with her boyfriend.

Thanksgiving came and went. A cold winter set in, and snow fell. Planning for Christmas and New Year's dominated December—red and green decorations, parties, presents, twinkling lights on pine trees, and . . . midterm exams.

"It was no use," Joan said. "I knew it was hopeless. I never would have left Stephens otherwise. I didn't mind the work or the snobs. I'd known nothing else since I could remember. It made no sense to stay and fail the exams. I never had a chance."

Shortly before school closed down for the holidays, she wired Ray collect to meet her. Without telling anyone else, Billie left Stephens College and walked to the railroad station. Standing on the platform, waiting for the train, she recognized Dr. James Wood, the distinguished-looking principal of Stephens. Billie tried to look inconspicuous, standing with her back to him from a safe distance.

"Lucille Cassin, isn't it?" he asked politely.

"Yes, sir."

"Going home early for the holidays?"

"Yes, sir."

"Good. I'll have someone to talk to on the ride to Kansas City."

Billie might have kept her secret from him, but Wood was suspicious and she knew it. There was nothing to be ashamed of, she decided, and blurted out, "I'm not coming back to Stephens."

He nodded. "Would you like to tell me about it?"

She told Dr. Wood about Rockingham. "I wasn't allowed to attend classes until my work was finished. How could I learn anything?"

"That's no excuse to quit, Lucille."

"I know when I'm licked," she sobbed.

"You can do anything if you want to. I've heard that you're a very ambitious young lady."

"Dr. Wood, I want to be a dancer."

"There's nothing wrong with that, Lucille, but you'll have to make a living in the meantime."

"That's why I came to Stephens."

They discussed her future on the way to Kansas City, and with all the drawbacks, he wanted her to try again. "I have three rules for successful living," he said. "Never quit a job until you finish it. That's number one. Number two? The world isn't interested in your problems. When your problems are the greatest, let your laughter be the merriest. And number three is, if you find you can do a job, let it alone, because you're already bigger than the job, and that means you will shrink down to its size. If the job is impossible, you may never get it accomplished, but you'll grow by trying. I'll jot them down for you."

Billie said she'd think about it over the holidays.

"Dr. Wood was a wonderful person," Joan said. "He had a heart of gold. Everyone liked him. I think he was responsible for the working scholarships, although he was too modest a man to take credit. He was a dear soul—I'd refer to him as Daddy Wood. We corresponded long after I arrived in Hollywood."

Financial problems had forced Anna to give up her lovely apartment. She and Hal moved back to the laundry, and Billie didn't care. She would help her mother, go out at night, and see as much of Ray as possible. He had met her at the train and spoken to Dr. Wood, who said everything would be all right.

Anna told her daughter, "One of these days you'll realize this school shit is a waste of time. Money for clothes, money for the train, money, money, money!"

"I used what I earned at Kline's."

"Yeah, but that wasn't enough, and you know it!"

"The principal wants me to go back."

"Yeah? Well, let him pay your way."

Hal offered his usual comment: "Don't expect to have a swell time over the holidays, college girl. We need help here at the laundry."

Billie could handle her nagging mother and sarcastic brother, but when Harry Hough shuffled out of the bedroom, her mind was made up.

She was going back to Stephens.

"You have a friend in Dr. Wood," Ray emphasized. "He'll do all he can to guide you."

"I feel better about the whole thing, knowin' he's there, but I can't stand shorthand and English and typing and . . ."

"That's nothing to be ashamed of. Discuss it with the counselor, and she'll change your courses next semester."

But there was no need to revise Billie's schedule. Frustrated and terrified of failing her midterm exams, she went to Dr. Wood, who looked over her records carefully. He also checked with St Agnes and Rockingham. "I have only admiration for you, Lucille," he said. "It's inconceivable how you got this far academically. I can see what you're up against, and I'm sorry I didn't know the details when I insisted you come back."

"Now you know why I can't face those exams and fail."

"There is no failure when one can face one's self in the mirror and say, 'I tried as hard as I could.' Remember that. Kipling wrote that success and failure are imposters. Treat both the same." Dr. Wood processed Billie's discharge papers; he was sincere about wanting to hear from her. "Get a job," he said, "take dancing lessons, and believe in yourself, Lucille."

For the second and last time she left Stephens College. Anna knew nothing about her daughter's problems. She assumed it was money. "My mother always thought about the almighty dollar," Joan said. "She thought of me as a workhorse, someone to pay the bills. She had faith in Hal and failed to see that he couldn't get along without her."

Billie went back to the laundry despite Anna's reconciliation with Harry Hough. Her salvation was Ray Sterling. They were closer than ever, but their long drives did not end up in the backseat of his car. His friends agreed he was in love with her. Billie probably would not have settled down even if Ray had confessed his feelings for her. In several interviews, Joan gave the impression that she was never intimate with her "childhood sweetheart." "I would never have gotten to Hollywood if he'd wanted me, but he didn't."

Billie thought it was both corny and amusing when Ray won an essay contest sponsored by the Women's Christian Temperance Union. His topic was alcohol's contribution to the deterioration of Western culture. She never laughed behind his back, however, and defended Ray when the fast crowd made fun of him.

It didn't take Billie Cassin long to catch up with her old friends. She worked diligently at the laundry and partied late into the night. Harry considered his stepdaughter to be a cheap whore. It seems likely that he wanted her, too. They fought every day until she told him, "I'm nineteen years old, making a livin' and payin' rent!"

"People are talking about you, Billie. I don't like it."

"Tough shit!"

"As long as you're livin' with us, I have a right to . . ."

"A right to me?" she laughed. "You filthy bastard! I'd rather move out!"

"If you don't," he raged, looking at her deep cleavage, "I'll throw you out!"

A job wrapping packages at Kline's Department Store didn't last long. She applied at the Bell Telephone Company and hated it. Next, Billie tried the department stores—salesgirl, package wrapper, clerk—but making enough money to afford a place of her own was impossible. No girls were willing to share an apartment with the notorious Billie Cassin. Their parents wouldn't allow it.

She detested going home to the laundry apartment even for a few hours of sleep. Anna demanded she give up the idea of being a dancer "and get to work!" Harry demanded she stop drinking and running around with boys. "I can smell booze on your breath!" He sneered. "And I hate what you look like."

"So don't look," Billie snapped.

"Harry worries about you," Anna exclaimed.

"I know. He's worried about not gettin' his share of the rent."

"Your brother's got a job at the Pitt Company and he's movin' out. With all your talk and braggin', he's makin' something of himself."

"As a clerk?" Billie laughed.

"At least he's on his own!" Anna said.

"Don't cry, Mother. He'll be back"

Billie began staying out all night, managing to avoid Hough, who left at dawn to deliver laundry. Anna either didn't notice or preferred not to be bothered. The tension mounted until Harry threatened to lock the door when he went to sleep. One night, Billie found the warning to be a reality, but she shrugged it off and went back to a party. After the last dance, she went to the ladies' room for the night. She sobbed herself to sleep and didn't hear voices until someone touched her shoulder and asked, "Are you all right?"

Looking up, she recognized the two singers who had entertained that evening. "I'm Billie Cassin, and I don't have a home anymore," she cried.

"We're the Cook sisters. I'm Nellie and this is Lucille."

"Do you think the cleaning lady will throw me out?"

"Why don't you come home with us?" Nellie smiled. "Mother won't mind. She's used to it."

"Are you sure?" Billie asked, getting up from the dirty floor.

"Yes. C'mon."

Despite the late hour, Daisy Cook greeted them at the door. They sat around the kitchen table drinking coffee. Billie listened to the girls describe the crowd's reaction to their show. "We've been asked to sing at the Ivanhoe next week," Nellie exclaimed.

"Oh, I'm delighted," her mother said. "I'll get to work on your dresses tomorrow." Daisy said very little to shy Billie but was warm and friendly. In the morning Billie found herself alone with Daisy, who was making breakfast. "You have a nice house, Mrs. Cook."

"It's all right. Lots of room, so you're welcome to stay."

"But you don't know anything about me, Mrs. Cook."

"Call me Daisy."

"You have a right to know somethin'. I want to be a dancer, but my mother isn't nice like you are, Daisy. She fights me all the time. I worked my way through three schools until I couldn't take it anymore. I came home and my stepfather tried to . . . tried to . . ."

"You poor thing," Daisy said, giving her a warm hug.

"How did Nell and Lucille get started?"

"Singing in places like the Edward Hotel, where you met them last night. They studied and practiced very hard. They still do. In this business you never stop rehearsing."

Billie looked around the big house, which was located in an exclusive neighborhood. "Guess the girls make big money," she sighed.

"Not yet, but I figure it's worth the sacrifice to impress men who can help the girls. You have to look successful to be successful. I design their gowns. Beautiful, aren't they?"

"Very. Nell and Lucille are very lucky to have a mother like you. I wish I did."

"Then you'll have to do it on your own."

Billie's eyes filled with tears. "I've tried," she wept. "I don't know what to do, where to go . . ."

"You stay here for a while." Daisy smiled.

Ray brought Billie's clothes to the Cook house. "I told Anna where you are," he said.

"As if she cares."

"It was the decent thing to do."

"I'm not sending her money, Ray. Don't ask me to."

"That's up to you," he said, "but I hope you won't give up the job at Emery, Bird and Thayer's Department Store."

"I hate it, but knowing Harry isn't going to get a cent of my pay makes it almost fun."

"Would you like to go to the Ivanhoe for the girls' opening?"

"Would I?"

"I made reservations."

"Reservations? Nell and Lucille are really in the big time!"

"They're talented," he reminded her.

"So am I, but my mother isn't like Daisy!"

Ray wanted to tell Billie that the Cook girls didn't run around with boys all night, that they had little money, but used it wisely. Billie had found a family at last, but the envy she had for Nellie and Lucille overshadowed her good fortune. Daisy was willing to give, and Billie was ready to take advantage of her.

Ray, however, invited Mrs. Cook to join them at the Ivanhoe and picked up the tab. He didn't think Billie was paying room and board, and he wanted to show his gratitude. She was already wearing the sisters' hand-me-downs, and he approved of Daisy's good taste.

The Kansas City elite crowded into the ballroom of the Ivanhoe to enjoy fine food served by Negro waiters wearing red tuxedos. The orchestra played a variety of music, and Billie danced the fast ones while Ray watched.

"She's pretty good," Daisy commented.

"I think so," he said.

"Popular with the boys, too, and they all seem to know her. Don't you dance the Black Bottom?"

Ray shrugged. "Too fast for me."

Just as Daisy was about to change his mind, a middle-aged, flashy-looking man came over to the table. She introduced him to Ray. "Mr. Belasco is a theatrical producer. He's here to see Lucille and Nellie."

"I'd like to handle their bookings," he said, looking out at the dance floor.

"They'll be thrilled!" Daisy said.

"By the way," David Belasco said. "Who's the girl dancing like a tornado out there? She's with you, isn't she?"

"Billie Cassin. She wants to dance professionally."

"I can use her."

When the orchestra played a slow song, Billie sat down. The "old man" asked her to dance. "Not a waltz," she scowled. Belasco told Daisy he would be in touch with her regarding the contract. That was her cue to take him aside "What about Billie?" she whispered.

"It's too bad her manners aren't as pleasing as her dancing," he replied, "but I'm still interested."

Daisy sat down again and smiled at Billie, who asked, "Who's yer square friend? A waltz! Christ!"

Ray cringed.

"Belasco's an influential man in the theater," Daisy replied. "He's going to handle the girls, and I can't wait to tell them."

"Yeah?"

"He'd like to audition you, too, Billie."

"You kiddin'?"

"No."

"I'll be damned!"

Ray took her hand. "Mr. Belasco was watching you very intently," he said. "I think he liked the dress, too. Why don't you wear it for the audition?"

"Is it jazzy enough?"

"He obviously liked everything about you."

"Yes," Daisy said, "and maybe the dress will bring you good luck."

"I'm glad we didn't waltz," Billie said. "I might have stepped all over his feet!"

"Your name, honey?" Belasco asked, sucking on a cigar butt.

"Lucille LeSueur."

"You sure picked a good one," he laughed. "Okay, show me what you can do." After a few steps he said, "You'll do. Twenty bucks a week. We open in Springfield, Missouri, next week. Maybe we'll be in Chicago before Thanksgiving."

Billie called Ray to pick her up in front of Emery, Bird and Thayer's Department Store. "I quit my job," she told him. "Tomorrow I'm posin' with the chorus girls to promote cars or somethin'. Five bucks, Ray! Five bucks for standin' still!"

He was happy for her, but, as with every good-bye, there was a feeling of loneliness and frustration. Regardless of the outcome, they would never be the same couple again. He knew the taste of dancing onstage would change Billie. He also knew this final parting would give him the strength to pursue his own goals without the interruptions of wanting to tame the tiger with a Bible.

Ray drove her to Union Station and said, "Go for it!"

The Cooks, however, were in for a shock. "It was probably the next day when we realized what Billie had done," Nellie said. "She had taken not only the dress I lent her but all the costumes we had been working so hard to finish for our orchestra tour. She robbed us blind." The next time they saw Billie Cassin was on the silver screen.

Billie was one of sixteen chorus girls who danced behind Katharine Emerine's vocal interpretation of New York operettas. The show folded two weeks later. Joan said Miss Emerine singled her out. "If you ever get to Chicago, look me up. I can help you find work." The other girls, however, were grateful for the same offer.

Billie had no choice but to return to Kansas City; however, she did not call Ray or Anna. Instead, she moved in with a young man who had been a frequent all-night date for several years. Although Joan never mentioned him, her relationship with E. S. was a blur of steamy sex, booze, torrid dancing, drugs, and laughter. Like Ray, he was a friend, but not as reliable or understanding. E. S. wanted no obligations or complications. Billie said her aim was Chicago, and she would do anything for the train fare.

E. S. had shady connections. One of them made risqué vignettes for vending machines. Billie danced in the nude but didn't realize she would have to wait for her money. "I get paid, you get paid," she was told.

"I did it for a fast buck."

"I get paid, you get paid!"

E. S. apparently gave her money and put her on the train to Chicago.

Ray Sterling never married.

3

FROM CHORUS LINE
TO TINSELTOWN

In the fall of 1923 Billie arrived in Chicago. Clutching Miss Emerine's card, she hailed a cab, asked to be dropped off a few blocks from the actual address, and ran away without paying the driver. Her expectations of a grand residence befitting a lady of the theater were shattered. The neighborhood reminded her of downtown Kansas City. Miss Emerine's rooming house was a dismal sight.

"She's on tour," the landlady said.

"But Miss Emerine told me to come here!" Billie said. "I . . ."

"I don't know when she'll be back!" The door closed.

Billie sat on the steps and gathered her thoughts. Having only a few dollars, she might have panicked. The shock woke her up, and she remembered the name of an agent-producer whom Miss Emerine often mentioned—Ernie Young. She carried her borrowed suitcase filled with stolen outfits to a corner drugstore and scanned the telephone book. "How do I get to this address?" she asked the druggist.

"You'll have to take a bus and a streetcar downtown to The Loop."

She arrived two hours later to find a long line of girls waiting to see Ernie Young. Billie hadn't eaten and had no place to sleep.

"The outer office was filled with the most attractively dressed, beautiful girls I had ever seen, all slim and chic," Joan recalled. "And here I was in a cheap blue suit too tight at the seams, service-weight hose, and with a hole in my glove. Unless I got into that office before those other girls did, I was sunk. The next time the inner door opened, I raced through it like a guided missile and burst into the room, tears streaming down my face. 'I know I'm not as tall or pretty as those other girls out there, but I have less than two dollars and no experience, and I can't go back to Kansas City!' I cried without introducing myself. 'Please, won't you give me a tryout?' "

Ernie Young was startled, amused, and curious. "Have a seat," he said. "Take a deep breath and tell me all about it." While Billie gave him her usual well-rehearsed sob story, he looked her over. She was too short for a chorus girl and a bit overweight, but he was drawn to her big eyes, provocative smile, and tenacity. "I'm desperate," she concluded.

"How about dancing for me?" he asked, putting a record on the phonograph. Young valued her enthusiasm more than her dancing. "That's enough, Lucille. We'll have to work out some routines."

"Routines?"

"I can't offer you a permanent job right now. You'll have to dance in bars and strip joints until . . ."

"Strip joints?"

"Not all the way," he scowled. "One of the girls will show you the bumps and grinds."

"Bumps and grinds?"

"Do you want to eat, Lucille?"

She nodded.

Young made a call. "It's all set. Twenty-five bucks a week."

"What do I have to do?"

"Nothin' much in this dive. Smile at the customers and dance up a storm. The men are only interested in your body, anyway."

"Do I have to . . .?"

"That's up to you, Lucille. Some girls do and some don't."

"I'm too hungry to worry about it now."

"Here's an advance on your salary. I'll get you a room in a cheap hotel."

Lucille LeSueur learned quickly and had her own ideas, too. By responding to the customers in strip joints and bars, she knew what kept their attention and "turned them on." Her act was lustful and fleshy. Her age made her even more desirable—she claimed to be only sixteen. Joan never explained why she lied about her age because, according to her, sixteen was her true age. Her wide-eyed look of innocence and layer of baby fat prompted men to fantasize about her. The other dancers liked Lucille; they saw her as an "unwanted child" who smiled despite her problems. It was a part Joan would play all her life—"reluctantly" discussing the hopelessness of her youth, a doctor's prediction that she would never walk again, the beatings and the cruel stepfather, crowned with a frosting of laughter.

She danced with five other girls at a salesmen's convention in Oklahoma City, but as 1924 was blooming, Lucille was becoming disgusted with the smell of stale cigar smoke and pudgy fingers pawing at her. Not all of the men were displeasing, however, and she played with those who had money and could afford the finer restaurants and trinkets. According to people who knew her at the time, she got venereal disease and had the first series of botched-up abortions in Chicago. Billie had the experience but knew little about the consequences. Her girlfriends in the chorus were accustomed to such "inconveniences" and looked after her.

"I'm sending you to Detroit," Ernie Young told her. "One of the dancing girls in the floor show at the Oriole Terrace is sick. This is the big time, Lucille, but understand you're only a replacement."

"What's big-time to you?"

"Thirty-two chorus girls don't fit on a small stage," he said. "The Oriole

Terrace is elegant. Top dog. Big orchestra and revolving platform . . . that kinda thing."

"Swell, Ernie."

"Eight routines a night ain't no picnic."

"Eight?"

"You'll learn fast."

Lucille wasn't prepared for the assignment, but worse obstacles faced her in Detroit—thirty-one chorus girls who had no intention of showing a new-comer the steps or the proper makeup. Her costumes were too big, but no one cared. Joan said, "They made sure I couldn't dress with them. When I asked a question, no one gave me an answer. They used show business lingo that was foreign to me. During rehearsals I kept up with them, but I needed more practice and advice. I felt like a hick and an idiot."

One of the chorines, however, took pity on Lucille and offered to work with her. "We have tricks in the chorus," the girl explained, "ways to get attention and be singled out. We work together and keep in step, but each one of us wants to be noticed."

"How do I do that?"

"By eyeing the good-looking customers. Not by winking or doing anything as obvious. Smile and stare right at them. Moisten your lips and pucker—like this."

"I get the idea."

"And always save the best for last," the girl said.

Lucille picked up the rest on her own. Eight weeks later she was moved to the front row. She had confidence now and nothing or no one could stand in her way. The only question was "Where to now?" Her ambition had been fulfilled just six months after leaving Kansas City. Some of the girls got married. Others went on tour with a road show for a change of scenery. Very few were sorted out for New York.

"I didn't know what I wanted to do," Joan related. "I was happy at the Oriole Terrace. We changed routines regularly, and our costumes were lovely. It was such a relief to entertain the upper class. I never got complacent because I wanted to learn and practice. I found out quickly enough that every new girl—and each of the regulars—was ready and eager to take my place. This meant I had to be the best and continue getting better. I remembered part of Daddy Wood's philosophy for a successful life: 'If you find you can do a job, let it alone, because you're already bigger than the job, and that means you will shrink down to its size.' Well, I wasn't bigger than the front row at the plush Oriole Terrace yet. I wanted to kick higher, to strengthen my ankles and thighs. My bad foot ached occasionally. I was only beginning and couldn't afford to be hasty."

Ironically, one of Lucille's favorite numbers was a gypsy routine. It reminded her of Daddy Cassin's Opera House and her electrifying gathered, full-flowered skirt, and oversize gold jewelry. The citizens of Lawton had criticized her for prancing around town in "gypsy rags," but that dress had been her favorite, and she had worn it for her show in the Cassins' backyard.

In April 1924, with poppies in her hair, bracelets jingling on both arms, necklaces bouncing on her breasts, and a full gypsy skirt flying wildly over the heads of wealthy patrons, Lucille knocked over a glass of water. It landed in the lap of a distinguished gentleman.

"It was an accident," Joan recalled. "I had no idea who he was. Besides, I didn't have that much sense."

When the number was over and the girls were making a fast change, they tried to convince Lucille not to worry.

"I'll be fired," she sighed. "I just know it."

"Maybe he won't complain to the manager," her chorine friend panted, trying to squeeze into her costume.

"I've never seen them before, but they got the best table in the house. They looked awful rich."

"Don't worry about it, Lucille. Smile at the guy. Glance over your shoulder and give him the business."

"Then his wife will have me fired!"

After the show, he came backstage looking for "the little fat girl with the blue eyes." Thirty-one dancers looked at Lucille, who paled when he spoke to the stage manager and they walked toward her. The gentleman's suit was wet, but he had a grin on his face.

There was silence for a few seconds that seemed like an eternity.

"Miss LeSueur, I'm J. J. Shubert."

"I'm very sorry," she said.

"May I speak to you privately?"

They strolled away from the others. Nervously she said, "I'll be glad to pay for the dry cleanin'."

"That won't be necessary."

"I've never done anything like this before, Mr. . . . Mr. . . ."

"J. J. Shubert."

"Mr. Sherbet."

"Shubert," he corrected her. "I'm a Broadway producer. We're trying out a new show, *Innocent Eyes,* here in Detroit and I'm looking for chorus girls."

"Me?"

"Could you attend the matinee tomorrow? I'll leave your name at the box office."

"Sure. Sure, I can make it!"

He tipped his hat and left.

Lucille went back to the dressing room and told her friend about J. J. Shubert. "I don't get it," she said. "Why me?"

"Same old line" was the casual reply. "He'll make all kinds of promises and try to get into your pants. We've all been through it. If I were you, I'd forget about it."

"But I've never seen a real show."

"Okay, but don't say I didn't warn you."

Another chorine said, "J. J. Shubert's a big Broadway producer. I've seen his picture in the newspaper. It's worth sleepin' with him. Nothin' to lose, honey."

"I sat in the audience, but I was in heaven," Joan said. "Sigmund Romberg wrote the music, and the leading lady was Mistinguett, a French entertainer. The showgirls wore sequins and feathers. They were separated according to size and danced in perfect rhythm. The show was opulent. It was dazzling. During the curtain calls, the audience threw roses at Mistinguett's feet."

J. J. Shubert was waiting for Lucille LeSueur in the lobby. "How did you like it?"

"Swell. Just swell."

"Can you learn the steps?"

"Sure."

"Our train leaves for New York at two A.M."

"Tomorrow morning?"

"You'll have to be on it."

Lucille felt light-headed, and her heart was pounding. "I don't have the train fare."

He laughed. "Don't worry about it, Lucille, and don't be late."

She told no one at the Oriole Terrace; she did the show that night, picked up her suitcase, and took a taxi to the station. She had committed a theatrical crime by jumping the show, but she had no regrets. Sitting on the train to New York, Lucille thought about letting down the Oriole Terrace management and Ernie Young, who had recommended her in the first place, but she felt no guilt. Getting ahead meant taking advantage of people who would do the same to her for a good break. Sentiment was a waste of time. She had to think of herself first and keep going. Getting ahead meant climbing a staircase to the stars. People were steps, that's all.

Lucille decided to never look down. Anna and Hal could go to hell. Ray was worth only the encouragement he gave her. Not marrying her would be his problem, and she would send letters to him about fame, excitement, and beautiful New York. She wrote to Ray, "I didn't think big enough. All I wanted was to be a dancer, but I wasn't aiming for anything. A glass of water taught me I can turn disaster into success."

J. J. Shubert said it all: "The girl had something I couldn't define, but she stood out. She wasn't particularly sexy, but she enjoyed herself onstage, and the audience, especially men, stared. I spotted her right away."

He spoke to Lucille briefly on the trip to New York. The chorus girls were friendly, too. They showed her the steps and practiced in the train vestibule. "At last I was understood by other girls who wanted to be understood, also," Joan recalled. "People think chorus girls are a gaudy crew bent upon becoming Wall Street's collective mistress. I thought so, too, until I became one of them. Hard? Yes, they're hard. They can't be sensitive and be successful. It just isn't in the Broadway racket."

Unlike the Detroit chorines, Shubert's dancers wanted Billie to make good. She was their "baby." They arranged for her to share a room with four girls in an old brownstone on Fiftieth Street just off Fifth Avenue. They introduced her to rich "stage-door Johnnies" and made sure she got a free dinner every night.

Innocent Eyes opened at the Winter Garden Theater on May 20, 1924, to excellent reviews. Two weeks later Billie was promoted from the back row of the chorus to a position in the front row. She took advantage of this miracle to write glowing letters to Anna, Ray, and Dr. Wood.

"Things were working out very well for me at last," Joan recalled. "Francis Williams, one of the principals in the cast, thought I should get out of that small room with five beds. She used her influence to get me into a theatrical boardinghouse. I moved in with another chorus girl, Mitzie DuBois, who knew the ropes. We had good times with those Johnnies, times filled with diamonds and dinner, but there was little chance for a steady relationship.

"A member of the boys' chorus, Lew Offield, became a very good friend. He was from Missouri, too. There was nothing romantic between us, but we spent a lot of time together walking through Central Park and down Fifth Avenue. It was against Shubert's rules to fraternize with members of the cast, so we had to be careful. He wanted to be a musical comedy star. We were standing on Broadway one day, and I saw Fred and Adele Astaire's names in lights—*Lady Be Good*. I told Lew I wanted to be a ballroom dancer. I guess he was thinking about Eddie Cantor in *Kid Boots*. Lew was like a brother. He went on the road with *Innocent Eyes*. I stayed in New York. The next time we saw each other was in Hollywood at Graumann's Chinese Theater. Lew hadn't changed, except he was now known as Jack Oakie. We had a good laugh. He sang, 'When hearts are young in organdy gowns . . .'—one of the songs from *Innocent Eyes*."

Lucille LeSueur dated a variety of men aside from those who lined up at the stage door every night. She fell hard for an actor who proved to be as fickle as she was. This was a new experience for her, however, because he professed love and devotion. She believed him. There was talk of marriage. Her friends thought it was the real thing when he sent flowers every night. Although the actor did not become famous, he had great potential in 1924 and was popular on Broadway. Lucille was thrilled to be seen with him. She allowed herself to be vulnerable and gave in completely. When the romance appeared to be serious, the actor's fiancée visited Lucille. "I thought we were engaged," the girl said. "We've been going together for over a year. If he wants you, no one can do anything about that. I just don't want you to get hurt, too."

Deeply hurt, Lucille broke up with him. With Lew gone, she turned to Ray and described her broken heart as completely shattered. She would never get over it. "My roommate, Mitzi, is very understanding, but she's been through this before and says it's part of life," Lucille wrote. "But I will never forget the brutal lies. How could I have believed them? Believed him? How can I ever trust anyone again?"

Ray consoled her. "New York is like a melting pot of all classes, a cesspool of licentiousness, Billie. There are bound to be flies gathering around a sugar bowl like show business; but there must be many good people in the city, too. May God keep you and give you the aid I cannot."

Considering her lifetime of setbacks and tragedies, it is hard to believe that a broken love affair would almost destroy Lucille LeSueur. It was, however, the beginning of a breakdown that she blamed on hard work instead of a tender heart.

When *Innocent Eyes* went on the road, Lucille stayed in New York with Shubert's next production, *The Passing Show of 1924*. Her salary was raised to $35 a week, very good money in those days, but she spent it all on clothes. Lucille never thought or cared about money until she was broke.

According to Patricia Fox-Sheinwold in her book *Gone But Not Forgotten* (Bell, 1981), Lucille secretly married James Welton, a saxophonist with the pit orchestra of *The Passing Show of 1924*. (This story was also reported in the January 29, 1982, edition of the *New York Post*.) They were divorced in Los Angeles during the late 1920s. There is no record of a New York marriage license issued to them. Possibly they drove to another state. Joan Crawford had already died when this information was disclosed. If she had married Welton, it was on the rebound; the union was brief because Lucille ran faster and wilder than ever before.

She asked her dates to take her to nightclubs in Harlem, where a new dance called the Charleston was the rage. She watched the blacks do the complex variations, and she made up her mind to learn the steps. She had the energy for it, and maybe this crazy new dance would catch on. If it did, she would be the best.

Lucille drove herself to exhaustion. She craved love but wasn't clever or coy enough for the men she chose. The holidays were coming, and with each letter from Ray she became more obsessed with seeing him. Knowing Hal was married and settled down made her feel more comfortable about going back to Kansas City for a vacation. Her problem, as usual, was money. Lucille approached Nils Granlund, whom she had met backstage. A half-partner in Club Richman, a new speakeasy on West Fifty-sixth Street, he was an influential man in show business. Granlund said Lucille came to him in tears. She needed money to get home. Her mother was very sick. He listened to her sob story and noticed how beautiful she was—". . . big blue eyes and voluptuous lips. She was one of the prettiest girls I'd ever seen."

Lucille rambled on about *The Passing Show of 1924*. "It's not doing very well," she wept. "I might be out of a job. In the meantime, I could use some extra money to get me home for the holidays to see my sick mother."

Granlund wasn't taken in by her story, but he was taken with Lucille. "Go down to the club and audition," he said.

Billie did the Charleston to the tune of "When My Sweetie Walks Down the Street." Harry Richman, a crony of Al Capone's, hired her for fifty dollars a week to dance in his speakeasy. She had little time to think about "stage-door Johnnies" or paunchy rich men who sent orchids to her dressing room. She played up to Granlund, however, because she needed a new dress.

"That's not my problem," he said. "You're making almost a hundred dollars a week!"

"I have lots of debts, and then there's my mother's doctor bills."

"If you're working so hard, why do you need a new evening dress?"

"Mr. Richman wants me to mix with the customers, and he told me to wear a knock-out gown. I don't have one!"

Granlund gave her the money, and she came right back to his office. "Thought you'd like to see what you bought," she laughed, taking off her clothes to model the expensive dress.

"Not here!" he shouted.

"So what?"

Before he could stop her, theater tycoon Marcus Loew walked in with a broad grin on his face. Granlund stammered an explanation while Lucille finished dressing. She wasn't the least bit embarrassed.

"Aren't you going to introduce me?" Loew asked.

"This is Lucille LeSueur," Granlund said nervously. "Just what M-G-M is looking for."

"M-G-M?" Billie asked, stuffing a fresh wad of chewing gum into her mouth.

"A movie studio in Hollywood. Marcus just bought it."

"Oh, yeah?"

Loew suggested a screen test.

"I can't act," she blurted out arrogantly. "I'm a dancer!"

"You can do that in the movies," Granlund said, trying to believe his ears.

"No music!" she exclaimed, taking off the evening dress. "I gotta be on my way."

Loew watched her rush out the door without a backward glance. "Is she for real?" he asked Granlund.

"She's a teenage hick, but a beauty, and she can dance, too. The kid's only been in New York for six months or so."

"I'd be glad to arrange a screen test," Loew said. "She has perfect features."

"I'll talk to her."

Granlund went to the Club Richman and saw Lucille mixing with the wealthy clientele in the new evening gown that he had bought. Instead of the laughing and frivolous flapper, she appeared weary and lonely. He invited her to his table. "What's troubling you, honey?"

"Nothin'."

"Bored already?"

"Tired, I guess."

"Sit with me for a while and we'll talk."

"Not about the movies."

"Give it a shot. You have nothing to lose."

"I'm not interested."

"All you have to do is pose for a camera. The whole thing takes a few minutes."

"Sounds too easy."

"Chance of a lifetime."

"No such thing."

"How do you know if you don't try?" he asked, taking her hand.

"How many times do I have to say that I want to be a dancer!"

"Is that all?" he asked, getting up from the table and still holding her hand. She looked up at him knowingly, and they left together. Granlund said he dated her often. Their closeness convinced Lucille to do the screen test. She did little more than smile in the camera full face, to the left, and to the right. Her legs were important, too. The film test was sent to Hollywood. The reply: "She doesn't have what we're looking for."

Granlund convinced Loew to give her a second test. She agreed unenthusiastically. The reply from M-G-M was the same: no good. Although Lucille wasn't interested in Hollywood, two rejections and the closing of *The Passing Show of 1924* reminded her of St. Agnes, Rockingham, and Stephens. Her past haunted her, and, for once, Lucille wasn't able to hide the burden. Granlund was worried about her. "Honey, go home for Christmas. Get some rest, visit your old friends. You need a vacation."

"What about my job at the club?" she asked in tears.

"Richman agrees with me. You're not yourself."

Joan said in an interview early in her Hollywood career, "The nervous strain of my work in the chorus and in the nightclub whipped me, and I had a breakdown."

Lucille LeSueur was a mixed-up young lady when she returned to Kansas City. It was a shock to Anna and Hal. Ray got the impression Lucille was disillusioned enough to stay for a while. She arrived at the laundry apartment on Monday, December 22, 1924, and made an effort to be chatty with Anna, who was, as always, suspicious. "Did you get fired, Lucille?"

"No."

"From what I hear, New York's busy this time of year. How did you get time off?"

"I'm sick."

"You don't look sick, Lucille."

"Sick and tired."

"If you came home to bellyache . . ."

"I came home to sleep! If Hal and Jesse had room, I'd stay with them."

"We're havin' Christmas dinner there. Try to get along with your brother."

"Yeah, yeah. I'm goin' Christmas shopping tomorrow."

"You have money, Lucille?"

"Jesus, yes!"

"Don't be sassy. I take enough bitchin' from Harry."

"Why don't you leave the bastard?"

"I am. Hal wants me to live with him and Jesse."

"Does he know he asked you?"

"He and I have no gripes, so don't you start up! Everything was goin' okay, but you had to come home."

"You won't see much of me."

"Things have changed since you left Kansas City," Anna said. "Your boyfriends have gotten married or moved away. What's left don't think much of you anymore."

"What're you talkin' about?"

"Stories got back from Chicago and Detroit, Lucille."

"I'm going to bed."

"I hope you'll be able to sleep alone," Anna said sarcastically.

Lucille was too tired to think. She woke up to the familiar stench of lye. The bedsheets were sticky and damp from the steam floating through the cracks in the door. She lay for a few minutes staring at the ceiling and wondering how she had lived there. She dressed quickly and walked in the crisp, cold air. Having money in her pocketbook made Christmas shopping a pleasure for a change. Hal's wife, Jesse, was excited about making the holiday dinner. "I hope we can be a family at last," she said over the telephone.

Lucille made numerous calls but could find no one to take her dancing. Ray apologized for being so busy, saying he would let her know. She went to the Jack O'Lantern alone and was ignored except for new boys who were anxious to dance with the Cassin girl. She found them silly and juvenile. Several old beaus barely acknowledged her and stayed close to their dates.

Anna did not say, "I told you so," when her daughter came home early.

"I know you're dying to spit it out," Lucille said, putting her feet up on the kitchen table.

Anna was busy sorting laundry. Without turning around she said, "You made a lot of enemies when you ran out on that show in Detroit, Lucille."

"Jealous ones."

"You can't run away any more than Henry could. He thought if we moved to Kansas City, nobody would know about the gold coins, but the news traveled faster than the train that brought us here."

"I didn't run away!"

"You're dirt, Lucille. That's why no one will have anything to do with you. Those naked pictures. Dancing without a stitch!"

Lucille glared at her mother. "That's how desperate I was."

"And bein' a prostitute in New York?"

"I was a Roseland girl for a while. Men paid to dance with me."

"And more," Anna said, wearily sinking into a chair. "What's done is done."

"I don't have to apologize to you or to anyone else."

"What about Ray Sterling?"

"What about him?"

"He's not hangin' around or callin'."

"Ray has family obligations."

"Like hell! He's in local politics and tryin' to clean up this town. He won't be seen with you."

"Shut up!" Lucille screamed. She ran into the bedroom, slammed the door, fell on the bed, and cried herself to sleep. Sick and weak, she stayed in bed the next day. Ray called to wish her a "Merry Christmas," but he did not ask her to go out. Anna made hot soup and fresh bread for her pale, feverish daughter. They barely spoke.

On Christmas Day Lucille was feeling better. Dinner at Hal's was pleasant. There were no arguments. Jesse was anxious to hear about New York, and Lucille told glamorous stories about *Innocent Eyes* and the famous stars who appeared across the street and around the corner—George M. Cohan, Fanny Brice, Gertrude Lawrence, and, of course, the famous Ziegfeld Follies. Hal made no sarcastic remarks, but when he looked at his sister, she got the message. He knew all about her scarlet life. After exchanging Christmas presents, Lucille lied about having a date and went back to the laundry apartment to rest. She felt nauseous and dizzy. She missed Ray taking her for drives and discussing their problems and their dreams. "I *am* dirt," Lucille mumbled to herself. "Poor Daddy Cassin, wherever you are. I know how tortured you were. Maybe we're both better off dead."

When the doorbell rang, she ignored it. Harry had probably forgotten his key. Good! Let him stand out in the subzero weather for a while. The doorbell rang again. She turned over in bed and buried her head in the pillow. The doorbell rang again. And again. "Who is it?" she yelled, putting on a robe.

"Telegram for Lucille LeSueur," the man replied.

She took her time answering the door.

"Lucille LeSueur?"

"Yeah?"

"Sign here."

She looked around for some change, handed it to the deliveryman, and closed the door. For a moment she hesitated before opening the envelope. Was it from Granlund telling her not to come back to New York? Was she out of a job? Where would she go? What would she do?

The telegram did indeed come from Granlund:

YOU ARE PUT UNDER A FIVE-YEAR CONTRACT STARTING AT SEVEN-
TY-FIVE DOLLARS A WEEK. LEAVE IMMEDIATELY FOR CULVER CITY,
CALIFORNIA. CONTACT M-G-M KANSAS CITY FOR TRAVEL EXPENSES.

LOVE,

GRANLUND

She read the telegram ten . . . twenty times. "It's true! It's really true!" she screamed, dancing around the laundry.

The next day, Lucille called Granlund collect. "I'm so happy! I can't believe it. Tell me it's the truth."

"Honey, I wouldn't kid you about a movie contract. Good thing you gave me your mother's address. Is she feeling any better?"

"About the same, but when she hears the good news, I'm sure the old girl will feel a lot different."

"I'm going to miss you," he said, "but this is your golden opportunity. When are you leaving?"

"Early New Year's Day. Think of me at midnight because I'll be waiting for the Sunset Limited to roll in."

"If you need anything, let me know, but M-G-M will greet you like a princess. Good luck, honey."

"What do I do when I get there?"

"Someone from M-G-M will be at the station to meet you, honey. I'm gonna miss you, Billie."

She called Ray. "I wanted you to be the first to know."

"God bless you" was all he could manage to say.

She hung up the telephone and wondered what God had to do with it.

"The movies?" Anna gasped, looking at the telegram.

"That's right, Mother. Seventy-five bucks a week."

"A fortune . . ."

Harry studied the telegram but wasn't convinced. "Where's the expense money?" he asked.

Billie waved the $400 under his nose.

"Why didn't you tell us about the screen test?" Hal asked.

"Nobody gave me a chance. I walked in the door, and Mother threw dirt in my face."

Anna bowed her head. "I don't know what to say."

"Try keepin' your trap shut," Lucille said, cracking her chewing gum. "I'm gonna get my ticket and buy some new clothes."

"Hollywood . . ." Harry mumbled, shaking his head back and forth.

"Yeah, warm breezes, Charlie Chaplin, Clara Bow, Mary Pickford, sunshine, and Valentino," Lucille said, putting on her coat.

"We'll take you to the station." Hal smiled.

"You've never done me any favors before, so don't start now. I've been on my own since I can remember and nothin's changed."

It was bitterly cold on New Year's Day 1925. "I'll never forget that trip," Joan said. "I spent all the money and had to take a coach. I sat up all the way to California. The closer I got to Hollywood, the more I missed New York and Granlund. I thought about Harry Richman and J. J. Shubert and my roommate, Mitzi. For a week I'd been in a daze, but riding the Missouri Pacific west I wondered what I was getting into. I was a dancer, and that's all I ever wanted to be. I didn't have the class or talent for acting. Nobody told me why I'd been signed to a contract. I began to worry."

For almost three days Lucille LeSueur, M-G-M starlet, shivered from the cold in an uncomfortable, narrow seat. She cursed herself for spending her expense money on pretty clothes that did nothing to keep her warm on the train. She washed her hands and face only once because the water froze in the lavatories. M-G-M had paid for a comfortable sleeper. Lucille was still learning the hard way, but she had had the foresight to save a few dollars for food.

On January 3, 1925, she stepped off the train and thawed out in the bright California sunshine. She expected to see Harry Rapf waiting for her with a bouquet of flowers. Lucille, standing alone on the platform with one new suitcase and a heavy coat, tried to act sophisticated. She thought she was on another planet. Was it actually seventy degrees in January?

"Are you Lucille LeSueur?"

She turned around. "Yeah. Who are you?"

"Larry Barbier, M-G-M publicity."

"I figured you were too young to be Harry Rapf."

"I'll get the rest of your luggage."

"This is it," she said, picking up the suitcase.

"Please, allow me. The limousine's right over here."

"I heard a lot about California from my roommate back in New York, but I didn't believe it. I'm dressed for winter."

"The hotel's not far. After you get settled, we'll go to Mr. Rapf's office. He'll go over the contract with you."

"First time I ever saw a palm tree except in the moving pictures. Everything's so bright and cheerful here. Never saw a pink house, either," she exclaimed, staring out of the window.

"It's like this all year round," he said.

Lucille got over her homesickness for New York in a matter of minutes. She had never been warm enough at St. Agnes or Rockingham. Either she didn't have the proper clothing or enough blankets. Running from the Winter Garden Theater to Club Richman in the bitter rain or snow didn't give her shoes and feet a chance to dry.

This place had to be real because Lucille didn't have enough imagination to dream about a place like Los Angeles. Larry Barbier was talking, but she wasn't listening. The limousine stopped. She watched slim, long-legged girls in tight shorts riding bicycles. "Miss LeSueur, we're here," he said, opening the car door.

"M-G-M?"

"No. The Hotel Washington."

"Oh." She winced.

"It's not swanky," he said kindly, "but you can walk the six blocks to the studio, and it's inexpensive."

He waited for her downstairs while she checked into her room. The hotel was shabby. It reminded her of the cheap dives in Detroit and Chicago. She carefully applied another thick layer of makeup. Remembering Daddy Wood's philosophy, she smiled contentedly at Larry Barbier, who took her through the gates of Metro-Goldwyn-Mayer. "I'll show you around," he said. Lucille hadn't seen many movies and asked if Mary Pickford was working anywhere that day. "Miss Pickford is with United Artists," he replied, "with Charlie Chaplin and Douglas Fairbanks."

"Who's that over there?"

"Norma Shearer and John Gilbert."

"Never heard of them," she said.

"They're top stars at M-G-M."

Although Lucille wasn't thrilled, she felt the exhilaration of action, hastily made movie sets, and costumed players in wigs and hats.

Harry Rapf smiled. "Welcome to M-G-M. Did you have a nice trip, Lucille?"

"Not bad."

"The sleepers are very comfortable, aren't they? I always feel like a million bucks at the end of those three days. We're going to do more tests, Lucille, but with rehearsals and production help. The ones you did in New York don't do you justice."

"I came all the way out here just to do another test?" she asked.

"As you can see in the agreement, M-G-M has the option to break your contract after six-month intervals. Until we know how well you photograph and more about your talent . . ."

"Are you tellin' me I can be fired in six months if you don't like me?"

"It's the same for all newcomers."

"Nobody told me."

"I wouldn't worry about it."

"I gave up a good job in New York. The telegram said a five-year contract!"

"We want you to succeed, Lucille. The crew working on your test tomorrow will be very understanding and patient. Come to me if you have any questions or problems."

She signed the contract and walked back to the Hotel Washington. By talking to another girl who was also doing a screen test, Lucille found out how very important this one would be. M-G-M would drop her in six months if she wasn't acceptable.

"Why didn't you ask questions?" the girl inquired.

"I trusted the person who told me it was a golden opportunity. He made it sound ideal, but I should have known better."

"Can you act?"

"No. I'm a dancer."

"I hate to make you feel bad, Lucille, but there are hundreds of dancers out here. Can't you do anything else. Sing, maybe?"

"Nothing, and if I don't make it, I have nowhere to go."

She chatted with the stagehands until it was her turn to face the camera. "I'm nervous as hell," she said. One of the stagehands whispered, "When the director tells you to do something, concentrate on an incident in your past. Relive it."

"Why can't I just dance?"

"And take the gum out of your mouth."

"I don't think I can stand still without it!"

"Use your eyes. They're beautiful."

She was posed by the director, who asked her to smile, laugh, tilt her head, and turn right and left. The stagehands stood behind the lights, urging her on. "All right, Lucille," the director yawned. "Cry!" She thought about Rockingham and the tears flowed.

"Show me some anger, Lucille."

She tried to stop crying, but the horrible memories of childhood imprisonment enveloped her. "Anger!" the director repeated.

Still sobbing, she heard another voice. "Hey, Lucille, can you do the cakewalk?" She looked up at Tommy Shagrue, an electrician. "Fun, isn't it?" he smiled, doing a few steps. The restless director repeated for the last time, "Anger, Lucille!!"

She thought about her mother and about being blackballed from the sorority at Stephens. Her eyes filled with rage, and her lips trembled.

She finished the test and hugged Shagrue. "Thank you, Tommy. I'll never forget what you did."

"Whatever tore you apart a few minutes ago, forget it. I think you passed."

"Do you think so?"

"I'm only an electrician."

"Don't ever say that," she exclaimed. "As far as I'm concerned you guys are as important as anyone else around here!"

Joan Crawford gave Shagrue a job on all of her movies and faithfully befriended stagehands throughout her career. They would prove invaluable to her transformation from common chorus girl to star.

*   *   *

Lucille's screen test showed promise. She was kept on salary but ignored. With only six months to prove herself again, she got up early every morning and reported to the studio. Everyone except the producers and moguls knew her by name. No pass was required at the gate. The security guards, prop men, lighting directors, electricians, cameramen, and extras were always glad to see her. Although she studied and was in awe of Norma Shearer, Lucille was bored with the star's three expressions. This was acting?

Her behind-the-scenes friends explained Norma's success. "Ever heard of Irving Thalberg?" they asked.

"No."

"He's vice-president and production assistant to L. B. Mayer, head of M-G-M. Mr. Thalberg's the well-dressed, frail-looking fellow always tossing a coin. Brilliant young man."

"Is he screwing her?" Lucille asked, sharing a cigarette with one of the prop men.

"They're seeing each other. He's been guiding her career for two years."

"She's a phony."

"Miss Shearer works very hard assuming charm," the technician said. "With Mr. Thalberg's power, she'll be given the choice roles."

"She has a long way to go before she's an actress," Lucille glowered. "Maybe I should see one of her movies instead of judgin' her after a dozen takes."

"Do that, Lucille. She comes over very, very well on the screen. What you watch being filmed has to be edited, and music makes a big difference, too."

"She uses a lotta makeup tricks."

"Everyone does," the propman laughed.

"Yeah, but Shearer's small eyes are crossed, her nose is too long, her forehead's too high, and her face has no bone structure. She looks different in movie magazines."

"Her pictures are touched up. They all are because the studio has final approval."

"Shit! Is anything for real around here?"

"Not for long. You'll find out."

"Think so?"

"There are two categories of stars," he explained. "The experienced ones, who were spotted in the theater, and the ones like you, who are attractive and vivacious but have no experience."

"You forgot a third category."

"What's that?"

"The ones who had stage mothers, like Mary Pickford and Norma Shearer."

"How do you know so much?" he laughed.

"I have nothin' else to do but read fan magazines and listen. Someone once told me to shut up and listen."

"One thing you don't need is a stage mother, Lucille. They're usually banned from the studio."

"They'd never let mine in!"

He laughed. "Then fight for yourself! Talk to your agent. Tell him you're a professional and feel guilty about getting paid for doing nothing."

"His secretary made an appointment for me."

Lucille watched the handsome, all-American movie actor Billy Haines playing opposite Norma Shearer in A *Tower of Lies*. She adored Haines. Always smiling and friendly, he knew Lucille was trying to lure him with her well-rehearsed crooked smile. One morning he asked if she were an extra. "No, I'm under contract," she said.

He winked. "You're one of the fortunate ones."

"Yeah, I see the extras lined up at the gate early in the morning. Hundreds of them. How much do they make?"

"Five dollars."

"When I feel sorry for myself, I watch them begging for a walk-on."

"Why in heaven's name would you feel sorry for yourself?"

"Because if they get in at least they get on camera. I'm always behind it."

"That's your fault, my dear girl. Emphasize whatever it is they liked about you in the first place and face them head-on. Go back every day as a reminder. Do it big. Do it right and give it class."

Lucille was on Haines's set often. The propman asked her if she had a crush on the actor. "I'm not sure," she sighed, "but I feel good just being around him. Is he married?"

"No."

"I hear the studio prefers their big stars to remain single. It makes them available to their fans."

"That's true, but don't worry about Haines. He's not the marrying kind."

"Playboy, huh?"

"He plays with boys, yes."

"A swish?"

"The biggest."

"Holy shit!"

Lucille worked diligently with makeup early in the morning and before retiring. She chose her clothes carefully and though overweight, she carried herself with ease and assurance. Regardless of the tricks she picked up at the studio, her astonishing eyes were compelling. In spite of her shyness, Lucille had a twinkle and knowing grin. The technicians liked her spirit and curiosity. She was, they recognized, willing to play for good or for no good reason.

Underneath the frowns of innocence was fire!

* * *

Harry Rapf looked up from his cluttered desk. "Sit down, Miss . . . Miss . . . ah . . ."

"LeSueur."

"Yes, of course. Lucille LeSueur," he said, glancing at her file. "How did you come by that name?"

"Why?"

"It's appropriate for a dancer at Maxim's in Paris."

"My father is French-Canadian."

"Are you saying Lucille LeSueur is your real name?"

"Yes."

He read over her vital information. She was seventeen. (Actually, she was twenty-one.) Height, 5'4". (Actually she was 5'1".) Weight, 145 pounds. Brunette. Good carriage. Plain appearance. Class: ingenue. Screen test was fair. "Have you been assigned to anything?" he asked between telephone calls.

"No, and I'm sick and tired of doing nothin'. How come those crummy-lookin' extras get parts and I sit on my ass?"

"Those people are starving, Lucille. They sleep across the street to be first in line. And for what? Three or five dollars? Maybe ten? They fight, they beg . . . they'll do anything to be in a crowd scene."

"So will I."

"What have you been doing with yourself?"

"Observing every goddamn day. Would you like me to recite Norma Shearer's lines? Billy Haines's lines? I could even fill in for Lillian Gish."

"I'll have Larry Barbier introduce you to Pete Smith, our publicity chief."

"And?"

"We'll need some action shots of you playing tennis, swimming . . ."

"Dancing?" she asked, eagerly leaning over his desk.

"Eventually. Get over to publicity right now, and I'll call Pete."

Lucille began long days of posing in the California sunshine. She loved every minute of it. Many of the pictures appeared in the newspapers. Pete Smith enjoyed working with Lucille and used his influence to get her an appearance in a film with no credit. He liked her easygoing approach and suggested that she double for Norma Shearer, who was playing a dual role in *Lady of the Night*.

"Double for her?" Lucille growled. "We don't look alike."

"Don't worry about it," Smith said. "They'll only see the back of your head."

"Swell."

Lucille came face-to-face with Norma Shearer and was more disillusioned than ever. "Our noses were almost touching," she told her technician friend.

"Have you changed your mind about her?" he asked.

"Her acting stinks, but she moves effortlessly. That dame wasn't nervous! My legs were like jelly. I could feel the camera on my head and those damn lights were as hot as hell!"

"Was Miss Shearer sweating?"

"No."

"You are, kid."

"I know. I felt it rolling down my scalp!"

Lucille watched Norma Shearer finish for the day. She walked over to a young man who was tossing a coin. "Is that her boyfriend?" Lucille asked.

Pete Smith put his arm around Lucille. "We refer to him as Mr. Irving Thalberg if we want to work here," he whispered in her ear.

"He has a nice smile," she said, taking a good look. "A gentleman."

"And a genius."

"Who's the funny little man standing beside him?"

"Paul Bern, another brilliant production man. He's more outgoing than Mr. Thalberg, who is shy, not haughty, Lucille."

"Where's the bigwig, L. B. Mayer?"

The stagehands laughed. "In his office handling everyone's problems, complaints, and contracts. He comes on the set occasionally."

"Who's single?"

"Mayer's married. Shame on you, Lucille LeSueur."

"Mr. Thalberg doesn't look as if he's too anxious to get hitched. His girlfriend's all over him."

"Shhhh. Don't talk like that," Smith snapped.

"I hear he's a mama's boy," she whispered.

"Mr. Thalberg was born with a slight heart ailment, and he lives with his mother. Is that what you want to know?"

"If I'm gonna work here, I want to know who's who and what's goin' on. Is that wrong?"

"Not if you lower your voice and keep it to yourself," Smith winked.

"Where's my next assignment?" she asked, grabbing his arm.

"That's up to Harry Rapf."

"Back and forth. Back and forth!"

"I'll put together a portfolio of your pictures and have a long talk with Harry. When you get your feet wet, I can take over from there."

"I'd love to dance, Pete."

"You'll walk, stand on your head, or hang from a rope. Lucille, be nice to Harry. Be ladylike but firm."

She waited a few days and went to Rapf's office. "I've been expecting you," he smiled. "These pictures are good, and I understand you've worked twice."

"You call that work?"

He laughed and sat on the edge of his desk where he could look her over very carefully. "You have good friends in New York, Lucille. I received a call from one of them who asked that his name not be mentioned."

"Granlund?"

"I can understand your restlessness after such a hectic schedule in New York."

"How is Gran—"

"I also had a long chat with Pete Smith," Rapf interrupted, his eyes scanning her bosom.

She crossed her legs and made no attempt to pull down her skirt when it rose far above her knees. At that moment Lucille knew she had his interest and undivided attention. When she looked up at him with her irresistible big blue eyes, he lost his train of thought. "You were saying?" she blinked.

"There *might* be a small part for you in *Pretty Ladies*."

"Do I comb the front or back of my hair?" she smiled coyly.

"Both. And you might limber up for a dance number."

"Whatever you say, Mr. . . ."

"Harry," he said, taking her hand.

"Thank you, Harry. There's only one problem."

"What's that?" he asked, leaning over to look deeper into her eyes.

"You said, 'There *might* be a part for you in *Pretty Ladies*.' When will I know for sure?"

"Suppose we make it definite this time."

She smiled and squeezed his hand, which was resting on her thigh. "I'm very grateful, Harry," she sighed. "I owe you so much."

As she stood up, he put his arms around her. "Don't worry about a thing, Lucille. I'll be with you all the way."

"I thought so, Harry."

A source very close to Crawford said, "Joan rarely told a story the same way twice. She often said that Rapf discovered her dancing in *Innocent Eyes*. Another version was that he never saw her dance. She played down Granlund for some reason. He was the one who had faith in her and was in love with her. It was not a deep, everlasting kind of relationship, sincere and passionate. Rapf, however, became known as the man who discovered Joan Crawford, and he was very, very fond of her. Although M-G-M was far from being pure, Mayer was strict and did not believe in the casting couch. He was no saint, but when it came to making and building top stars, it was talent and hard work all the way. Joan was very ambitious, however, and she'd been around. If Harry Rapf could get her the break she needed, I'm sure she showed her appreciation behind closed doors. The way he looked at her made me think so. Otherwise, why would she give him the credit for getting her a Hollywood contract?"

Pretty Ladies imitated the style of the Ziegfeld Follies. ZaSu Pitts and Tom Moore had the lead roles. Norma Shearer and Conrad Nagel made brief appearances. Lucille LeSueur was a chorus girl covered with imitation snow and was on camera in a dressing-room scene with ZaSu Pitts.

Myrna Williams, another chorine in the film, befriended Lucille. She came from Montana and danced in the chorus of Graumann's Chinese Theater's prologues. "I also teach dancing," she said.

"That doesn't leave much time for fun."

"I didn't come all the way here for fun, or to dance."

"That's all I want to do."

"I've had offers to play gypsy girls, native girls, Spanish girls, and God knows what else. Nothing dramatic."

"Do you get around town?"

"Never."

"Christ, I'm dying to hit the spots. Some of the technicians take me out, but my agent doesn't think it's a good idea for me to be seen with them."

"I don't care for nightclubs."

"I live for them."

"That's not the only way to get noticed, Lucille."

"You're so goddamn calm."

"I never thought about it."

"I have enough energy for both of us. Met any interestin' men in Hollywood?"

"No. I live with my mother."

Lucille glared at Myrna. "You don't act like one of those."

"Who?"

"Never mind. You're a swell kid, and I'm glad to have you for a friend."

"I've been offered a contract with Warner Brothers."

"Stay here!" Lucille pleaded.

"I had my chance," Myrna smiled contentedly. "Valentino and his wife, Natasha Rambova, asked me to test for *Cobra*. I was so terrible they couldn't convince the studio to use me."

"Valentino!" Lucille gasped.

"He's very sweet. Very kind."

"Yeah, but not strong enough to fight for you. Just goes to show, you gotta do it yourself!"

Myrna was cast as an Oriental girl, slave girl, native girl, Indian girl, and chorus girl in more than sixty films. Irving Thalberg brought her back to M-G-M as Myrna Loy in 1932, but it wasn't until *The Thin Man* that she became a star and was crowned "Queen of the Movies." "Myrna and I didn't have much going for us in *Pretty Ladies*," Joan said. "We both had freckles, and she had piano legs and slant eyes. I was too fat. It took her sixty movies to reach the top. It took me only nineteen. Crazy . . ."

Pete Smith and Harry Rapf were busy promoting many M-G-M contract players. They did, however, enjoy Lucille's open-mindedness, her raunchy language, and her boundless energy. Unlike the other young girls, she did not consider herself a future femme fatale or Sarah Bernhardt. The heavy makeup and daring wardrobe were attention-getting devices. Above all else, she wanted to be liked. That's all she ever wanted. When the world was at her feet, Joan's greatest fear was not being accepted, admired, and liked. She went out of her way, and often too far, in attaining friendship. On occasion, this eagerness was mistaken for perseverance. Lucille dated the technicians at night, went to Harry Rapf's office every morning, and hounded Pete Smith, who confided in her one day, "I've been talking to Harry about you, and we both agree your name's too stagy. It rhymes with sewer, too. No good."

"So?"

"So, we'll change it."

"To what?"

"I'm going to put your picture in *Movie Weekly* and sponsor a contest to find the right name. This will be a sensational publicity stunt not only for the studio but also for you. We'll make a big deal over the winner, and movie fans will identify themselves with you."

"Don't I have anything to say about my name?"

"Not much."

"What about a film in the meantime, Pete?"

"We want your new name on the credits. Be patient for a little while longer."

"Shit."

The winning name was "Joan Arden," but a few days later it was discovered that a bit player went by the same name. "Joan Crawford" was second choice. "It's awful!" she told Smith.

"You'll get used to it."

"LeSueur may sound like sewer, but Crawford reminds me of crawfish!"

Smith gave her a reassuring hug. "This is only the beginning, honey. You belong to M-G-M now, heart and soul."

"I don't look like a Joan Crawford," she pouted.

"You will."

She wandered out to the set and saw Billy Haines resting between scenes. He grinned and motioned for her to sit down. "What's today's tragedy, Lucille?"

"That's not my name today."

"Introduce yourself."

"Mr. Haines, meet Joan Crawford."

"How do you do?"

"Sounds like crawfish!"

"It might have been worse," he said. "Suppose they chose 'Cranberry' and served you every Thanksgiving with the turkey?"

"This is serious," she sighed. "It's my life!"

"Okay, Cranberry, how about dinner tonight? We'll celebrate."

"I don't feel much like it."

"Coogan's been asking about you."

"That brat?"

"Jackie's father." Haines smiled. "He's producing *Old Clothes* and thinks you'd be good in the part of a destitute young girl who befriends his son."

"How come Harry didn't tell me?" she asked, powdering her nose and applying more lipstick.

"I've never met such an impatient little tart. Be excited! It's a good film, and you'll probably get second billing."

"To a kid?"

"A boy's who's been in over a dozen films. Forget about Jackie and concentrate on your new name. Stand in front of a mirror and repeat it a hundred times."

"Billie Cassin . . . Lucille LeSueur . . . Joan Arden . . . Joan Crawford. And they're probably all illegitimate," she moaned.

"Keep talking like that, and you'll have yourself convinced. Listen to me, Cranberry, it's time for you to be seen around town—at the Montmartre, the Coconut Grove, the tea dances and luncheons, and the Pom Pom Club. Go everywhere. Tell Pete you want to be seen at premieres. He'll arrange for escorts."

"What'll I wear?"

"Haven't you saved any money?"

"I have mostly dancin' clothes."

"That's what you'll be doing, Cranberry! Didn't you say something about the Charleston?"

"I'm the best!"

"It's catching on out here."

"Swell!"

Old Clothes, starring Jackie Coogan, introduced Joan Crawford to moviegoers. Louella Parsons wrote in the *New York Journal–American:* "The girl, Joan Crawford, is a discovery of Jack Coogan, Sr. She is very attractive and shows promise."

Harry Rapf congratulated Joan. "Maybe the kid stole the movie, but you held your own," he said with a lingering kiss. "Ready for another?"

She smirked. "French kiss or movie?"

"Small part of Lady Catherine, a member of the court in *The Only Thing.* You'll work with Eleanor Boardman and Conrad Nagel."

"What do I do? Curtsy?"

"Don't be a snob, Lucille."

"Joan."

"The costumes are splendorous!"

The film was a horrid mess and a blur for Joan, who was tired and hung over during the ordeal. She had wasted no time making the rounds of clubs and entering dance contests. She was the star Charleston dancer at Loew's State Theater. Silver- and gold-toned trophies dressed up her drab room at the Hotel Washington, which she no longer hated because she was never there. As Haines predicted, Joan became the talk of Hollywood. Reporters said, "Everything about the young hotcha girl from M-G-M is real. Her energy is abundant. She dances through lunch, tea, and dinner, long into the night. Joan Crawford is the hottest and most daring girl in town. She hasn't a care in the world and is frank about her love of dancing and how she mastered the Charleston. Saying she learned the sizzling steps in Harlem is a devilish admission, but no one can keep up with her. She is to the Charleston what Valentino is to the tango."

M-G-M could not ignore Joan. Pete Smith and Billy Haines encouraged her. Harry Rapf waited for Joan not to show up at the studio or to appear with dark circles and bloodshot eyes. Neither happened. Mogul Mayer knew her on sight and wanted to know why she wasn't scheduled for a film. "Isn't she the kid who got her name from a fan-magazine contest?" he asked Rapf.

"Yes. We've put her in a few films, but she needs refining. She's a chorus girl from the wrong side of the tracks."

"Any family?" Mayer asked.

"She never talks about them."

"What and whom does she talk about?"

"Dancing and a childhood sweetheart."

"We don't want a hick showing up with a wedding ring, though from what I'm told she's not the marrying kind."

Rapf shrugged. "They come and go, but this girl is the busiest pest I've met. She is mesmerizing, though. On film with a dozen beautiful girls, Lucille LeSueur stands out. She stares you down with passion and evil. She's not as obvious as Clara Bow because she doesn't try the way Clara does."

"M-G-M is not a flophouse for flappers," Mayer bellowed. "The girl, Lucille or Joan . . . whatever her name is, has the right idea. So far, anyway. I want a clean image, Harry. I don't care what people think she was or is as long as they can't prove it. Can she act?"

"She has remarkable eyes and . . ."

". . . and she dances," Mayer interrupted. "Think she can handle *Sally, Irene, and Mary?*"

"I know she can."

"Tell her to knock off the nightclubs during production."

"Cranberry—co-stars at last!"

"I know, Billy! I haven't slept a wink since I heard the news."

"You haven't slept a wink because you've been up all night," he said, squeezing her plump cheek.

"How did you get started in movies?" she asked, sitting on the floor by his feet.

"I entered a 'New Faces' contest sponsored by Sam Goldwyn and won. Metro and Goldwyn merged, and here I am."

"The fan magazines were right about you, Billy—tall, dark, and handsome. The wisecracking playboy."

"Took three years for them to notice, but I doubt it'll take you that long, Cranberry."

"You were born with charm. Everyone loves you and not just because you're a star, Billy. I've never heard anyone say a bad thing about you."

"Not even a whisper about my being queer?" he asked, chucking her under the chin.

"One of the technicians told me because I had a terrible crush on you."

"It wasn't a disgusting shock?"

"You're the sweetest man I've ever known, Billy. Men probably line up at your threshold. Will you do me a favor?"

"Anything, Cranberry."

"Save the leftovers for me."

Sally (Constance Bennett), Irene (Joan Crawford), and Mary (Sally O'Neil) were showgirls in a Broadway revue. James Quirk wrote in *Photoplay*: "One of the nicest pictures of backstage chorus girl life that it has been our lot to see. For a change we see the tinseled creatures as they really are— hardworking, ambitious youngsters who go home to corned beef and cabbage, usually, instead of to nightclubs and broiled lobster. The picture as a whole is very well cast, the title roles perfectly so. Joan Crawford, as Irene, the sentimental one, gives a good performance."

Edmund Goulding, who had directed Greta Garbo and Gloria Swanson, was a patient, gentle Englishman. He saw the devoted Irene in Joan's eyes, but not in her temperament. In private he told Joan she was overanxious. "Pace yourself, Joan. Walk slower. Pause in the doorway before you enter. The camera grinding away makes a second feel like a minute—a minute seem like an hour. It's most difficult to stand still because you're an impatient and energetic young lady. As they say, you come on too strong. Think first, pause, and then—act!"

She knew exactly what he meant, but found it difficult to stand still or to walk slowly with knees of jelly. Goulding spent time with Joan, and Haines waited to give her a hug of encouragement. These two men trying to groom her for more important roles gave Joan a sense of direction and timing. But it was cameraman Johnny Arnold who created the first mold of Joan Crawford.

"You photograph very well," he told her. "Your face reminds me of Garbo's."

"No shit!"

"I'm referring to bone structure," Arnold explained. "If you lost a few pounds your face would be perfect from any angle."

Intrigued but bewildered, she consulted Haines, who shook his head. "I've been telling you that for weeks, Cranberry, but you got mad."

"I've never been on a diet!"

"It's divine," he swooned. "Steak and vegetables three times a day. No bread, potatoes, or desserts, and no nibbling between meals."

"That's it?"

"You'll be broke, but thin."

"I've always been broke, but never thin." She laughed.

Joan discovered that the protein diet gave her more energy, and the lingering baby fat began to disappear.

Harry Rapf, pleased with *Sally, Irene, and Mary*, gave his "protégé" a $25 weekly raise and a kiss. "What do you plan to do with all the money?" he asked.

"Move out of that dump."

"Don't go crazy," he warned. "That's a contagious disease in Hollywood."

"I've been lookin' for a tiny bungalow to rent, and I think I've found what I want."

"Furnished?"

"No, but what the hell do I need? A bed, a table, and some chairs, right?"

"Honey, there are no guarantees out here. You understand that."

"Harry, I've never had a guarantee in my life."

The Boob with George Arthur and Charles Murray was "a piece of junk" according to the *Baltimore Sun*. *Tramp, Tramp, Tramp* starring Harry Langdon was almost as bad. Joan had little to do in either movie, but she received second billing.

In *Paris* with Charles Ray and Douglas Gilmore, the results of Joan's diet began to show. A waistline and high cheekbones were vaguely apparent. According to *Variety*, "Advance information on Miss Crawford among the picture mob has her strongly heralded as a 'comer.' Undoubtedly a 'looker' (when profiled she can double for Norma Shearer in a close-up), Miss Crawford nevertheless will have to show more talent than in this instance to make that billing entirely unanimous."

Director Edmund Goulding gave Joan a chance to let go. She admitted it was a mistake. "I overacted, but it was a good lesson," she said.

Decorating the little bungalow took her mind off the cheap movies she was forced to do. Hanging tacky pink taffeta draperies, she grumbled to herself about Norma Shearer. "I don't know why *Variety* had to mention her. We look nothing alike!" she told Haines.

"Why don't you forget about the curtains." He winced. "In fact, why don't you take them back?"

"Johnny Arnold said I resembled Garbo, and he should know."

"All the frills and tassels and lace and sequins in this tiny place, Cranberry. It's unbearable. I have spots before my eyes."

"Am I going to be compared to Norma Shearer because I doubled for her?"

"Not when it comes to decorating," he said, putting on a pair of dark glasses.

If Joan's bungalow resembled a bordello, her face and body were taking shape beautifully. She had lost almost 20 pounds, plucked her eyebrows, and dyed her hair according to her mood. She preferred carrot red. *Photoplay* featured pictures of Joan before and after. "Joan, does that beautiful strength in mouth and chin tell the story of your transfiguration? Compare the butterfly with the grub. Can you believe they are the same?"

She thanked Pete Smith for choosing her as one of the four actresses featured in *Photoplay*. "Yes," he sighed, leaning back in his leather chair. "I don't think Swanson changed, but she's always news. Garbo, too. She was very plump, too, you know."

Joan put a wad of gum in her mouth. "And Shearer, of course. She combs her hair off her face and becomes Venus."

"You have Shearer-itis and M-G-M considers that the plague. Norma's engaged to Thalberg, and they plan to marry next year."

"I hear his Jewish mama doesn't want a goy for a daughter-in-law. I also hear titless is pushing like mad."

Haines, dozing on the couch in Smith's office, jumped up and gasped, "Shut up, you naughty girl! Never, never, never talk like that again."

"If you'll excuse me," Pete said, leaving the room. "I think my telephone's about to ring."

Joan laughed. "Pooh! It's all over town that normal Norma has her traps set for innocent Irving."

"Not rolling over your tongue, dear one," Haines said. "Promise you'll not discuss this matter with anyone. Promise, Cranberry!"

"I suppose so."

"Thalberg is responsible for my career, and if anyone deserves happiness, he does. When you get to know him . . ."

"Sounds like you love him."

"Not that way."

"He's slim and pretty."

"I don't go for that type."

"How come every time I find a guy who understands me, he's not available."

"You were too wicked for Ray and not wicked enough for Granlund, but I don't think you loved either one, Cranberry. As for that actor in New York, it wasn't meant to be. He was a louse, and now he's a failure."

"You and I could get married." She winked. "I go my way and you go yours. We'd have a lotta fun."

"That's not uncommon in Hollywood."

"I was kiddin', Billy. Why ruin a great friendship? That's been my greatest problem . . . making friends and then going to bed with them."

"If you turn a good trick, that's talent in this town. There are all kinds of worthwhile institutions in Hollywood, but marriage isn't one of them. The more we fuck around, the more we're adulated. The more we get married, the faster they lose respect for us."

"Why?"

"Vows, Cranberry."

"We understand each other because marriage isn't one of our goals."

"Clever little tart, changing the subject. You made a promise, remember?"

"No."

"About Norma and Irving."

"I'll try, but honestly, Billy, he sounds like the kind of guy who puts on his pants to answer the telephone!"

The little man referred to as "Father Confessor and Adviser to the Stars," Paul Bern, began to appear on the sets where Joan was working. Occasionally he came with Thalberg, but most often he came alone. He chatted with the director and cameraman, script in hand. She might have been nervous, but Joan was getting used to M-G-M officials roaming the studio. She knew Bern dated the most beautiful actresses in Hollywood, and although they were taller than the small, balding, middle-aged mogul, he seemed to tower over them.

Feigning concern over his presence, she asked a technician why Bern was particularly interested in *The Taxi Dancer*.

"He's been watching you, Joan."

"Why me?"

"He's looking for star material now that Barbara La Marr is gone."

"Did she commit suicide?"

"Who knows? She took an overdose of drugs . . . hopeless addict. She used cocaine, Benares blend."

"Ben . . . what?"

"Opium."

Joan lit a cigarette and gazed up at the smoke clouding the lights overhead. "God, I love Barbara La Marr. She was labeled 'The Girl Who Was Too Beautiful.' No wonder she gave up!"

"After six husbands any woman would be exhausted."

"Six?" Joan exclaimed. "Jesus, she was only thirty!"

"Not to mention so many lovers in between."

"Was Paul Bern one of them?"

"He wanted to marry Barbara. When she turned him down, he tried to drown himself in the toilet, but his head got stuck and . . ."

Joan laughed hysterically. "You're kiddin'! This is another one of your jokes!"

"No. A plumber had to unscrew the seat. Paul looked like he'd just won the Derby!"

"I don't believe it."

"He was living with Thalberg at the time, but it was the plumber who told the story."

"Did he supply her with drugs, Billy?"

"No, no. Bern was desperately trying to help Barbara. He doesn't get too involved with production. Casting, maybe, and he has a calming influence on temperamental players . . . sort of a self-made psychiatrist."

The reviews of *The Taxi Driver* were fair. Again, *Photoplay* gave Joan a boost: "She rides high over the inferior material. Here is a girl of singular beauty and promise. And she certainly has IT. Just now she is very much in need of good direction."

Carrying a scrapbook with clippings and reviews that barely filled three pages, Joan approached the Father Confessor. "Mr. Bern, may I have a word with you?" She smiled politely.

"Good morning, Joan. How lovely you look today."

"Thank you."

"How can I be of help?"

"Maybe you can explain the rotton studio system. It stinks. I've had only one good part, got swell reviews, and they put me back in crap. It doesn't give a girl much incen . . ."

"Incentive? No, it doesn't. Incentive is vital. I know that."

"When do I get a break?"

He smiled. "Losing a few pounds gives you a classic appearance."

"A *few* pounds! Twenty big ones. I expect to wake up one morning and find a steak sleepin' in my bed."

"I'm going to arrange a picture session for you. I'm anxious to see the results."

"You mean stills?"

He nodded.

"Christ! What do I wear? How do I pose?"

"All you need is that wonderful symmetrical face."

"Is that good?"

"It means the photographer should pay you. Are you free for dinner this evening?"

"I am now."

Joan could have toned down her makeup and daring neckline. Instead, she accentuated the eye shadow and rouge, chose a favorite flapper gown, and met Bern at the door. The wise old owl never blinked when he complimented her. "I thought we'd go to the Montmartre," he said in the limousine.

"How come you chose that place?" she asked. "Can you do the Charleston?"

"Tonight is white tie and violins. More conducive to talking," he said, glancing over at her.

Bern was treated like royalty at the Montmartre. As the evening progressed, Joan felt cheap sitting opposite the soft-spoken, quiet-mannered, well-groomed gentleman who reminded her of Henry Cassin. It was not easy for Joan to communicate with Paul, whose wisdom overwhelmed her. They discussed the future; he wanted her to understand it would take more than a few fine reviews to prove she was a good actress.

"You're doing very, very well," he stressed, "but it's important that you get as many hours before the camera as possible. It isn't only talent, Joan. It's a state of mind, a placid body, an immunity to people milling about and a director's harsh tongue. It's complete and utter concentration on the role you're playing, with all thoughts of overdue bills and boyfriends shut off until you so choose to think about them far away from the movie set. It's knowing which side of your face photographs best and where the markers are located . . . how *not* to let another actor upstage you and eventually how to steal a scene.

"These are only a few pointers, Joan. Experience is the vital commodity. You'll always have butterflies in your stomach, but when you feel more at home on the set than you do in your own living room, you'll blend into the scene with no effort. And don't be quite so sensitive. If you're assigned to a mediocre film, don't take it personally. Remember that your face is on the screen, and moviegoers are becoming acquainted with it."

"I feel like I'm being punished when they put me in crap like *The Boob*."

"When Mr. Mayer or Mr. Thalberg decides to teach you a lesson, Joan, you'll know it."

Joan moved uneasily in her chair, crossed and uncrossed her legs, and scanned the room without seeing or caring. Bern patted her hand and said he had faith in her. "I know what it is to be impatient," he said, trying to take Joan's mind off her problems. Although he rarely talked about himself, Bern wanted her to know that no matter how difficult it might have been for Lucille LeSueur, others had suffered more.

Bern was born in Wandsbek, Germany. His parents emigrated to America and settled in a New York slum. He changed his name from Levy to Bern and enrolled at the American Academy of Dramatic Arts.

She giggled. "You wanted to be an actor?"

He looked away with a hint of embarrassment. "Yes, but I soon discovered my interests were broader than an actor's." He was enthralled with all aspects of production, and for the next four years worked as a stage manager and assistant director of plays. Then he made up his mind to take a chance in Hollywood. M-G-M hired him as a supervisor until Irving Thalberg asked him to join his staff.

"Irving this and Thalberg that." Joan scowled. "What does L. B. Mayer do around the studio? Sign paychecks?"

Bern ignored the remark and asked about her fan mail. She perked up and said she answered each letter personally, bought her own stamps, and mailed them on the way to work. Bern hinted that this was a waste of her time. M-G-M had personnel who handled such trivial matters.

"I don't trust no one!" she emphasized. "Those letters might get thrown out. After all, if people take the time to sit down and write to me . . . well, goddamn it, it's only right that I answer. I'll do anything."

Bern was impressed but not surprised. She had gotten her name in the newspapers by winning so many dance contests, and Louella Parsons knew Joan was the brightest young star at M-G-M. L. B. Mayer knew her by name although he had yet to introduce himself. Bern explained to Joan that she had arrived in Hollywood at a very unusual time. The merger of Metro Pictures Corp., Louis B. Mayer Pictures, and Goldwyn Co. had made M-G-M the most powerful studio in the world, but the death of Marcus Loew had been a shock to the company. Also, rumor had it that the first sound movie, Warner Brothers' *The Jazz Singer,* would revolutionize the motion picture business. Sound might only be a phase, but M-G-M had to prepare its players, consider new equipment, put aside future projects, and begin again.

Abruptly, Bern stopped talking and apologized for discussing business. Joan appeared to be frightened and confused. Suppose sound ruined her? If M-G-M procrastinated, would it recoup its losses? Joan was genuinely upset and asked Paul how he could be so calm knowing he might be out of a job. He told her to study her scripts and leave the legalities to the head office. Just as important was her wardrobe, and there was no reason why she couldn't borrow the proper clothes from the studio; however, he would choose what she would wear because they would attend premieres, parties, concerts, and plays together.

Joan nodded. She had no choice.

"Bern is the one who can make you, Cranberry." Haines insisted.

"But he's puny."

"Has he made any advances?"

"No."

"Go to his apartment if he asks you."

"I'll have to get stinkin' drunk!"

"Trust me."

Bern kept his promises. He provided Joan with fashionable gowns that clung elegantly to her well-developed body. He esorted her to exclusive dinner parties, opening nights at the opera, and premieres sparkling with floodlights that illuminated the sky. In spite of their frequent dates, Joan felt inferior to this intellectual. She never forgot the night he had a drink in her apartment. "Paul looked around and said nothing," she recalled, "but he was paralyzed by a black velvet painting studded with rhinestones. What did I know? I thought he was admiring it. He just stared and smiled weakly. I got to know that look, and it meant 'dreadful.' I left my chewing gum at home and improved my speech with the help of a drama coach."

Winners of the Wilderness belonged to Tim McCoy, but Bern emphasized the importance of working with good directors such as W. S. Van Dyke. "And Jack Conway is another," Paul said. "That's why I want you to play opposite Francis X. Bushman, Jr., in *The Understanding Heart.*"

"Seems to me a girl around here would do better going to bed with the director instead of her leading man," Joan remarked.

"You might try talent," he said with a tinge of sarcasm.

Bushman took a liking to Joan and gave her the edge in *The Understanding Heart.* The *New York Evening Graphic* reported: "Miss Crawford screens remarkably well and shows development so far beyond her previous work that one may expect important tidings of this young player."

Although Rapf stepped forward as the one responsible for Joan's progress, it was Bern's manipulation that gave her the chance to work with Lon Chaney in *The Unknown.* Chaney was very demanding of himself, particularly in this role, as an armless knife-thrower in a circus who used his feet to hurl knives at his assistant, played by Joan. "If I had to name one person who taught me not only how to act and how to concentrate but also how to master a role that was practically impossible, it was Lon Chaney. He practiced in his dressing room every spare minute. On the set, nothing distracted him. He became that armless man. Lon Chaney did not exist. I was terrified, but the man was a perfectionist. Working after hours he was shy and sweet, so unlike the character in *The Unknown.*"

Bern kept a watchful eye on Joan but did not interfere. If she could hold her own with Chaney, her future was promising.

Haines was very busy, too. His popularity was firmly established, and M-G-M was immensely pleased with his work. Visiting Joan on the set of *The Unknown,* he noticed her preoccupation with Chaney. "He's a genius with makeup," she told Billy.

"As they say, 'Don't step on that spider, it might be Lon Chaney!' "

"You made that up."

"I wish I had. Speaking of spiders, how's Bern?"

"I owe him so much."

"Have you been to his apartment?"

"Often."

"Beethoven?"

"Yes."

"Cranberry, you could have the other half of M-G-M if Bern could 'get it up.' "

"Who owns the other half?"

"N-O-R-M-A!"

Joan stormed off the set, turned around, and threw a tube of lipstick at

Billy. "I hope it's your shade!" She laughed, and the members of the crew joined in. The one who enjoyed the joke most was Haines.

The *New York Evening World*'s review of *The Unknown* was a breakthrough for Joan: "Miss Crawford's one of the screen's acknowledged artists, and each picture seems to merely justify the characterization. Certainly her performance in this picture is a most impressive one."

"Congratulations!"

"Thank you, Mr. Mayer."

"I hardly recognize you these days. What have you done to yourself?"

"Everything."

He smiled. "I can see that, but you've become an actress—quite a contrast to the hustling little flapper-about-town."

"I do both," she said proudly.

"I thought it was time we got to know each other. We're a family at M-G-M and I want you to come to me with your problems, troubles, and any other burdens that weigh heavily on your heart."

"Thank you, sir. Thank you."

"On my desk is a new contract. Is two hundred fifty dollars a week adequate?"

"Is . . . how much . . . ad . . . ?"

"Two hundred fifty dollars."

"Yes, I can live on that. I mean, can I!"

"Paul tells me you send money to your mother who lives in Kansas City."

"It's no one's business."

"As I said, Joan, we're a loving family here, and I'd like you to think of me as your father. We don't have secrets."

"My mother and I don't get along."

"And your father?"

"Which one?"

"Pardon me?"

"My real father deserted us, sir."

"Well," Mayer beamed as he rolled out of his chair, "I won't desert you. Now, Joan, what do you want more than anything?"

Joan hadn't expected a gift from him. The raise was more than enough. "A roadster!" she exclaimed.

"Good," he said, embracing her hands. "You can well afford to buy one now!"

Joan was elated but perplexed. Had she assumed he was offering her a car, or did he purposely tease her into thinking so? She felt as if she had been kissed and kicked at the same time! It was a good indication, however, that she had as much to learn off-camera as on. Joan would find out that L. B. Mayer was the greatest actor of them all.

Bern did not take the credit for Joan's raise, although his squiring her

around Hollywood and recommending that she co-star with Chaney had influenced Mayer considerably. "The Great White Father," however, knew that
Joan was dating handsome nineteen-year-old Mike Cudahy, alcoholic heir to
a Chicago meat-packing fortune. Then there was Tommy Lee, son of auto and
radio millionaire Don Lee. Mayer relished this publicity, and he recognized a
future star in Joan, but there was no pattern to her dating habits. He knew
about Haines, the bums who helped Joan win her dancing trophies, Bern, and
the rich heirs with their gold-plated flasks and Pierce Arrows. Mayer did not
need proof that Joan was a wildcat. He'd done his homework, and the folks
back in Kansas City had used many adjectives to describe the Cassin girl, and
none was pure.

Money was power, but despite his dedication to a family of exceptional
stars, Mayer needed ammunition for heated contract negotiations. He had his
little back room for starlets who would never make the grade, but he did not
have a casting couch for the promising ones. Mayer fondled and hugged (Joan
said he usually managed to "accidentally" touch her right breast), but there
was no trading of sex for stardom. Supposedly, he had offered Jean Harlow a
mink coat for a few hours in bed. Reliable sources insist the story is true,
although Hollywood insiders doubt it. If true, it is one of the very few
exceptions for Mayer.

Renowned for his harsh language and threats, he was also famous for his
tender approach and solemn promises. With Joan he would use all tactics. In
her he saw a workhorse, a go-getter, a hustler, and a beautiful tramp. There
was no need to have Joan watched. His flunkies said she was more concerned
about her image than furs, cars, jewelry, and marriage. "As long as she doesn't
get laid on Sunset, I don't care," Mayer said. One of his staff jotted down, "at
sunset," and the story got around.

"Did he mean on Sunset or at sunset?" Joan asked Haines.

"Mayer's really saying he knows you're sleeping around."

"So what?"

"The studios run this town. They've covered up more dirt than a Montana blizzard. It's inconvenient to get up in the middle of the night to prevent
a scandal, to make payoffs, and to slap us down a peg."

"Mayer knows about you?"

"He'll get around to arranging a marriage if there are any concrete
rumors."

"Maybe we have a chance after all," she teased.

"Not unless you're a lesbian, Cranberry. That's how it's done."

"Is that why Valentino got married?"

"That was more psychological than essential."

"Don't bother explaining it to me."

"I wouldn't dream of it. Besides, I don't think of you as the type of girl
who would allow the studio to play matchmaker. Did Mayer ask you about the
playboys in love with you?"

"No."

"I'm asking you then. What about Cudahy? He's handsome, rich, and in love with you."

"He's also a drunk, Billy."

"I've seen you handle him with ease, Cranberry."

"We kinda love each other."

"What are you going to do about it?"

"Try to get him off booze. A few nights ago, he didn't drink at all."

"With you, that is."

"I'm gonna try, Billy. I'm gonna try because Mike and I have a chance, but most important, I want to help him."

Adela Rogers St. John wrote that Joan and Cudahy made a beautiful couple. "Joan wore black a lot in those days, with big picture hats and much too much makeup. Scarlet lips, mascaraed lashes, flaming hair—hard, haughty, pitifully defiant. Substituting excitement for happiness, drama for contentment, and laughing just a little too loudly in the face of Hollywood's disapproval."

F. Scott Fitzgerald said, "Joan Crawford is doubtless the best example of the flapper, the girl you see at smart nightclubs, gowned to the apex of sophistication, toying with iced glasses with a remote, faintly bitter expression, dancing deliciously, laughing a great deal, with wide, hurt eyes."

Mrs. Cudahy did not approve of Joan and said so over tea one afternoon in the family mansion. "I don't think you're good enough for my son, and I blame you for his drinking."

Thoughts of being blackballed from the sorority at Stephens spun around in Joan's head. Not good enough. Not good enough. Not good enough. She cared little about what Mrs. Cudahy thought and expressed what had been on her mind for more than a year. "You give Michael almost two thousand dollars a month," she retorted. "He squanders it. He has no purpose in life. No goal. No ambition. He's an alcoholic. I can't help him if you don't care enough to try."

Joan never saw Mrs. Cudahy again nor did she give up on Michael regardless of the many nights she had to carry him to his door. "When a love affair begins," Joan reflected, "it's like a new dress. It may be your favorite. There's an accident. You tear it. You love it, so you patch it—cleverly, daintily—so that no one can see it. Yet *you* know you have patched it. The next time, perhaps, you burn it. Again you patch it and conceal it, but you know it is no longer perfect. Finally, after much patching and mending you can no longer pretend, even to yourself, that the dress is 'as good as new.' You may still think it is the prettiest dress of your wardrobe, but it is patched beyond wearing. The only thing to do, then, is to be brave and discard it! Bury the shreds in the prison of your heart as you bury the shreds of your dress in your mending basket. Remember only its first beauty, when it was new and glittering and attractive!"

This Crawford interview sounded as patched and mended as the dress, but Joan most certainly was not explaining a broken love affair to the Vanderbilts or the Huttons, who discarded their gowns after an evening's gala. No, Joan communicated with her public, and M-G-M merely added a few adjectives. She was not brokenhearted over Cudahy, but her inability to make a man out of him was disappointing. She told a friend, "Maybe he didn't love me enough to change. I'll never know."

Paul Bern began to court Joan seriously. He gave her an ermine coat, but she gave it back. "I couldn't afford to lose his friendship," she said. "We were in a nightclub with another couple, and I admired the woman's fur coat. Paul asked me if I wanted one like it. 'Of course!' I said. 'What woman wouldn't?' He left the table for a while, returned for the entertainment, and then we left. Instead of the polo coat he had checked earlier, Paul put a full-length ermine over my shoulders."

Bern talked very little about himself. She knew nothing of his sexual desires and habits. He reminded her of Ray Sterling, who wanted only to talk, to listen to her problems, to correct her diction, to discuss literature, to meditate to Bach, and to avoid any kind of intimacy. The only difference was that Joan had been attracted to Ray.

When Joan was given the lead opposite John Gilbert in *Twelve Miles Out,* Hollywood took it for granted that Bern was responsible. The two men had lived together and were still close friends. Gilbert was caught up in the eye of Hurricane Garbo at the time; he had been arrested and jailed for drunk driving while trying to find his beloved Greta after her third attempt to escape marriage to him. Beside himself with frustration and remorse, Gilbert arrived at the studio every day with an empty heart and blank face. Joan recalled the many phone calls to Garbo and how his mood depended on the conversations. Joan was strongly attracted to Gilbert during their scenes together. There was magic between them, and she experienced her first feeling of sexual desire in an actor's arms before the camera. "A woman can tell if a man responds, and John did," she said, "but he was obsessed with Garbo. He was a beautiful person . . . a warm and gentle human being. Within a few short years this great star would be destroyed. I know how, but I don't know why."

Gilbert, earning $10,000 a week, was M-G-M's hottest property, but he was the one member of the M-G-M family whom Mayer hated most. One reason was Garbo, who not only followed Gilbert's advice in money matters but threatened to become an American citizen by marrying John when Mayer wanted to have her deported for failing to show up at the studio. Many guests at the wedding of Eleanor Boardman and King Vidor in 1926 heard Mayer say to Gilbert when Garbo's name was mentioned, "What do you have to marry her for? Why don't you just fuck her and forget about it?" Gilbert pounced on his boss with both fists, and the two men drew blood. The other guests pulled them apart. When Mayer got to his feet holding a pair of broken eyeglasses, he shouted, "You're through, Gilbert! I'll destroy you if it costs me a million dollars!"

It would take L. B. Mayer a few years, but a threat was as good as a promise—it was just a matter of time.

"Cranberry, forget about Gilbert. Finish the picture and walk away. His life is a mess. Don't get involved. You'll rile Mayer and he'll find out. So will Bern and Thalberg. Garbo's signing for five thousand dollars a week thanks to Gilbert. She's gaining on him."

"She doesn't want John!"

Haines sighed. ". . . a very strange woman. Not dangerous, Cranberry. Just strange and unpredictable. Gilbert will be on a merry-go-round for a long, long time, and you'll find yourself with another Cudahy."

"I'd like to help John."

"Then leave him alone. You haven't got a chance."

Gilbert admitted *Twelve Miles Out* was a terrible picture, and he had no intention of seeing it or attending the premiere. Mayer was furious that this statement was made directly to the press. John said publicly that one of his best scenes had been cut out and he did not know why. Had Mayer done it deliberately? Was he pushing Joan? Did Joan influence Bern? Was Bern trying to impress Mayer? Was Mayer sleeping with Joan? Was Joan angry at Garbo for causing Gilbert anguish? Was Garbo jealous of Joan's trying to seduce Gilbert? There were many questions but no answers.

Twelve Miles Out was a success; it received rave reviews. Mayer complimented Joan personally. "I'm so sorry, my dear, that you had to be exposed to such temperament," he sighed. "I understand you worked under extreme pressure."

Joan said director Jack Conway handled matters smoothly.

"I'm surprised he didn't throw that bastard off the set! I apologize for using profanity, my dear."

"Mr. Gilbert was a gentleman despite . . ."

"Despite his selfish ass!"

"Mr. Mayer, why did you cut out that scene? It was very good. John wrote it himself."

"Who the hell are you to accuse me of editing? I pay people to do that! Gilbert's not a writer. He's not even an actor!"

"Then how come I make two hundred fifty dollars a week and he makes ten thousand dollars?"

Mayer growled. "You have no idea what I have to contend with—no idea at all. Thalberg was still wearing woolen underwear when he came to work here because Mama was afraid he'd catch cold. And Gilbert, that son of a bitch, was married to the lovely and sweet Leatrice Joy, who wept while he and Irving ran around every night. I warned them! When Leatrice sued for divorce, my heart was shattered. Joan, it was torn to shreds. My studio involved in a divorce. Unthinkable. And a poor wife and mother with a beautiful baby girl thrown into the street. Shameful! Motherhood is sacred. I'll never forgive that lousy bastard. Never!"

"Doesn't she get alimony?"

"Can money replace a cozy home and loving family and the holy vows of wedlock? Can money do that?" Mayer asked.

"It helps."

"I can imagine how you feel, working twice as hard as that jackass and earning so much less. Don't worry about anything, Joan. That's why I'm here."

She glanced casually at his desk for a new contract.

He was aware of her searching eyes. "Money can't replace a prime role in a choice film with one's dearest friend." Mayer winked.

"It can't?"

"William Haines and Joan Crawford in *Spring Fever!*"

"Thank you, Mr. Mayer. Working with Billy is always a treat."

"You'll have everything you want. If only my other girls were like you— loyal, religious, wise, and talented. Perhaps that's why Irving chose Norma. She's very demure. They're getting married, you know. I'm looking around for the perfect gift."

"How about matching woollies?"

Mayer threw his head back and laughed. "God gave you a rare sense of humor, Joan."

"I pray for it every morning at St. Augustine's Church. I'll even say a prayer for Mr. Thalberg tomorrow," she said.

In 1926, the Western Association of Motion Picture Advertisers, a fraternal organization of press agents, selected the dozen most promising young movie actresses. Among them were Joan Crawford, Dolores Costello, Mary Astor, Janet Gaynor, Dolores Del Rio, and Fay Wray. For the first time in her life, Joan became friendly with a group of girls and was determined to keep them together. The "Wampas Babies" became her substitute for a sorority. Joan arranged weekly luncheons at Montmartre, demanding the best table by charming the headwaiters. If her chosen table wasn't set up properly, the management heard about it.

When Jane Peters, another girl-about-town, planted herself at the "royal table," Joan told her to move.

"I prefer sitting here," the cute blonde said.

"I've seen you before."

"The Charleston contests, remember?"

"Oh, yeah, well, move your ass, kid. The first table near the palm is reserved."

"I recall your winning trophies, Miss Crawford, but not Montmartre!"

Joan screamed for the headwaiter and made a scene. Miss Peters, later known as Carole Lombard, stood up, adjusted her veiled hat, put on her gloves, looked Joan in the eye, smiled politely, and said, "Fuck you!"

Joan, of course, dressed elegantly for these luncheons and tea dances. She had a Ford roadster and loved to pick up the girls for a few hours of chatter about their careers. Joan, with her fashionable dresses and daring hats, heavy makeup, abounding energy, and constant table-hopping, was the undisputed queen. Any new acquaintances, such as the Young sisters, Polly Ann and Betty Jane, were written up in the columns as being seen at Miss Crawford's table. One afternoon, teenager Loretta Young tagged along. Her beauty captivated everyone, and Joan, annoyed, refused to allow the girl to join her tea parties. Loretta stayed home alone, answered the telephone, and accepted her first movie part, which had been meant for Polly Ann. Miss Young was only fifteen when her long and successful career began, thanks to Joan.

West Point, starring Joan and Billy Haines, quickly followed *Spring Fever.* It was a grueling schedule, but Joan wanted to go out dancing every night. Bern managed a quiet evening with her once a week. He admitted being serious, but also expressed his one great fear. "I hope you're not on dope, Joan."

"Who's been spreading rumors?"

"Please don't be offended. It's common out here."

"Do you have me confused with Miss La Marr?"

"Barbara wasn't the only one. Remember Olive Thomas?"

"Yeah. I saw her in *The Flapper.*"

"Olive was a Ziegfeld girl when she was sixteen, then came to Hollywood and married Mary Pickford's brother, Jack. They were the ideal couple. They were also cocaine and heroine addicts. Olive was twenty when she committed suicide."

"What am I supposed to do, put a rose on her grave?"

"Then poor Virginia Rappe was murdered by Arbuckle."

"I heard she had the clap and he wouldn't touch her."

Bern sat down next to Joan and held her hand. "Poor Wally Reid, the All-American boy, had to take morphine to keep up with the exhausting pace of making films. He died in a padded cell. Wally was only thirty."

"Jesus, you're morbid!"

"And Barbara . . ."

"You're still in love with her!"

"I am more concerned about those who will follow in her footsteps, and it pains me to watch their self-destruction."

"I'm not one of them."

"Joan, you've got to be on something! How do you stay out all night and work all day . . . on and on. What are you taking?"

"A lotta crap from you! Nobody can accuse me of taking dope and get away with it."

"I was asking, not accusing. Please, Joan. If anything happened to you . . ."

She smirked. "Wally Reid got his morphine from the studio."

"Paramount," he said calmly, "not M-G-M."

"Look, I smoke and hate booze but drink it socially. That's all."

"Beautiful women are like beautiful flowers. I hate to see them trampled to death."

"Don't worry about me, Paul."

He squeezed her hand. "By the way, I forgot to congratulate you on *Rose-Marie.*"

"*Rose-Marie!*" she screamed.

"Without the music, my love."

"No wonder everyone in this town's on dope!"

"Top billing, Joan."

"Top billing?"

"Top billing."

Joan rushed out the next day and bought a small box camera to take pictures of her name on the marquees. *Rose-Marie* with James Murray was well received, but before Joan had a chance to protest, she was cast opposite Ramon Novarro in *Across to Singapore.* When the film was completed, she decided to take matters into her own hands. She was tired of Bern's classical music and preaching, tired of Mayer's fatherly hugs, and tired of being the most promising newcomer. Without hesitation or fear, she approached Irving Thalberg on the set. She made small talk, but he paid little attention and barely acknowledged her.

"Why does your wife always get the choice parts?" she blurted out. "It's not fair."

He said nothing at first. Nor did he look at her. It was a long minute before he said, "You're progressing nicely and will continue to do so."

"I can't play Juliet in a wheelchair."

"Somehow that role doesn't suit you," he said coldly.

"I'd like to know how long it takes to get a good part in a good picture, that's all!"

"You wouldn't want to make a fool of yourself, I'm sure," he said.

Before she could challenge him, Thalberg walked away without glancing at her once. Joan could not remember an emptier feeling.

"You did what?" Haines exploded.

"I had to, Billy!"

"You'll pay a high price for it."

"Like what, for example."

"Thalberg could put you on suspension without pay."

"Or?"

"Put you in a film you'll try to forget for the rest of your life."

The name of that picture was a Tim McCoy western, *The Law of the Range*. Whether Thalberg knew Joan was terrified of horses isn't known, but she was determined to go through with it. She told McCoy, "I'm going to enjoy working with you and your cowboys if it kills me!" Joan was the first one on the set every day and made friends with everyone as if this were the happiest time of her life. If Thalberg was anywhere nearby, he saw only a smiling Joan Crawford. She did not complain once or say an unkind word about *The Law of the Range*. Haines and Bern kept their distance because this was one battle Joan had to fight alone. She came through it with fine reviews and prayed a little longer at St. Augustine's: "Please God, get that lousy mama's boy off my back! Give me another chance."

PART TWO

4

CINDERELLA AT THE PALACE

Joan waited. Thalberg continued to ignore her, Bern always had a new gown for her, the luncheons and tea dances continued, but she had no idea what type of role M-G-M was planning for her.

John Gilbert met Joan on the lot one day with a warm embrace. "I think we'll be reunited very soon." He smiled handsomely. "They gave me a script called *Four Walls,* an underworld drama, and your name was mentioned."

"I'm overjoyed," she said seductively.

"I am, too, Joan."

"You look wonderful!"

"I feel wonderful."

Was it possible she was going to work with Gilbert again? The next morning she prayed for it, and the script of *Four Walls* was in her hands. Word got around the studio that Joan had "paid her dues" and was being considered for other worthwile properties.

Joan was more thrilled about trying her luck again with Gilbert than being off probation. "The chemistry between John and me was still there," she said, "but so was Garbo. They were living together, but there was no talk of marriage. He was so vibrant, dynamic, and passionate. I followed, I responded, and, oh, I wanted him. We spoke to each other with our eyes. Making love to John was so natural. We could have gone all the way each time we touched."

One of the crew members who worked on *Four Walls* said, "The kisses shared by Crawford and Gilbert were sizzling. We all knew it and were rooting for her not only as a dramatic actress but to rival Garbo, who was ruining Gilbert's life. We thought Joan was clever enough to be discreet if Jack were led properly. He hadn't been happier in a long time. Though he and Joan couldn't get enough of each other when the camera was rolling, he didn't follow through. Joan, not one to give up, asked for extra run-throughs to keep the fire going. I'm sure she could have made Gilbert forget about Garbo. That was the word that got around. She was a very sexually potent girl."

Photoplay summed it up: "For getting down to earth with the practical sort of love-making that folks like, our hat is off to John Gilbert and Joan Crawford. John certainly takes that girl in hand, and boy, how she loves to be taken!"

The *New York Evening World* gave Joan a standing ovation: "It isn't often that a supporting player manages to steal a picture right from under the nose of John Gilbert . . . But that's what happens in *Four Walls* . . . For Joan Crawford simply walks off with it. The picture will go a long way toward lifting Miss Crawford to a point nearer the top in Hollywood circles, a point toward which she has been rapidly climbing in the last year or two."

Bern hinted that Joan's next picture would be one written with her in mind. She forgot about Gilbert, forgot about Tim McCoy's *The Law of the Range,* and forgot about Norma and Irving Thalberg. Unfortunately, she could never forget Murphy's law . . .

"Hi, Billie! Surprise, huh?"

"What the hell are you doin' here?"

"I figured Hollywood might change my luck."

"Get your dirty feet off my couch, you son of a bitch!"

"Mom sends her love."

"I send her enough checks! Listen, Hal, I haven't got time to show you around town. Give me some notice if you decide to come back, and I hope you don't."

"I'm stayin', Billie."

"Not in my house!"

"I'm broke but willin' to work in the movies."

"Willing?!"

"Yep," he said, looking through the icebox. "What's for dinner?"

"Nothing."

"That's okay." He lay back on the couch. "Pick up some pork chops. A salad's okay unless you want potatoes, too."

Joan put her hands on her hips and stood over him. "Where's Jesse?"

"That's all over. Hey, I'm hungry."

Shocked at seeing him, Joan drove in a trancelike state to the store. Tired, furious, and speechless, she cooked dinner, washed the dishes, and watched her brother unpack. "You can't stay here long, Hal."

"There's room," he said, pushing her clothes aside in the small closet.

"The way Mom was talking I thought you'd be mayor of Kansas City by now," she hissed.

"Do you really want to know the truth? Why I came out here?"

She chomped on some chewing gum and began filing her nails.

"I figured," he continued, "if you could make good out here, I'd have a chance, too."

"I'll see what I can do because you'll need money to live somewhere else or get your ass back to Kansas City."

She spoke to Bern, who got Hal work as an extra and bit player. He was good-looking and came across well on the screen, but had no concept of what it was to become an actor or how to play the game. "My brother was a lazy

Crawford—before her protein diet—as a Broadway showgirl in *Sally, Irene, and Mary* (1925).

The flapper at M-G-M (1926). Joan's energetic Charleston got L. B. Mayer's attention.

Billy Haines with Joan in *West Point* (1928). Haines would remain her closest confidant throughout her career.

The fairy tale couple: Douglas Fairbanks, Jr., and his bride in 1929.

Crawford and Gable in *Possessed* (1931). Their on-screen chemistry had moviegoers begging for more and touched off a thirty-year love affair.

Doug and Joan back from their six-week European vacation (1932). It didn't save their marriage, as L. B. Mayer had hoped.

The electricity with Gable continued in *Dancing Lady* (1933).

Joan with second husband Franchot Tone. Co-starring with his famous wife in seven films did little for Tone's ego or their marriage.

Crawford with her most enduring love—her fans.

With Spencer Tracy in *Mannequin* (1938).
He made her laugh despite her failing marriage, but his clowning, criticism, and
drinking ended their brief romance.

Norma Shearer, Joan, and Rosalind Russell in *The Women* (1939). This chummy
pose was solely for the camera's benefit—
Shearer and Crawford competed bitterly
for star status.

Robert Taylor, Joan Crawford, and Louis B.
Mayer at a party for Taylor in 1941. Mayer
ruled M-G-M with an iron hand and tried to
control his stars' personal lives as well.

Crawford and Gable in *Strange Cargo* (1940), their last, and best, picture together.

Crawford with her third husband, Phillip Terry. When her career resumed she left the household chores to Terry but carefully scheduled every activity, including sex.

Joan and director Michael Curtiz with her Academy Award for *Mildred Pierce* (1945).

"Mommie Dearest" showing off her adopted children, Christina and Christopher.

Crawford with her fourth husband, Pepsi president Alfred Steele.

Bette Davis and Joan on the set of *What Ever Happened to Baby Jane* (1962). The fireworks started soon after production began.

Joan as the shapely ringmaster in *Berserk* (1968). At age sixty-four, she was still every inch the glamorous star.

drunk," Joan recalled. "He got work at M-G-M because I ran my ass off begging for favors. I had my own career to think about, and I felt I was on the brink of what I'd been waiting for and that meant campaigning on my own behalf. But I cooked for the bastard, cleaned up after him, and tried to get some sleep while he partied with friends all night in my house. Finally I sent for my mother. I was supporting her anyway, and she'd gotten rid of Harry. It was a disaster having them both, but I was damn sick of cooking and cleaning up after Hal. He and I fought worse than ever. Being broke was better than having a nervous breakdown."

Bern was worried about Joan. He knew all about her family problems and resented the intrusion of Hal and Anna, too. "We're just about ready to go ahead with Hunt Stromberg's *Our Dancing Daughters,*" he said. "The part of Diana is you, Joan . . . the misunderstood flapper who dances the nights away with a broken and lonely heart."

She read the script, and there was no doubt it had been written for her. With fine support from Johnny Mack Brown and Nils Asther, *Our Dancing Daughters* was a smash. The *New York World* wrote: "Of Miss Crawford it may be predicted that in case her managers continue to find such breezy little comedies for her, she will realize what apparently has been her ambition for at least two years, and get going as a star in her own right. She has good looks, sprightliness, intelligence, and a good sense of humor. She dances with great grace and versatility and she knows when— and how—to call a halt."

"Bravo!" Mayer cheered, greeting Joan personally at his office door. "How does it feel to be a star?"

"Nothing much has changed."

"Look at this review in the *World.*"

"Yeah. Can you beat that?" she scowled, grabbing the paper. " '. . . she will realize what apparently has been her ambition for at least two years, and get going as a star in her own right.' As if I've been playing house with Gilbert and Bushman or raising horses with Tim McCoy! I *will* realize!"

"You take these things too seriously, Joan. It's the meaning that counts."

"That's good because I haven't got any money to count."

He waved a piece of paper at her. "New contract, my dear."

"And . . . ?"

"I'm doubling your salary."

"You wouldn't kid a girl," she said with a sly look.

"Read it for yourself."

Tears flowed down her face. "Do you know what this means?" she sniffled.

"You tell me," he said, sitting next to her on the couch.

"It means I can get a place of my own. It means I don't have to live with my fuckin' brother and mother any longer."

Mayer's mouth dropped. "Please, Joan . . ."

"I want to buy a house," she said excitedly, ". . . a bungalow on Roxbury Drive in Beverly Hills."

"What a nice thing to do for your family."

"My family?" she piped up. "They can live in the dump we're in now. I'm moving into the new place alone, Mr. Mayer."

"How much?"

"Eighteen thousand bucks."

"Can you afford it?"

"Not unless you can lend me the down payment."

"On one condition."

"I don't like conditions, but let's hear it."

"That you continue to support your dear mother."

"Did it ever occur to you that some mothers are bitches?"

"No, and I won't listen to such talk."

"Haven't I been sending her money for almost three lousy years?"

"I have your word?" he asked.

"You'll lend me the down payment?"

"Yes."

She threw her arms around him. "God, thank you! Or is it the other way around?"

"Cranberry, you can't allow your mother and brother to live in that tiny hole," Haines exclaimed. "Do you know what people in Hollywood will say?"

"What the hell do I care?"

"When you're a star you have to live like one."

"The house on Roxbury is delicious," she said.

"Your mother's been getting around town wearing the latest creations, and your brother's dating some pretty chic girls. When they get their names in the columns, then what?"

"The gossip columns!" Joan huffed. "Who wants to read about a wash woman and a drunk?"

"They're Joan Crawford's family."

"Jesus Christ! It's bad enough trying to keep up my image. Am I expected to do the same for them?"

Haines looked at her as if to say, "You naughty, selfish girl . . ."

"I get a raise and it's gone already!" she mumbled, lighting a cigarette.

"There's a nice bungalow over on Genesee. Two or three bedrooms, I think. Not expensive, Cranberry."

"I was hoping to use the extra dough on my own place."

"Instead of cramming it full of cheap nonsense, buy a few quality items," he said. "I'd be glad to help. Give the old stuff to your family."

"All right. All right. All right."

"I don't know what you're complaining about, Cranberry. If you want your mother to wear expensive clothes, why protest over a decent place for her to live?"

"Because I didn't give her any damn money to buy a new wardrobe!"

"She probably used her life's savings," he said sadly.

"Bullshit. I had to send her a train ticket!"

"Charge accounts?" he asked.

Joan"s face turned gray. "That's it! She's been buyin' stuff and not tellin' me."

"I guess you'll have to have a little talk with Mama," he smiled.

Joan straightened out the overdue bills and made sure Anna could not charge anything without permission. Shortly before she moved into her own house on Roxbury, Hal wrecked her Ford roadster. "Live your own lives and don't bug me," she told them. "If you can't live on what money I give you, go back where you came from!"

Although Joan did not live that far from her family, she wanted privacy. Her dream world had been shattered when Hal showed up at a time when everything was working out so nicely. She was honest with Pete Smith and Harry Rapf. An official family portrait was allowed, but under no circumstances would she permit any publicity about her mother and Hal. No interviews, either. "I don't want it known they live in Los Angeles," she explained, "because I have no intention of having cozy family Christmas and Thanksgiving dinners. I can't stop them from using the name LeSueur, but few remember Lucille, anyway. If they want a cent from me, that's the way it is."

Bern invited Joan to the opening night of *Young Woodley* at the Vine Street Playhouse on October 27, 1927. After the performance he took her backstage to meet the leading man, Douglas Fairbanks, Jr. "We'd been introduced casually several months before," Joan recalled. "He seemed stuffy. Too pompous. I thought he was splendid in *Young Woodley* and told him so. Paul and I had planned to have a late supper, but I wasn't hungry. I went home, got into bed, and thought about *Young Woodley*. In the middle of the night I picked up the telephone and sent Douglas a congratulatory telegram. He answered in person the next day. I invited him for tea. That's how our romance started. He was tall, very thin and boyish but also the epitome of suaveness. Douglas had been educated in France and England, and possessed a marvelous sense of humor, impeccable manners, and a gentle nature."

He invited her to watch the play from the wings. She was there almost every night. They dined in gourmet restaurants, enjoyed golf and tennis together, and bronzed on the beach. Fairbanks was everything Joan wanted in a husband. It was she who fell hopelessly in love with him. According to her daughter Christina Crawford, Joan chased young Doug relentlessly until she got him. Whether he was being gallant or truthful, he maintained that it was Joan who avoided him. "That aroused my curiosity," he claimed.

Despite his famous name, Douglas Fairbanks, Jr., was not a successful actor when he met Joan.

He was born on December 9, 1907, in New York. His mother, Beth Sully, was heiress to a cotton fortune, and his father, Douglas Fairbanks, Sr., was a well-known stage actor. His parents' divorce in 1918 was blamed on his father's success in Hollywood. Beth received a $400,000 settlement and squandered it in a rebound marriage.

A family friend felt the swashbuckling idol was ashamed of his fat and timid son, who preferred oil painting to athletics. Douglas Jr. remembered little if any father-son relationship. "I was never cut out to be a father," the elder Fairbanks admitted. "It isn't that I don't like Junior, but I can't feel about him the way that I should."

Mary Pickford became Junior's stepmother in 1920. While Fairbanks and America's Sweetheart became the most beloved couple in the world, Beth and Junior lived in Paris on a limited budget until Jesse Lasky of Paramount decided to cash in on the Fairbanks name by offering the fifteen-year-old a part in *Stephen Steps Out* for $1,000 a week. When Fairbanks Sr. found out he forbade Beth to go through with it. Threats were exchanged until Junior said he had every intention of doing the movie. The elder Fairbanks was furious; he resented being defied by a son who was no longer the stubby bore he remembered.

Fairbanks made it known in Hollywood that all he wanted for the boy was a good European education. *Stephen Steps Out* was a dismal failure, and Beth took what money her son had made and went back to Paris until the disaster was forgotten. A year later, a much wiser Beth returned to Hollywood with her son. Young Doug started at the bottom, playing small roles in films, to the dismay of his father, who, seeing a young and vibrant Fairbanks on the screen, felt old.

Mary Pickford understood that her famous husband was in his mid-forties and resented every wrinkle and extra pound. She tried to make peace and succeeded somewhat. Besides, it was quite apparent that Junior wasn't going to make it in the movies and was seriously considering acting in the theater. He did fairly well in a number of plays, including *Romeo and Juliet* and *The Jest*. Mary persuaded her husband to attend the opening night of *Young Woodley*. Dad thought Junior was a "pretty good actor." Film producers agreed, and the movie career of Douglas Fairbanks, Jr., began.

It was at this stage in his life that he met Joan Crawford, the feisty and ambitious actress who had enough spunk for both of them. Doug had been sheltered and smothered by Beth. He was a very young and innocent twenty, and Joan was a very mature and experienced twenty-five. She was his first love.

"I was 'Billie,' and he was 'Dodo,' " Joan said. "We invented a language of our own, like 'Opi lopove yopou.' He sent love poems and flowers to my dressing room every day. When he worked at First National Pictures, we'd rush across the street to meet for lunch. Two months after we met, Douglas proposed marriage. It was almost midnight on New Year's Eve. Two days later we went shopping for my platinum wedding band. He said I'd get my engagement ring when we got married. Both the wedding ring and diamond anklet were engraved 'To my darling wife' and I wore them from that minute. We were naive enough to think we were keeping it a secret!"

Supposedly Joan was only nineteen. Doug subtracted two years from his real birth date and became nineteen also. "Just two innocent teenagers," she repeated throughout the years. Reporters followed the couple everywhere. There was no need to beg for kisses. If they were separated for more than ten minutes, the lovers staged a tearful reunion. Garbo and Gilbert were moved to page two of the newspapers if their names were mentioned at all. The movie fans wanted Crawford and Fairbanks, the fairy-tale romance of the decade.

Joan gave up chewing gum and raucous laughter. She danced the Charleston, but with a little less pizzazz. The luncheons and tea dances became fashion shows, but Joan's girlfriends could not keep up with her tailored trend. She was never seen in the same outfit twice. The waiters noticed a difference in her appearance but not her attitude. "Instead of barging in," one of them said, "Miss Crawford entered, paused to look around, and walked slowly to her table. The place settings had to be p-e-r-f-e-c-t. Her complaints were amusing, actually. She did not make a scene or shatter an eardrum. We were graciously led to a secluded corner, and, with her back to the dining room, she cursed about how this was wrong, that was missing, and how dare we embarrass her. When she returned to her table, she changed into Her Serene Highness."

Joan yearned to impress Douglas, but she wanted to be eligible to walk the red carpet into Pickfair, America's version of Buckingham Palace. Then there was the critical Beth, who had sacrificed the best years of her life for the royal heir. Hollywood columnists assumed Joan was approaching her twentieth birthday, so they attributed her radical change to maturity.

A source close to "the royal family" said, "The elder Fairbanks was sick over the fact that his son was going out with Crawford. He was vehemently opposed to the impending marriage." There was nothing Joan could do about her past, but she would make sure there were no flaws in her present conduct.

After *Dream of Love* with Nils Asther, she co-starred with Billy Haines in *The Duke Steps Out*. "Cranberry, you're the talk of the town," he grinned. "Everyone's buzzing about poor Mary's curls drooping at the thought of a flapper scratching her terra-cotta tile."

"Please don't tease me about it," she mumbled.

"I hear mothers all over America are telling their kids bedtime stories about Princess Joan instead of reading *Cinderella*."

"Can I help it if Douglas and I fell in love? He's a wonderful guy, isn't he?"

"And a likable one, too, but only you could end up with two mothers-in-law."

"I never thought about that. Shit!"

"Mary Pickford's a lot like you, Cranberry. She's barged into a few offices unannounced, too. You rolled your stockings down, and she rolled her hair up. I believe she was thirty-two years old when she played a twelve-year-old girl in *Little Annie Rooney*. She's tried to play adult roles, but the public protested. When she's too old to play Alice in Wonderland, Mary Pickford is finished in films."

"How old is she now?"

"Around thirty-five."

God, Joan thought to herself. My future mother-in-law is only ten years older than I am!

"I would approach the situation this way," Haines continued. "You're making a transition from jazz baby to dramatic actress. I predict your career will last longer than Mary's."

"What do you know about Pickfair? And her marriage to Robin Hood?" Joan asked, sneaking a wad of chewing gum into her mouth.

"There are sixteen servants cluttering up the place and more are needed at formal dinner parties. Douglas doesn't allow Mary to dance with another man. She has to phone him wherever she is."

"Bore."

"Pickfair looks like a museum, but I know for a fact that a good deal of the furniture came from local department stores. It would be fun trying to pick it out."

"Who are their friends, Billy?"

"Chaplin and D. W. Griffith, of course. Lord and Lady Mountbatten, the Crown Prince of Japan, the King and Queen of Siam, the Duke of York and . . ."

"I don't want to hear any more."

"Don't get discouraged, dear heart. Fairbanks was quite a rascal before he got caught up in crowns and palaces. He used to have chairs wired with electric shocks, serve drinks in dribble glasses at formal dinner settings, and frequently crawl underneath the dining-room table to nibble on a lady's ankle."

"He doesn't seem the type."

"How do you know, Cranberry? Maybe he's got some fun left in him yet."

"I hear he's quite European."

"Trying to be, anyway. When your Douglas spends enough time at Pickfair, he'll get in with nobility, too. In fact, I've noticed that both father and son resemble country gentlemen."

"I want them to get along," Joan said sincerely.

"Your future husband is several inches taller than his father, who is only five feet eight."

"That's all?" Joan gasped.

"He's always flying through the air. Divine illusion."

"What do they eat at Pickfair? I don't want to throw up."

"You won't be invited, so why worry?" he laughed.

"Just in case!"

"Duck, beef, chicken, caviar, halibut . . ."

"That's not so fancy."

"But the chicken is *à la poulet* and the beef is *à la jardinière* and the coffee is *café noir*. A friend framed one of the menus."

"My Doug wasn't brought up that way. He's sweet and unpretentious."

"How can anyone be unpretentious in a glass-enclosed, custom-made Rolls-Royce roadster?" he bellowed. "Goldilocks had to get permission from Lady Mountbatten and the Prince of Wales before having a third one made."

"Dodo says . . ."

"Who in heaven's name is Dodo?"

"Douglas," she exclaimed.

"You're playing house, Cranberry! What does Mayer think about all this?"

"He's very, very happy. We have his blessing."

"Did you kneel and kiss his ring?"

She laughed. "Here we are joking about Pickfair and we should be spending every minute of our spare time going over our diction."

"We're talking, aren't we?"

"Billy, if *Hollywood Revue of 1929* flops, so does M-G-M."

"With Norma Shearer and Marion Davies in it?" Haines teased.

"Do you have that much faith in their sponsors, Thalberg and Hearst?"

"Thalberg, genius that he is, had no faith in talkies but went ahead with *Broadway Melody,* anyway. I predict it will win an Oscar. He can't lose with *Hollywood Revue of 1929.*"

Joan glared at him. "Have you seen the script?"

"Why?"

"Norma plays Juliet to John Gilbert's Romeo. I sing, 'I've Got a Feeling for You.' How's that for casting?"

M-G-M officials were very proud of Joan. *The Duke Steps Out* with Haines was a success, and when Joan officially announced her engagement to Douglas Fairbanks, Jr., on October 8, 1928, Mayer asked the future groom to co-star with Joan in *Our Modern Maidens.* Not only would pairing the much-publicized romantic couple onscreen attract droves of moviegoers, it would also help Doug's career, which had been crawling since he left the theater. Mayer gave Joan a raise and another loan to buy a white stucco Moorish house at 426 North Bristol Avenue in Brentwood for $40,000.

The decision to buy the house does not appear to have had anything to do with her engagement to Fairbanks. It was simply a case of the bigger the star, the bigger the house. Mayer did not quibble with Joan about the matter because he did not want it known that the Prince of Pickfair was in debt. Joan saw great potential in the man she loved. His name had been exploited and little else. With her encouragment, he would thrive on his own ability.

Although she moved into the Bristol Avenue house, Joan had little time for redecorating. Besides, she wanted to consult her husband about everything from furniture to the finger bowls. "I'm tired of doing everything myself," she told a friend. "It's been tough making my own decisions, fighting for my rights, and running around to escape loneliness. I can't even visit my mother and Hal without bickering, and I have to look after them, too. All I've ever wanted was a man to stand by my side. Doug and I will help each other. What a wonderful feeling!"

Joan was accommodating to the press, and it was common knowledge that the residents of Pickfair did not approve. The doors were closed to her. Mary Pickford was too gracious to comment, but her husband made it clear he did not want to discuss his son's plans. The press sided with Joan, the poor young girl who'd worked her way through school and danced to stardom. She had been abused by her stepfather, beaten by a headmistress, and blackballed by a sorority. Poor Joan. She'd known starvation, worn rags, and sacrificed marriage to her childhood sweetheart. She prayed every morning at St. Augustine's Church. She corresponded with the president of Stephens College because he believed in her. A hopeless cripple as a child, she rose above her handicap by dancing until she collapsed from pain and won more Charleston trophies than any girl in Hollywood.

By the time fan magazines flashed her picture on their covers with the heartrending stories of her pitiful background, moviegoers might not have shed too many tears if Pickfair had burned to the ground and its occupants been stranded in the servants' quarters. Although Joan would always be friendly with the press, she went out of her way during her engagement. Her fan mail was answered personally, and she granted all interviews patiently.

Mayer watched her progress daily. She was one member of his famous family who would make the transition from silent films to talkies. It didn't matter if Joan ever entered Pickfair. The forthcoming marriage was the sort of publicity money could not buy. She was a winner either way. Mayer's indirect message to Pickfair was *Our Modern Maidens*. Translated it went, "If we've accepted your son, why can't you accept our daughter?" The reviews were excellent. *Photoplay* summed up the film as follows: "Joan Crawford and Douglas Fairbanks, Jr., in a sequel to *Our Dancing Daughters*. Must you be told this is a sure-fire hit?"

It seemed only fitting for the couple to place their footprints in the courtyard of Graumann's Chinese Theater.

Doug's mother, Beth, had finally recognized his love for Joan, who begged her not to reveal the time and place of their marriage. The press blamed Pickfair for the couple's elopement instead of a beautiful church wedding in Hollywood. In the rectory of St. Malachy's Roman Catholic Church in New York City on June 3, 1929, Joan and Doug became man and wife. She gave him a wafer-thin platinum watch with diamond-studded hands. His gift to her was a gold cigarette box and lighter. Beth and her fiancé, Jack Whiting, attended the wedding.

According to the bride in *Portrait of Joan*, her autobiography, she sent a telegram to the studio:

IF I HAVE WORKED HARD IN THE PAST WATCH ME NOW

Douglas's telegram read:

JOAN AND I WERE MARRIED YESTERDAY. NOW THAT I HAVE A WIFE TO SUPPORT NEED RAISE IN SALARY.

They spent their brief honeymoon at the Algonquin Hotel in Manhattan. M-G-M was rushing *Hollywood Revue of 1929*, and Joan had yet to take singing lessons. Her first day at the studio, she was handed a sheet of music, and with the Biltmore Trio backing her up, she was told to sing. "I don't know how!" she wailed. The conductor urged her to try a few bars. "I like it!" he said.

She winced. "But I sound like a man."

"Very earthy quality, Joan. Let's try it again."

Several weeks later she did the final take with a little tap dancing thrown in—the first audible tap dance on the screen. Wearing a rain hat and coat in the final "downpour," "Singing in the Rain," Joan joined the cast while Cliff Edwards (Ukulele Ike) sang M-G-M's theme song.

As predicted by Haines, *Broadway Melody* won an Oscar and *Hollywood Revue of 1929* was nominated for Best Picture. But the stock market crash changed the attitude of moviegoers at a time when sound was causing expensive havoc and destruction in Hollywood. Motion pictures would play a big part in uplifting the saddened heart of a nation. Movie themes would blend tears with laughter, there would be romance in a meadow or in the arms of a gangster, and the westerns would mosey along. Joan said M-G-M was so concerned whether Garbo, Shearer, and Gilbert would make the transition to sound that she was almost forgotten. "I had tap-danced and sung on the screen but not talked," she said. "I was scheduled for *Untamed* with Robert Montgomery, and given a diction book and told to study it. Mostly, I read out loud to myself, and Doug helped me tremendously. If I had difficulty pronouncing a word, I repeated it over and over again. I talked to myself a lot. I read newspapers aloud.

"*Untamed* opened with me singing, 'Languid and plain-tive, hear the chant of the jun-gle!' I was horrified until Paul Bern explained that my husky voice was what people expected from a girl with my torrid looks. I wasn't sure what that meant. How is anyone's voice identified with their face?"

John Gilbert didn't make it. His high-pitched "I love you" in *His Glorious Night* had apparently been meddled with. Over the years the sound of these three words has been grossly exaggerated, but his masculine image was shattered in a few brief seconds. It would not have taken much tampering with the sound equipment to destroy the tone of his voice.

Greta Garbo spoke for the first time in *Anna Christie*: "Gimme a visky with chincher aile on the saide—and don't be stingy, baby."

Norma Shearer was successful in talkies. Thalberg decided to cast her in more ultrasophisticated roles. She won the 1930 Oscar for Best Actress in *The Divorcée* while Joan seethed.

Ninety percent of the silent stars faded. Charles Farrell's voice was displeasing. Norma Talmadge and Marie Prevost simply "retired." Mary Pickford, Colleen Moore, Douglas Fairbanks, Sr., Lon Chaney, Sr., and Gloria Swanson could have made the transition, but their exaggerated facial and body expressions could not be toned down.

William Boyd flourished. Gary Cooper was more popular in talkies. Edward G. Robinson, Charles Boyer, Douglas Fairbanks, Jr., Laurel and Hardy, and the Marx Brothers crossed over the bridge with ease.

Silent films brought in $60 million in 1927, but with sound, despite the Depression, the box offices collected $110 million in 1929. Though people stood in breadlines, they found a few pennies to go to the movies.

Joan Crawford's first talkie, *Untamed*, was a hit. The *New York Star* wrote: "Miss Crawford sings appealingly and dances thrillingly as usual; her voice is alluring and her dramatic efforts in the difficult role she portrays are at all times convincing."

The *Brooklyn Eagle* said: "If *Untamed* does little else for Miss Crawford, it proves that she is an actress for whom the microphones should hold no fear. Her diction is clear and unaffected and while there is nothing in the lines that offers her opportunity for exceptional acting, she managed to make the impulsive heroine of the story somewhat more credible than the part deserves."

Although M-G-M and Joan's fans were relieved that she succeeded, most publicity was aimed at her fairy-tale marriage. Every magazine and newspaper carried the official photo of her sitting beside Doug, holding his hand in hers, her head on his left shoulder, and his right hand in his jacket pocket. Joan wore a simple, frilly, spotted dress. Her sweet smile and dreamy eyes blended into a look never again to be caught by a camera. This was Joan's first and last chance at puppy love with no motive, perhaps the one alliance that captivated her body, mind, and soul with complete faith in togetherness forever.

As she had for Ray Sterling and Paul Bern, Joan tried to appreciate Shaw, Wells, and Beethoven. She often carried a leather book and either pretended or was trying to become interested in the contents. Doug introduced her to Shakespeare. He read out loud while she sewed and knitted. "It was a dollhouse marriage," she said. They called their ten-room home "El Jodo"

(Joan and Doug). Billy Haines was in a faint when he saw the rose, ivory, and green brocaded silk drapes hanging from ceiling to floor, gold brocaded settees, and a large picture of the couple hung next to a vase of fresh flowers that rested on a Burmese cover, which was draped over the grand piano. The rest of the living room was done in green.

The sun porch was crammed with toy gifts—Doug's electric train, Joan's teddy bears and dolls. Joan was proud of her handmade hooked rugs and delicate curtains. She handled the finances because Doug's were a mess. "We're on a budget!" she announced shortly after their marriage. Until her husband was the breadwinner, Joan relished knitting his sweaters, initialing his handkerchiefs, and monogramming towels. "I had no concept of handling money, either," she admitted, "but Doug was fourteen thousand dollars in debt when I became his wife, so we had to set priorities and El Jodo came first. It was where we were happiest after a hard day at the studio. We were always touching. It was torture to be in the same room and not be close."

Observers thought Joan and Doug had created their own mini-version of Pickfair—a little castle of dreams and mementos. Being banned from the "royal house" brought them closer together. As a couple, they didn't care, but Doug wanted his father and Mary to accept Joan, who had endured far too many snubs in her lifetime. Although she was terrified of meeting her in-laws, Joan prayed that the elder Fairbanks would reconcile with his son. She had no illusions about Pickfair and dreaded the thought of going there—ever. Haines said he was surprised Joan's fans hadn't picketed the estate.

Eight months after the wedding, an engraved invitation arrived at 426 Bristol Avenue.

Mr. and Mrs. Douglas Fairbanks, Sr., request the honor of your presence at a dinner honoring Lord and Lady Mountbatten at Pickfair.

Mountbatten had asked to meet "Our Dancing Daughter." Apparently he was not aware of the tension, but his wish was granted. Joan was frantic. Wasn't it bad enough to meet Doug's family? Did the dinner have to include English royalty, too?

"I can't go," she told Doug. "I'll do everything wrong. I can't go and that's it."

"I'll be there with you, Billie," he grinned, hugging and kissing her.

Joan fretted for a week about choosing the appropriate dress and accessories and getting the proper hairdo. She asked Doug about Pickfair etiquette. She wore a virginal white gown and regretted it on the way to the dinner party. "I'm going to throw up," she moaned. When the limousine pulled up to the entrance, Joan gagged and leaned over. The chauffeur opened the car door, and Doug took his pale wife's hand. "We're here, Billie."

"Take me home, Dodo. Please take me home."

He took her arm and, as if the director had said "Action!" Joan Crawford stood erect. With her chin up, she entered the sacred portals of Pickfair. The butler said, "Good evening, Mrs. Fairbanks."

Acknowledgment at last! Butler or no butler, he accepted and referred to her as Mrs. Fairbanks.

After a few more steps, she spotted her swashbuckling father-in-law. They looked at each other. He didn't smile. Nor did she. Leaning against her husband, Joan got closer and closer to the son of a bitch who condemned his son for marrying "that cheap flapper." Yes, he was shorter than she expected, but still an imposing, fit, tanned gentleman. With one or two more steps to go before their introduction, Joan stopped.

"My shoelace is untied, Dodo," she whispered. "Do you mind?"

Doug got down on his knees while Mary Pickford waited and the elder Fairbanks grinned. Joan smiled nervously, but she looked very much in control to the other guests. They thought it was sweet as they watched the handsome young Doug on his knees before his flapper bride, trying to lace her shoe while royalty waited. This pause gave Joan a chance to get her bearings and to catch up to her heartbeat.

Mary Pickford, also in white, but shrouded in diamonds, extended her gloved hand. "Joan, dear, welcome to Pickfair." Joan said the occasion was a total blank to her in later years.

Although the two women would say very few words to one another during her marriage to Doug, Joan got along very well with "Uncle Douglas," who was, as Haines had related, a tease and prankster. He would deliberately embarrass Joan by asking which of his movies she liked best and why. She was speechless. He knew she had never seen a Fairbanks film, and he changed the subject when blushing red covered her freckles. Distinguished guests, even titled ones, might pick up a salad fork, stab a green, and have rubber tongs double up. Joan recalled a lady who didn't respond to the "hot seat." "Didn't you feel anything?" Uncle Douglas asked.

"Well, yes," the lady said, "but I thought that's how you felt meeting a movie star."

It wasn't always an honor if the host of Pickfair helped you personally with your chair. Most likely it was a breakaway.

Mary would occasionally smile and shake her head. "Oh, Douglas, you've done it again."

If Uncle Douglas saw Joan watching Miss Pickford and counting the forks, left to right, he'd attract her attention. "Oh, by the way, Billie . . ." he would say, getting her so confused that she once used a dessert spoon for the fish course. He burst into gales of laughter.

Despite his teasing, Uncle Douglas was on Joan's side. The night of her first great ball at Pickfair, Joan was descending the staircase on his arm when the lady behind stepped on the train of her dress. She felt the rip straight up her back. Horrified, Joan hesitated, but the elder Fairbanks never missed a step.

He swung the torn train over his arm and guided her down and through the long line of guests, who were taken aback by Joan's blazing scarlet gown and flaming red hair. As usual, Mary wore white, a diamond tiara, and a darling smile.

As difficult as it was for Joan to face these formal affairs, she detested even more the ritual Sunday visits to Pickfair. She and Doug arrived at ten in the morning. While she knitted alone in the living room, the men left for a game of golf or a long walk. Around noon the family gathered for an imposing gourmet luncheon. Afterward, Mary retired upstairs for a nap, and the two men went to United Artists for steam baths while Joan went back to her needlepoint or knitting alone in the living room. "Around six," she said, "the men returned, Mary would descend wearing a beautiful gown, guests would begin to arrive, and there I sat in that same damned chair in the same damned dress I'd put on in the morning, feeling gruesome."

It took Joan a few months to gather up enough nerve to bring along a cocktail dress and change for dinner in the downstairs powder room. She referred to Mary Pickford as "Ma'am."

"I was doing fine until I hit Pickfair," Joan admitted. "I was out to tear up the world in the fastest, brashest, quickest way possible. Then I saw myself through the Pickfair eyes—and every bit of my self-confidence dropped away from me. Shyness overwhelmed me, and I got a terrific inferiority complex. Immediately I set out to change myself in every way."

If Mary did not communicate with Joan, she made it clear that her wholesome "Little Mary" screen image must be maintained, and becoming a grandmother would surely shatter the illusion. During the first year of her marriage, Joan wanted to complete her dollhouse with a baby. She was outspoken about wanting children. When gossip columns and fan magazines wrote that Joan Crawford had had a miscarriage, fans sent letters urging her not to give up trying. Several close friends said Joan admitted to having an abortion, but not to save Miss Pickford's golden curls.

Joan knew her marriage was in trouble when she and Doug began following the formal tradition of gracious entertaining at El Jodo. He thrived on social life with the upper class and had the name. She had been a loner during her initial months in Hollywood and had made few friends other than Billy Haines, press agent Katherine Albert, and actress Dorothy Sebastian, who was married to William Boyd. Her other acquaintances scattered when she married Fairbanks.

To accommodate Douglas's friends, she had to have his birthday party at the Biltmore. Fearing someone would be slighted, Joan found herself surrounded by Norma Shearer and Irving Thalberg, Ruth and Leslie Howard, Constance Bennett and Hank de la Falaise, Florence and Fredric March, Laurence and Jill Olivier, Helen Hayes, and so on. Joan wasn't comfortable with the European set (or those who were working at getting in), but soon found her formal Saturday night dinners continuing the next day with Sunday brunch and swimming parties. The Bristol Avenue house was given a new name—"Cielito Lindo" (Little Heaven). Unable to handle the roles of actress and hostess, Joan acquired domestic help.

Her candle of happiness was gradually burning out.

At Doug's suggestion, Joan tried to learn French and Spanish. Having lived abroad, he was fluent in several languages while she had yet to master the King's English. His closeness to the elder Fairbanks brought out cultural and social leanings that had been dormant. Joan denied wanting to be like Mary Pickford. They were poles apart. But Dodo thrived on Pickfair, and adored his stepmother's graciousness and social status. Joan was expected to carry on the family tradition.

"I look forward to your soirees, Cranberry," Billy said, "but is it proper for the hostess to spend so much time in the kitchen?"

"In case you haven't noticed, I prepare most of the food myself."

"I wouldn't broadcast it," he whispered.

She heard laughter and peeked through the window. "As far as they're concerned, I supervise the help as every perfect hostess does."

"Don't play your snobbish little games with me."

"I'm tired, that's all. Our budget's shot to hell. I have no privacy, no time to concentrate on my scripts . . ."

"I thought you and Johnny Mack Brown were very good in *Montana Moon*."

"Oh, Jesus."

"And what about *Our Blushing Brides*? Timely, I'd say, though I doubt you were a blushing bride for real, Cranberry."

"I'm not in the mood for your jokes," she fumed, putting a layer of mustard on a slice of bread and eating it lustily.

"What would the other guests say if they walked in and saw you?"

"Lay off!"

"I love you, Cranberry, because I know you prefer the comics to Shakespeare and mustard sandwiches to lobster and Sundays at home instead of knitting at Pickfair."

"Don't you have any other juicy gossip, Billy?"

"It's possible your mother-in-law may not be a star much longer. She wants to play vampish roles and has shingled her hair. Have you seen the latest photos from London?"

"No."

"Her idyllic marriage is over."

"Nonsense!" Joan laughed.

"She never should have made *The Taming of the Shrew* with Fairbanks. He was very unprofessional. He showed up late, forgot his lines, and insisted on doing retakes of the scenes that displeased him but denied Mary the same consideration. It's the beginning of the end for them, Cranberry—their marriage and their careers. It's common knowledge your Uncle Douglas is a bit neurotic."

"What's happening to all of us? How can a sweet marriage turn sour?"

"Poor Cranberry. I bet you still believe what you read in movie magazines."

"Aren't you terrified of what sound might do to all of us?" she asked. "So what if we passed? The only good actors come from the stage; we in films talk with our hands and eyes. My God, Billy, is the public so fickle that they would turn their backs on Mary Pickford?"

"A facade is not everlasting," Haines sighed. "Why do you think your famous in-laws entertained at home instead of going out? Because Mary doesn't want the public to see her as she really is instead of the child they idolize on the screen. Suddenly she wants the world to accept her in Theda Bara roles. It can't be, Cranberry. Nor can Robin Hood remain forever young and vigorous. Can you imagine him playing Caesar or Hamlet? As for Miss Pickford, she eloped with a drunken actor in her youth, then divorced, and when she married Fairbanks, she became the Virgin Mary. Did you know she abandoned her next film, *Secrets*?"

Joan was preparing a bowl of fresh fruit. "Are you sure?" she asked, ignoring several oranges that rolled across the kitchen floor.

"I've been dying to tell you for days."

"Dodo didn't say a word about it."

"Maybe he doesn't know," Haines said. "And don't you be the one to break it to him. Stay out of it and think of yourself. This is not being selfish. In Hollywood, the good as well as the bad will bring you down if you let them."

Joan motioned to the maid. "Finish up here." She smiled. "Thanks, Billy. I know there's more you'd like to say, but even your devilish heart won't allow it."

Joan and Douglas remained the ideal couple. It became fashionable to attend one of their elegant dinner parties now that Pickfair's royal doors were open only occasionally. Dodo was anxious to cultivate rich and influential friends. Now that his famous and distinguished father was about to retire, the crème de la crème were eager to respond. He shocked readers of *Photoplay* by expressing his attitude toward marriage: "I don't think that people ought to be conscious of the fact that they are married. They ought to live in sin, so to speak."

The reporter warned, "That might be misinterpreted, you know."

Doug smiled. "I mean that after marriage it is a very good thing to attempt to keep up the same relationship that existed before marriage—to keep right on courting your wife."

As 1931 approached, there was little time for courting, however. Doug signed with First National for such trivial films as *Party Girls*, *The Forward Pass*, *Loose Ankles*, and *The Careless Age*. Joan's career, however, took off like a rocket when Norma Shearer became pregnant with her first child.

"How did that happen?" she asked L. B. Mayer, who swallowed a smile.

"Irving would like to postpone *Paid* for his wife," he said, "but I suggested you for the role of the innocent convict."

"I've read the script and I want the part!"

"You'll have to convince Irving, Joan. He's stalling."

Joan stuck out her neck once again, but this time her approach was professional and demure. She told Thalberg how proud she would be playing a role good enough for his beautiful Norma Shearer. "I've proven that I can handle dramatic parts and won't let you down," she said.

"Sam Wood is a very demanding director."

"I know and that's why I want to work with him."

"We'll give it a try," he said unenthusiastically.

Joan paid a visit to St. Augustine's and prayed that Norma would have a healthy full-term baby.

She wore no makeup in the jail sequences and refused to comb her hair. In the other scenes, she downplayed her looks and concentrated on camera angles, lighting, and timing. Joan had only the technicians to rely on for support and encouragement. A nod meant she was doing fine.

Paid revealed yet another Joan Crawford. *Photoplay* raved: "Just wait until you see her in this powerful dramatic role! The story is absorbing and Joan is simply grand." *Variety* confirmed: "Histrionically she impresses us as about ready to stand up under any sort of dramatic assignment."

Doug was given a chance in *The Dawn Patrol* with Richard Barthelmess and Neil Hamilton, directed by the great Howard Hawks. Fairbanks was, however, less than enthusiastic. He accepted whatever role he was offered. Joan was exhausted when she got home from the studio. Doug was busy either writing short stories, painting, or sculpting. "He was far more talented than Joan," a close friend said. "*Cosmopolitan* and *Vanity Fair* published his stories. If he had tried harder, Doug might have been a fine actor, but there was always a part for him because he had a famous name. Being married to Joan kept him working in films, too. She felt he had everything going for him but why not work harder, fight for better pictures and meaty parts?"

In 1931 Douglas made $72,790. Joan earned $145,750.

"He didn't want me to work," she said. "Isn't it strange—a man marries a woman for certain qualities and then wants to change them. And as much as I loved him, working was essential to me. Marriage gave me tremendous incentive. As one columnist wrote, 'Douglas Fairbanks, Jr.'s, name had been better known than Joan's but she became a box office star while he remained a leading man.' It's the rock 90 percent of the industry's ruined marriages split on."

Doug, who put little energy into his work at the studio, looked forward to entertaining during the week. Joan was drained. Regardless of the role, she gave of herself completely and wanted only a refreshing swim, a light dinner, and a quiet evening with her husband. "I'd remind him about his promise that we could spend a weekend alone," Joan said. "When I heard voices and the doorbell, I had to forgive him because I knew he hadn't forgotten intentionally."

After her success in *Paid*, Joan had everything she prayed for except a perpetual honeymoon. The pig Latin and touching ended. Nothing other than sharing the same house existed. Doug's friends were usually on hand to greet her in the evening. "I managed to get through it," she said, "because of my work."

And Clark Gable . . .

5

POSSESSED

The future "King of Hollywood" had not been crowned as yet. He wasn't even a star. After several bit parts, the thirty-year-old Gable played a laundryman in *The Easiest Way* with Constance Bennett and a bootlegging killer in *Dance, Fools, Dance* with Joan Crawford.

A burly man with big ears, huge hands, and bad teeth, Gable had drifted across the country from Ohio, working as a lumberjack, carnival hawker, and farmer. Drawn to the theater, he wanted to be a stage actor. Eager, but clumsy, his attempts failed miserably until he met Josephine Dillon, a drama teacher, in Portland, Oregon. She described Gable as a "gorgeous skeleton" and agreed to give him acting lessons. When she moved to Hollywood, he followed, and they were married in 1924. Josephine, thirteen years older than Clark, said it was a business arrangement and the marriage was never consummated. Their goal was Broadway.

Clark worked as an extra in films and hated it. After a break with a stock company in Houston, Texas, he was offered the lead in *Machinal* in New York, where he met a wealthy divorcée, Ria Langham, who was seventeen years his senior. While he waited for his divorce from Josephine, Ria supported him until Clark accepted the lead in *The Last Mile* at the Majestic Theater in Los Angeles. A clever agent convinced him to try motion pictures when the play closed. Gable wanted no part of Hollywood but could not turn down a one-year M-G-M contract for $650 a week.

When he was cast in *Dance, Fools, Dance,* the studio had not yet decided what to do with Clark. He wasn't suave or handsome enough to replace Gilbert or Valentino. Nor was he the boy-next-door type. But since he had played a vicious criminal on death row in *The Last Mile,* M-G-M knew he could fill in as a convincing gangster.

Gable said he wasn't looking forward to working with Joan Crawford. "She was a star and knew the ropes in pictures. I was afraid she'd laugh behind my back."

Joan was terrified of stage actors. "I was a wreck," she said. "I kept thinking he knows how to read lines. I'm suffering by comparison. In one scene where he grabbed me and threatened the life of my brother, his nearness had such an impact, my knees buckled. If he hadn't held me by both shoulders I'd have dropped. Every girl on the set noticed him."

Ria Gable, a Houston socialite, was delighted that her husband was co-starring with the wife of Douglas Fairbanks, Jr. Surely this would open the door to Pickfair. Clark groaned at the thought. He was, like Joan, an opportunist, and he liked the better things in life, but stuffy dinner parties bored him. Gable would appear in twelve films in 1931, co-starring with Fay Wray, Norma Shearer, Barbara Stanwyck, Joan Blondell, Madge Evans, Greta Garbo, and with Joan three times. He had no time for Ria's social climbing.

Joan was trying to save her marriage, but she was tired of Shakespeare, and Dodo had no free time to read poetry anyway. When they were not entertaining high society, they supped at Pickfair or spent the weekend at San Simeon, William Randolph Hearst's castle. Doug thrived, of course, but Joan dreaded these outings except for seeing her close friend Marion Davies, who was Hearst's mistress. Marion, a former chorus girl, was thoughtful, unpretentious, and sweet, but she had to sneak cocktails because W. R. forbade her to drink. On one occasion he walked in on the girls unexpectedly. Marion handed Joan the glass in time, but Hearst said, "I never saw you drink, Joan."

She smiled. "I thought I'd try it."

"Well, try it!" he bellowed.

She did. "Anything for a friend," she said. "I hated booze and had to choke it down gracefully to save dear Marion."

Ria would gladly have done the honors. She and Clark settled down in Beverly Hills not far from Pickfair and were beginning to have intimate dinner parties, although he often went to bed early. In his seventh major film, *A Free Soul*, Gable scored with a left to Miss Shearer, and America had a new hero and star. Gable balanced the tipped scale of the sexes. It was the beginning of the rough-diamond image—a man who was raw, crude, and hardened but had a heart of gold. If Gable couldn't get his woman, he either booted her in the fanny or carried her over his shoulder to the cave she'd never leave. Why? Because she didn't want to. Men cheered and women swooned. M-G-M raised Gable's salary to $850 a week.

Joan watched Gable's career intently. She had never requested a leading man before, nor had she been affected by one other than John Gilbert, who was a boy scout compared to Clark. She discussed her feelings with Billy Haines.

"I remember him six or seven years ago," Haines told her. "Gable was an extra in *The Pacemakers*. Always hanging around."

"Does he remember you?"

"I don't think he knows what day it is."

"He's getting almost as much mail as I am," Joan said. "There's something about him, Billy. After *Dance, Fools, Dance* he was in *Laughing Sinners* with me."

"Before he floored Norma?"

Joan took a deep breath. "I sang, 'What can I do?—I love that man!'"

Haines scowled. "How appropriate."

"He gives me chills."

"When he socked Norma or when you sang?"

"Damn it, Billy!"

"I went through this with Mike, Jerry, John, Dodo, and God knows how many other men."

She smiled seductively. "Not like this."

"Do you want him for a leading man or a lover, Cranberry? You can't have both."

"Why not? Garbo did."

"Yeah, and look what happened to Gilbert. He's an unemployed alcoholic."

"I feel terrible about that, but life goes on."

"Cranberry, you're a married woman and Gable's a married man."

"And you're living with Jimmy Shields. If we're all careful, who's gonna get hurt?"

"Jimmy's in business with me. You know how much I love interior decorating."

"Christ! Why beat around the bush with me? He's your wife! Why don't you bring him to my next party?"

"I won't flaunt Jimmy. That's against the rules."

Joan looked at Haines and nodded thoughtfully. "Maybe you're right. I gotta get back to the set. It's a thrill working with Pauline Frederick in *This Modern Age*. She's my favorite, you know."

Haines smiled. "Interesting . . ."

"Why?"

"She and Gable appeared on the stage together—in *Madam X*, I believe. Beautiful Pauline goes from one phase of youth to another."

"You're up to something, Billy."

"They had a wild affair, that's all. She paid for his gleaming smile."

"She's old enough to be his mother!" Joan snapped.

"So is his wife."

"How do you know so much about Clark and Pauline?"

"God, it was common knowledge. He was seen at her mansion on Sunset every night after the play."

"I've been told I resemble Pauline."

"It's true, Cranberry, but are you as exciting in bed?"

She lit a cigarette and blew smoke in his ear with a whisper—"I'll let you know."

Joan admired Pauline Frederick, whose unique ability to project emotion with her eyes and hands hypnotized critics. She was one of the first to use her shoulders effectively—one up and the other down, or one thrown back and the other forward. She knew more about lighting and camera angles than the experts, but she had a gentle, professional approach. An irresistible, full-figured, dark-haired, energetic, multitalented lady, she left behind a string of brokenhearted lovers. Exquisite, witty, and dramatic, she lived life to the ultimate.

When *This Modern Age* was finished, Joan had as much admiration for Mr. Gable as she did for Miss Frederick, but for different reasons. "I'd like to look like her when I'm fifty," she said, "and be able to lure young bucks into my bed."

In a 1931 *Photoplay* interview, Joan said she had no misgivings about her past—truth or fiction. She explained rumors of her wild life when she danced half-naked in Hollywood nightclubs and how it enabled her to choose a husband without question or regret. Confirming a happy marriage, she concentrated on her future as a dramatic actress. "I had to attract attention any way I could in the beginning," she said. "And continue doing so until I got better parts. Every experience I had and every mistake I made during my nightclub career has helped, if only to show me the things which I should avoid in the future. Also I learned to know men pretty thoroughly, and very few of them kept my confidence. Perhaps I was at fault, however. Due to an incident in my childhood I didn't dare trust anyone. As my need of faith grew intolerable, I reached out eagerly to believe and confide in all my various Hollywood acquaintances, with the usual results. Only in the last year have I developed an instinct for differentiating between sincerity and effusive protestations of loyalty undying.

"Yes, I learned a lot about men, all right. But if a woman knows nothing of men, how in heaven's name can she consider herself capable of judging for herself and choosing the one man she can trust implicitly, the man that could satisfy the many vagaries of a woman's heart and soul."

Doug was the hero of this story, of course. He averaged two films a year—enough to afford him the luxury of being with titled or rich friends who did not have to work for a living. Joan's patience was wearing thin. She was drifting at sea, going nowhere, and finding conversation with Doug a useless pastime. In her autobiography Joan said she was disappointed by her husband's lack of ambition. She needed to look up to a strong husband. He should be the breadwinner, too. Joan craved love and intimacy. During the brief moments the couple found themselves alone, she broached the subject of their empty marriage. Doug recognized it, too, but was convinced everything would work out.

Joan let it be known she wanted Gable to co-star with her in *Possessed*, the story of a small-town factory girl from the wrong side of the tracks who heads for New York and becomes the sophisticated mistress of a wealthy Park Avenue attorney. "I knew when Clark walked on the set," Joan recalled. "I didn't know which door he came through, but I knew he was there. He had presence. I knew I was falling into a trap that I warned young girls about—

not to fall in love with leading men or take romantic scenes to heart. Leave the set and forget about it because that marvelous feeling would pass. Boy, I had to eat those words, but they tasted very sweet."

Joan and Clark had worked together briefly in two quick films, but it wasn't until *Possessed* that the magic between them sparkled. The cast and crew noticed the strong attraction. Word spread throughout the studio. "Our relationship was physical," Joan said, "but it went beyond that. We came from similar backgrounds—crap! We had been unhappy kids and never had a real home in our teens. We were nobodies transformed into somebodies by Hollywood. We were unhappily married to people who tried to change us. We asked for it, bought it, and had to live with it, and we were scared shitless. He was relieved to know I felt the same even though I was an established star—if there is such a thing. God, how we talked and sometimes cried. Could we hold on to what we already had at M-G-M? Would the public see through us?

"Clark was the first damn friend I could talk to in Hollywood. Billy Haines was compassionate but thought I worried needlessly. Doug had no idea what fear was. Clark never—and I mean never—talked about me to anyone outside of a few people who were responsible for us in M-G-M's publicity department. They stood by and protected us. It took me a long time after he died to open up and tell the beautiful truth. When we first became involved, he told me it wasn't his thing to get involved with a married woman. I was the exception. We were both in and out of affairs, marriages, and divorces all the time, but we outlasted them all."

Joan said she cried every morning on her drive to the studio and wept all the way home. She couldn't sleep but dreaded her thoughts when awake. She feared for her future, she feared for her marriage, and she feared for her passionate love for Gable. "I no longer enjoyed parties and small talk," she confided. "There were times I wanted to get into my car and race through the night." Sometimes she did take drives along the road by the ocean and found peace. Occasionally she met Gable on the beach. He'd listen despite his own mounting problems.

Ria Gable had noticed a change in her husband who, from the sheer exhaustion of going from film to film without a break, had shuffled tediously off to the studio in the morning and studied his script as soon as he got home. Suddenly, however, when filming *Possessed*, he was a different man. It wasn't pleasant for him going home to Ria after romancing Joan, but he was happy and left in the morning with an eager wave and a smile.

One of the technicians on the movie set described the circumstances. "Crawford and Gable were attracted to each other instantly," he said. "He had what she wanted and she had what he wanted. Call it chemistry, call it love at first sight or physical attraction. The electricity between them sparked on the screen, too. It wasn't just acting. They meant every kiss and embrace. I hadn't seen anything like it since Garbo and Gilbert in *Flesh and the Devil*. In the script Gable said to Crawford, 'The surest way to lose a woman is to marry her, and I don't want to lose you . . . Even if I were married to you, I couldn't respect you more than I do.' One of Crawford's lines was 'A woman can do anything and get anywhere as long as she doesn't fall in love.' At the time, of course, no one knew they would have a long love affair and that *Possessed* was a preview of what lay ahead."

Moviegoers were thrilled with the screen lovers and wanted more. L. B. Mayer would have to accommodate them, but he had no intention of condoning an affair between a married ex-lumberjack and an ex-flapper married to a Fairbanks.

"Clark, you look as good in a tuxedo as a ten-dollar suit," Mayer said. "I'm very pleased with your performance in *Possessed,* but then the sizable raise you got out of me was incentive, I guess. Hiding out in Palm Springs is an old trick, by the way."

"It worked, didn't it?"

"I thought you'd be more original."

Gable laughed. "Are you sore about a few lousy bucks?"

"No, I'm sore about the shabby way you're treating your wife. I'm ashamed we deliberately kept her hidden from the press. She's a charming lady."

"Very," Gable said, lighting a cigarette.

"On her way to New York on the train she's been giving gracious interviews."

"Yeah?"

"When is Ria coming home?"

Gable shrugged.

"Before you leave this office we're going to find out because I'd like to know before Louella and Hedda."

"What's the beef?"

"Have you any idea what we went through when your first wife made herself known? What I had to go through to shut her up?"

Clark scowled. "I'm paying for it."

"If you think two hundred dollars a month is payment due, my friend, you're all wrong. Josephine should have consulted a lawyer. Fortunately I was able to reason with her. The woman lives in a slum, for Christ's sake, but your present wife is a smart lady . . . or so I thought."

"I guess my line is 'What's that supposed to mean?' "

"When it comes to lines, my boy, you've got 'em!" Mayer exclaimed. "But I thought Joan had heard them all. I know her better than you do, and she's good for only one thing."

"I love her," Gable said.

"A few years ago I told Gilbert to have fun with Garbo and forget about marriage. He punched me in the face."

"I think Ria will be civil about a divorce," Clark said. "As for Joan, her marriage to Fairbanks has been over for a long time."

Mayer's face turned crimson. "Divorce? Marriage! What the hell are you talking about?"

"Joan and I are going to get married."

"What about the others you've been sleeping with?"

Clark frowned. "You have a lively imagination."

"Not as lively as your sex life."

"That's my business!"

"As long as you work for M-G-M it's my business, and don't you forget it!"

"I'm in love."

Mayer laughed. "There's no such thing in this town. The wife you have is superior. She's been very, very understanding despite your indiscretions. Think about it."

"I don't have to. The marriage is over."

"You get on that damn telephone and ask your beloved wife to come home. You miss her!"

"She won't buy it."

"That's what she wants to hear. She'll buy it."

"Then what?" Gable asked, lighting another cigarette.

"You'll take her to nightclubs and parties. You'll laugh and dance and be happy."

"What am I trying to prove?"

"That your affair with Crawford was a fling. Maybe it never happened."

"I can't do it."

"You and Joan are finished, or you'll never work for this or any other studio in Hollywood. I'll see to that. Don't put me to the test."

Gable took a deep breath and then sighed with defeat. "How can I tell Joan?"

"I've known her for five years. Coming from me, she'll understand. All you have to do is call your wife and convince her to hurry home."

"Before I do, would you tell me what you have against Joan?"

"I have great admiration for her as an actress, but she's a tramp. This studio, with some help from Pickfair, fed Joan's ambition, but behind those expensive clothes and elegant dinner parties is a washerwoman's daughter. I know things I can't tell you, Clark. You're no saint, but separately you and Joan might have a chance—together, only scandal, pain, and regrets. If your marriage is bad, we'll discuss it some other time. No third parties. You'll thank me one day."

"I doubt that."

"Call your wife," Mayer said, "and give her my fondest regards."

Ria Gable did not believe Clark wanted her back, but she knew the studio had something to do with it, and she was eager to have Mayer in her corner.

She was seventeen years older than Gable and accepted the fact that the contrast was obvious. Not being photographed with him didn't bother her. She had one bad run-in with reporters and swore there would not be another. When Clark became involved with Joan, however, Ria came out of hiding and boarded a train for New York. At each station, she granted interviews with optimistic smiles and confirmations about her happy marriage. If there were any doubts about who Mrs. Clark Gable was, they were dispelled by the time she reached New York, where she flaunted his name in hotels, theaters, department stores, and restaurants.

Possessed was acclaimed by *Photoplay:* ". . . you really don't care if the story is old and some of the lines a little shopworn. For the Gable boy and the Crawford girl make you believe it . . . It's the best work Joan Crawford has done since *Paid* and Clark Gable—he's everybody's big moment. If Joan weren't so good, he'd have the picture. You'll like it. But while you're seeing it the kids should be doing their homework."

L. B. Mayer was impressed.

"Fabulous reviews, Joan. Whenever I assume you've done your very best, I discover your talents are endless. Boundless! In M-G-M's galaxy of stars, yours is the brightest. *Possessed* is another turning point for you."

"Clark and I are a good team. We work well together."

"To put it mildly."

"What's next?"

"That depends on you," Mayer said with a smile.

"Are you giving me script approval?" she asked eagerly.

"I have the script, but I don't need your approval. Only your solemn word."

"Don't keep me waiting, L. B."

"*Grand Hotel.*"

"Holy shit! With Garbo and Barrymore?"

"Maybe . . ."

Joan crossed her legs seductively and smiled. "So, the time has come at last. I knew it happened every day in this business but thought you were above trading sex for a good part."

He laughed. "Is that what you think?"

She glowered. "What else?"

"No, Joan. I'm not trying to get you in my bed, but I want you out of Gable's bed—or else."

"Oh, that . . ."

"How can you sit there and be so casual . . . as if he took you out for an ice cream soda?"

"Calm down," she said nervously. "Clark and I are in love, that's all."

"That's all!"

"I mean . . . it isn't shady or dirty. It's real and beautiful and . . ."

"Who do you think you're kidding? Me? Yourself? He can't be faithful to any woman. Do you want a list of girls he's been laying?"

"If he married me, that would stop," she announced.

"Hell, *you* don't know what it is to sleep in one bed."

"I beg your pardon!"

"Beg, plead, deny . . . let's get it over with."

Joan began to cry. "You've broken my heart."

"It'll mend."

"But I'll prove something to you," she sobbed. "My career always came first above anyone and everything else. I don't want *Grand Hotel*."

"What?!"

"You gave me a choice, L. B., Clark or . . ."

Mayer pointed a finger at her. "Give him up or you're fired, Joan, and you'll be blackballed from movies. That goes for your cocksman, too. But I suppose he can go back to the lumberyard and you can go back to the laundry."

She sobbed bitterly. He waited for the appropriate moment and put his arm around her. "You're like a daughter, Joan. You were the first M-G-M creation . . . the pattern for others to follow. A delightful, blessed experiment, and look what we created. A vision. An actress. A lady. A unique woman with a hunger for fame and praise and recognition. There's more—so much more to come."

She blew her nose daintily and sniffled. "I'm so confused," she wept. "So very confused."

"Take my advice," Mayer said, dabbing her cheeks with his handkerchief. "I warned you about Fairbanks. I wanted to help get you out of that one. We sat right here, and I offered to handle it personally. Goddamn it, Joan, I can't let you get hurt again. I'd rather destroy you myself than see you tortured by a scandal."

She nodded and sobbed. "What do you want me to do?"

"Dry those eyes, powder your nose, and promise you'll never see Gable again off the set. The affair is over. Finished. Done."

She moaned and wept.

He handed her a script and said softly, "Tidy up now and look this over. You'll feel much better." Joan took her time fixing her face. With moist eyes she read a few pages, then leaped off her chair and hissed, "A fuckin' whore!"

"I prefer to think of your character as a stenographer with ambition."

"Who goes around screwing sick old men?"

Mayer smirked. "Why don't you discuss it with your girlfriend, Billy Haines?"

Joan grabbed her purse and the script and glared at L. B. across his desk. "Don't you ever lose?" she asked.

"Pray that I don't, my dear. When I lose, everybody loses."

*   *   *

Joan and Clark were shaken but not defeated. They realized that Ria and Doug were suspicious, and Hollywood columnists had their pencils sharpened, but the lovers found a way to be together. "God, Clark had balls in those days," Joan recalled. He said the same thing about her.

Ria came back to her husband and was finally acknowledged and photographed with him at premieres and nightclubs. Joan and Doug were guests at the Gables' dinner parties. The members of this intimate group, which included Norma and Irving Thalberg, were all chums on the surface.

Joan invited Ria for lunch while rumors of the famous affair were still rumbling. A reporter spotted the two women and rushed over to their table. "I saw you in *Possessed*, Miss Crawford, you were wonderful, inspired. The way you look at Clark, anyone can tell you're crazy about him."

Joan looked up at the reporter and said, "May I introduce you to my good friend, Mrs. Clark Gable?"

Mayer didn't buy it, but he had no reason to believe his two stars were misbehaving. His few meetings with Joan had to do with *Grand Hotel*. He knew she feared appearing in a Garbo film, but she agreed professionally that any movie with Greta Garbo was, indeed a Garbo film. Joan was proud to be part of a great cast, which included Lionel and John Barrymore, Lewis Stone, Wallace Beery, and Jean Hersholt. Mayer encouraged her. "If you can hold your own in this one, Joan, you'll be hailed by your peers."

Joan had passed Garbo's dressing room every morning for three years, always calling out "Hello," but never receiving a reply. One day, Joan was in a rush and said nothing. Garbo's door opened and she sang out "Allooo?"

"I had no scenes with her in *Grand Hotel*," Joan recalled. "She worked all day until five o'clock. I came to work at six and worked all night. Garbo wanted strict privacy, and we were all told not to follow her or use the same stairways and so forth. One day, I decided to take a chance and we came face-to-face. She took my face in her hand and said, 'What a pity! Our first picture together, and we don't work with each other. I am so sorry. You have a marvelous face.' If there was ever a time in my life when I might have become a lesbian, that was it."

Joan was disappointed in John Barrymore and Wallace Beery, both of whom were hearty drinkers and rather gruff on the set. "They were usually hung over and resented rehearsing," she said. "There was a lot of profanity, too. Once the camera began to roll, they were perfectionists, but I can't say it was an easy film for me to do. John and Wally were notorious scene stealers, too. There I was fighting for recognition in a Garbo film and trying to nudge two famous actors aside so I could get into the act! Of course, it turned out beautifully and won an Academy Award for Best Picture. Many of my better scenes were cut by the censors, but I appeared throughout the entire film and the critics reviewed us as a cast, not individually. *Grand Hotel* was a highlight of my career."

Joan waited for a kind word from Mayer, who was too busy to see her.

When she was scheduled for *Letty Lynton,* which was to be directed by Clarence Brown, who had been supportive of Joan during the filming of *Possessed,* she insisted on seeing Mayer. "I'm excited about *Letty,*" she cooed. "With Adrian designing my wardrobe, it will be a delicious picture."

"Yes," he said, going over some documents on his desk. "Adrian seems to think shoulder pads will make you appear taller and less like a fullback. I've seen the sketches."

The insult about her broad shoulders indicated that he hadn't quite forgiven her. "L. B., have you finished casting *Letty?*"

"Why?"

"Because . . . well, I think Clark would be perfect for . . ."

"You have chutzpah!"

"What?"

"Nerve. Gall. You're a brazen hussy. I'm very busy, Joan."

"Are you going to ruin a marvelous role because you resent Clark?"

"Resent? Resent?!" Mayer shouted, throwing down his pen.

"Yes," she repeated. "Resent!"

"I resent Gable so much that he's doing *Red Dust* with Jean Harlow and *Strange Interlude* with Norma Shearer. How's that for resentment?"

"I thought John Gilbert was doing *Red Dust.*"

Mayer slumped in his chair and motioned for her to sit down. "I was willing to give John a chance," he said. "His marriage to Virginia Bruce seemed to have straightened him out. Thalberg's determined to save John's career, but after a few days of shooting, it was decided he was wrong for the part; he was replaced by Gable."

"And you had nothing to do with it?" she asked.

"Absolutely none of your business, Joan, but the question is an interesting one since it was Harlow's husband, Paul Bern, who thought Clark might be better. And we all know what good friends Paul, John, and Irving are, don't we?"

"Who do I get in *Letty?*"

"Robert Montgomery."

"Again? L. B., Clark is better suited for the role."

"Why don't you sit here at my desk, and I'll play Letty!"

Joan left Mayer's office in a huff. Director Clarence Brown understood the reason for her tears during the filming of *Letty Lynton,* and the cast sympathized with her, too.

While Joan fretted, Clark was soothing Jean Harlow's nerves on the set of *Red Dust.* Her marriage to Paul Bern had been a mistake; they fought bitterly when he found out Jean refused to wear a bathing suit during her bath in the rain-barrel scene. Bern had been one of those responsible for *Red Dust* and had recommended Gable as his wife's co-star.

"I thought Paul was above all that," Clark said. "He's a humble guy and a gentleman who apparently doesn't want a bunch of stagehands looking at his nude bride."

"I thought he liked me for me—not these," she said, rubbing ice cubes on her nipples.

"Baby, there are a lot of big boobs in this burg."

"Paul could sleep on a mound of 'em and not get aroused."

"Does Mayer know about this?" Gable asked.

"Yes, he knew about Paul's impotence and pleaded with me not to get married, but the son of a bitch wouldn't tell me the truth. After two months of wedded piss, I'll have to wait a year or so to get a divorce, according to Mayer."

"Maybe he plans to take the whole group to court at the same time?" Gable grinned, patting her on the fanny.

But on Labor Day, 1932, Paul Bern put a gun to his temple and pulled the trigger. He left a note of apology to Jean. Bern was impotent; he had the genitals of a young boy. He had attempted suicide before, when Barbara La Marr laughed at him. Harlow was more understanding, but she felt betrayed. It's possible she and Bern might have been able to conceal their problems until a friendly divorce was arranged by the studio; however, shortly after his death, it was established that Bern was already married. His first wife committed suicide a few days after he did. The fact that Jean Harlow's husband was a bigamist provided a bigger scandal than did his inability to function in bed. M-G-M arranged for Jean to fake suicide—proof of her love and utter despair.

Joan was saddened by Bern's death. "Such a terrible waste," she said. "He had so much to give and so much talent."

Gable took it upon himself to comfort Jean when she returned to work. She missed her cues and forgot her lines. Mary Astor, who was also in *Red Dust,* said the entire cast was patient and worked around her as much as possible.

Joan did not particularly care for Jean, who was rumored never to wear bras or panties. She saw for herself the closeness between Jean and Clark and wanted him to remain objective.

"Joanie," he said, "she's a lot like you. Her mother and stepfather spend all her money. She marries the wrong man, he knocks himself off, and she has to pay his debts. Surely you can feel her pain."

"I could have married Paul Bern, but it was obvious something was wrong."

"Well, maybe you got around more than she did," Gable said innocently.

"Spare me."

"Forget it. Let's not be petty at a time like this. How do you think I felt taking Gilbert's last role? I hear he's drinking and spitting up blood, for Christ's sake! And Bern with the body of a six-year-old boy—lying there being photographed . . ."

"I don't trust blond widows," Joan winked, leaning against him.

"Get hold of yourself!" he snapped. "If Mayer suspects anything, we'll never be in another picture together unless it's on the front porch of a farm in Kansas."

"Are you growing a mustache?" she asked, feeling his face.

"My part in *Strange Interlude* calls for it."

Joan giggled. "I can't imagine you with a soup strainer."

He kissed her passionately. Every minute was precious to them. They went to the same dinner parties. Ria and Joan were friendly at these gatherings. Fairbanks was gracious and attentive to his wife, but their togetherness was for show. They granted few interviews and, as Joan explained later, "We were taking separate roads. Neither path was wrong, but marriage is successful only when a man and woman stay on the same road and walk along it, hand-in-hand."

While Doug went off on a yachting trip and Gable went before the camera sporting the mustache that would become his trademark, Joan was ushered into Mayer's office.

He smiled. "Sorry I've been so busy. As you know, we've had our problems here."

"Replacing Paul Bern won't be easy," she said coldly.

"Joan, that's in the past, as are so many things. Am I right?"

"I didn't know any one person had a monopoly on yesterday."

"We're fencing and I don't like that."

"If you put down your sword, so will I."

He looked her over and smiled. "Damn it, I know now I made the right decision. When Joe Schenck asked to borrow you for *Rain,* I hesitated. Why, I don't know, because only Joan Crawford could play a realistic Sadie Thompson."

"You'd loan me out to United Artists?" she gasped. "I don't know anyone over there. I don't know the electricians or the lighting directors or the cameramen or . . ."

"But they know who Joan Crawford is, and you'll get the royal star treatment."

"I'd be lost, L. B. I can't do it. I can't."

"Playing Sadie Thompson will make you a great star, Joan. That's what you've always wanted, isn't it? To be great?"

"Do you want the truth?"

"If that's possible."

"I'm terrified."

"If you're dissatisfied, pick up the telephone and I'll make it all right again. Joe Schenck is very excited about your impending visit. He'll treat you like a queen."

"Let's forget it," she said with tears in her eyes.

"You'll be working on beautiful Catalina Island. It will be a glorious vacation."

"I have to live there?"

"They have cozy cottages, I understand."

"Who else is in the picture?"

"Walter Huston and William Gargan."

"They're stage actors!" she exclaimed.

"Get used to them, Joan. In desperation, Hollywood has turned to the theater for talent."

"How can I be an original after Jeanne Eagels played Sadie on the stage, and Gloria Swanson played her in the silent film version?"

"Forget about Eagels and Swanson. Joe Schenck wants an original Sadie, and he and I agreed that only Joan Crawford could do it."

"Well, when you put it that way . . ."

Mayer put his arm around Joan and walked her to the door. "In years to come many young actresses will be terrified to play Sadie because you did it superbly. Enjoy Catalina, Joan!"

Joan would remember *Rain* with disgust for the rest of her life. She did not get along with the cast. Gargan admitted he had never seen her on the screen, and Huston ignored her. "They did so many takes, my head was spinning," Joan recalled. "I was used to rehearsing and, when I was ready, going before the camera. My first take was always my best. Not in *Rain*. By the time everyone else was set for the real thing, I was tired and hardly at my best."

She spent every night alone in her cottage feeling unwanted, lonely, and abandoned by Doug and the studio. She kept in touch with Gable and Haines by telephone. "What I see in the mirror is Sadie," she told them, "but working with method actors is a horrid experience." Her timing was off. Although she had the upper hand because she was a pro at making movies, the other members of the cast treated her as if she were the infamous Miss Thompson. "I'm going to pieces," she told Mayer, "and plan to take a vacation when this crap is in the can!"

Critics considered Joan's performance in *Rain* to be only satisfactory. *Variety* opined, "It turns out to be a mistake to have assigned the Sadie Thompson role to Miss Crawford. It shows her off unfavorably. The dramatic significance of it all is beyond her range." Joan was prepared for the worst, but her fan mail hurt deeply. Loyal Crawford followers complained bitterly about her acting, her glaring lips, and her agreeing to portray Sadie in the first place.

Depressed and tired, she retreated to Malibu and spent a few weeks by herself. Joan had damaged her career with *Rain* and even though Douglas was sympathetic, he didn't come to her. Gable did. He, too, had fought with Mayer over every film. "If it hadn't been for Hearst, I would have been fired," he told her.

"Marion's doing, most likely," Joan said.

"Mayer wanted me to play a priest in *Polly of the Circus!*"
Crawford laughed.

"I settled for a minister and a raise."

"Marion's doing again, most likely."

He grinned. "Nice girl."

"Hands off. Hearst is more dangerous than Mayer."

"Joanie, you and I are still being punished by L. B. But I figure he's more
concerned about scandal than our affair. Does that make any sense?"

"None. By the way, I've decided to divorce Douglas."

"And marry me?"

"Is that a proposal?" she asked.

"Yes, but Ria's spending money faster than I can make it, and she'll take
me for every cent if I walk out. The next year or two will be tough."

She laughed. "What else is new?"

Joan returned to M-G-M refreshed and anxious to work. Doug had signed a
contract with Warner Brothers but continued making mediocre films. He and
Joan were seen together at important premieres, weekends at San Simeon, and
prestigious parties. Their formal dinners were few and far between. Joan kept
busy with interviews and luncheons until Mayer sent for her.

"I don't wish to discuss Catalina," she said sternly.

"I asked you here. Don't tell me what I have to say."

"Admit you made a mistake."

"Joan, one bad film isn't the end of the world. I know you're tired. That
brief holiday in Malibu only depressed you more, so I'd like to make it up to
you."

"Really?"

"You need a real vacation. How about a trip to Europe with Douglas?"

"Who?"

"Your husband."

"What about him?"

"A second honeymoon, compliments of M-G-M."

"Why?"

"Because you never had a first."

"I'd hate to take Douglas away from his work," she said.

"I made sure he has no commitments."

"What about me, L. B.? I need a good film desperately now."

"With *Letty Lynton* playing the circuit at the same time as *Rain,* you have
nothing to worry about. I have *Letty's* reviews right here. *Photoplay* says you
were at your very best. The *Motion Picture Herald*'s review will please you, too:
'The gowns which Miss Crawford wears will be the talk of the town for weeks
after—and how Joan wears them!' "

"I'm an actress, not a model. I want to work."

"After your romantic trip to Europe with Douglas."

"It sounds more like a command than a gift," she snapped.

"All arrangements have been made. You'll sail from New York on the SS *Bremen* to England. Douglas is anxious to show you Paris, too."

"I'd rather do a film," she mumbled.

"Our publicity staff in London has arranged for you to make a few appearances, Joan."

"They never heard of me in England!" she exclaimed.

He smiled. "Have a wonderful time and don't worry about a thing."

Joan found out Mayer's sudden generosity was his way of separating her from Gable. Fairbanks looked forward to the holiday. Not only did he want to share his childhood memories with Joan but he also was anxious for a complete reconciliation. His good friends Jill and Laurence Olivier were sailing on the SS *Bremen,* too, and Noel Coward promised to meet them in Southampton. Joan had mixed emotions. She'd never been to Europe and was adventurous enough to hope the trip might broaden her perspective. Also, Douglas was spending more time with her as they shopped and packed for their holiday.

In New York, Mayor Jimmy Walker sent eight police motorcycles to escort the famous couple to the pier; crowds tore at their clothes and tried to touch Doug's new mustache. When they thought they were safely on board, a man attempted to climb through a porthole for a glimpse of his favorite actress. Once at sea, their second honeymoon was romantically private and, for a while, fulfilling. Without forcing it, Joan was comfortable and loving with Doug. It had been three years since they shared a marriage, but both thrived on renewed happiness.

Joan forgot about *Rain* and had second thoughts about Gable. She could not conceive of a life without Clark. He would, however, not be free for a long time, which meant a drawn-out, dangerous affair. She knew there was no other man like him and probably never would be. In his own humble way, Gable knew this and cultivated a keen eye for women. Both Joan Blondell and Barbara Stanwyck said they had to sit down or faint when they met him for the first time. Then there was Mayer's list of women who had been intimate with Clark. Joan wasn't surprised. They meant nothing to him, but was he capable of love? And could she tolerate not knowing who was laughing behind her back?

Once Joan arrived in England she was too busy to think about anyone other than Doug. Noel Coward was at Southampton to accompany them to their suite at the Savoy. Then came a round of plays and theater suppers. Joan was totally unaware that she had so many fans in England. "There is no other movie audience in the world to compare with the English," she said. "They are more alert to personalities than people in New York or Hollywood. At Noel Coward's *Cavalcade,* they tore my evening coat off my back, and I basked in their fond attention. Noel, Douglas, and a corps of bobbies carried me into the theater on their shoulders. This is the public without which an actress cannot exist. I had a ball."

It was not unusual for a theater audience to rise when Joan was ushered to her seat. Fairbanks accepted the attention calmly, but Joan wept openly. She adored London and enjoyed her husband's friends in their home environment. Lady Mountbatten, Lady Ravensdale, the Duke of Kent, and Noel Coward invited London's stage and screen celebrities to their proper dinner parties. Joan was more at ease with Big Ben, Buckingham Palace, and Waterloo Bridge as a background for their English conversation and wit.

She was excited about making a speech before three thousand people, mostly working girls, who were fans of hers. With the help of M-G-M's publicity department, Joan rehearsed calmly; she arrived at the hall to the sound of love chants: "Our Joan! Our Joan!" The cheering crowd was well behaved and jubilant, but Joan froze. "God bless you" was all she could manage before she was escorted off the stage.

On the turbulent Channel crossing, Doug talked about "his" Paris and the many little cafés he wanted to show Joan . . . the outdoor restaurants where they would sip wine and watch people. She looked forward to the visit, also, but became extremely ill on the boat. He described France to her through the bathroom door. Poor Joan wanted only peace and quiet in Paris, but the press found the second-honeymooners staying at a friend's estate outside the city and pursued the couple to Montmartre, where Doug had studied painting. Joan's shopping plans were halted, too. She managed to buy a few gifts for friends despite American tourists following her everywhere.

Aside from a few days alone on the voyage to England, Joan and Doug were friends and little else. Whether the cause of their estrangement was his British friends' monopolizing their time in London, the dreadful Channel crossing to France, the lack of freedom to walk the streets of romantic Paris, or an attempt to mend a marriage torn beyond repair, one fact is certain. They had both changed. Douglas had yet to mature and could not fathom his wife's need for privacy. Joan had become not only a popular actress but also a box office star and needed time alone to survive.

Doug and Joan remained together but went their separate ways. She knew he was seeing other women, and he was almost certain about the Gable affair. Doug was busy at Warner Brothers, and Joan co-starred with Gary Cooper, Robert Young, and Franchot Tone in *Today We Live.* Despite Joan's elegant wardrobe and three handsome co-stars, she was miscast as an English girl. Two Crawford flops in succession bothered Mayer. Letters were still pouring in about *Possessed,* and even though Gable had shared the screen with Carole Lombard, Helen Hayes, and Jean Harlow, the public wanted to see him with Joan Crawford.

Mayer knew about Joan and Doug even though there had been no official announcement. Fairbanks was the target of a $50,000 alienation-of-affection suit. A man named Dietz claimed Doug had stolen "the love and affection, comfort and assistance" of his wife. Joan had planned to give her separation exclusive to *Modern Screen*, but Louella Parsons got the scoop. Joan told the columnist, "My God, Douglas doesn't even know. I wanted to ease out of it gracefully after he's settled the alienation-of-affection suit!"

"If you don't tell him, I will," Parsons insisted.

"Give me time to pack his things," Joan said.

"Where is he?"

"Working."

Parsons shook her head.

Douglas was amused. He told Louella, "I'm going to send Joan flowers, call her every day, and send her telegrams when I can't get her on the phone. We are still in love."

Mayer watched the publicity circus. He was forced to remain silent about Gable because Fairbanks was quite a ladies' man, also. The whole complicated situation was not messy, after all, when Joan filed for divorce on May 13, 1933. She told the judge, "He would sulk for days at a time and refuse to speak to me. Oh, I was unable to sleep because of it! Whenever I spent the day working at the studio, he would ask where I had been at various times, when I had taken luncheon, and what I had done. All the time he knew I was at work, too. He made uncomplimentary remarks about my friends. He was so unreasonable."

The divorce was granted.

Modern Screen wrote, "Of course, Joan will get the brunt of it all. Of course the envious will be saying, 'Sure, we knew it wouldn't last. Crawford is just reverting to type.' Joan knew this and that is why the separation has been postponed longer than it should have been for the peace of mind of both."

Joan testified in court that her doctor prescribed a three-month rest, and for appearances' sake she relaxed at Malibu. Mayer was satisfied she was able to handle her own divorce without M-G-M's interference. He decided to award her by casting Clark Gable in *Dancing Lady*. Fred Astaire made his screen debut, and Franchot Tone played the rich playboy who tried to lure Joan away from her stage director, played by Clark.

She broke her ankle during filming but did not let that stop her from dancing. Fortunately it happened after her strenuous numbers were finished, but she took off the cast to dance with Astaire.

Gable was not happy with *Dancing Lady*. He played an inferior part to Tone, whose believable portrayal of the sincere playboy ran away with the film. Because of his infrequent and insignificant roles, Clark was in a foul mood. His bad teeth were bothering him. He drank whiskey to deaden the pain of a minor role, infected gums, and Joan's constant reminder that she had kept her end of their deal.

"When are *you* getting off your ass?" she wanted to know.

"Ria will destroy me," he moaned.

"She's loaded. A smart lawyer will prove that."

"I don't want to hurt her, Joanie."

"Hurt *her*? What about me, for Christ's sake?"

He scowled. "Your divorce won't be final for a year. There's time, and, besides, I don't want to hurt the kids."

"*Her* kids."

"I've grown very fond of them."

She laughed. "You don't even know their names."

"All right, damn it! Ria will take me for everything, and I don't want to be broke again. I couldn't take it. The timing's all wrong. Josephine wants more money, too. She's been talking to the press."

"I thought you paid her to keep her mouth shut."

"I did."

"L. B. must be livid."

"Nothing he can do," Gable said, sweating.

"Does that mean you'll have to pay double alimony?"

He shrugged.

"In that case," she sighed, "we'll have to wait."

Gable took a leave of absence after he finished *Dancing Lady*. M-G-M said he was hospitalized for an appendectomy, but his infected teeth were removed. Josephine, meanwhile, wrote letters to Clark in fan magazines, criticizing his acting and referring to their life together. He ceased monthly payments to her, and by the time he returned to M-G-M with a new set of false teeth, Josephine's letters were passé.

He and Mayer had a vicious argument over his roles, particularly his part in *Dancing Lady*. "I know what you're doing," Clark complained. "Joan's dating Franchot, and you're building him up like you did with Fairbanks. Okay, but not in my pictures!"

As punishment, Gable was loaned to Columbia Pictures for a film no one else wanted—*It Happened One Night*. The move backfired on Mayer; the film won the Academy Award for Best Picture of 1934 and earned Oscars for Clark and his co-star Claudette Colbert. Everyone in Hollywood was shocked. Gable had threatened to leave town when he was given the assignment. Ria had talked him out of it, but he did the film braced with bourbon. "I didn't wear an undershirt," he said, "I was half-drunk, and I didn't seduce my leading lady, but I won an Oscar."

He was sent to New York for a round of premieres, press parties, dinner dances, and cocktail parties—the means of introducing every major star to the American public. Publicity was grossly exaggerated, but unless one had been mobbed and touched and kissed and grabbed and poked, one was not a full-fledged star. Gable hated it, but found the world at his feet. Girls were a dime a dozen, and he didn't turn them all down. More than once Ria found her husband kissing another woman or in the arms of one. Seventeen years older, she could understand how he was overwhelmed by this experience. Her love for him would endure these indiscretions until he grew tired of it.

Clark returned to Hollywood with more confidence. He had outwitted Mayer by winning an Oscar and had seen the reality of his charm outside the protective walls of M-G-M. He knew his days with Ria were limited, and, knowing his popularity had more power than Mayer's wrath, his fear began to wane.

Joan had been dating Franchot Tone, who proposed marriage to her every day. In an interview for *Photoplay* she said, "It isn't fair for a woman who wants a career as much as I do to marry. It wouldn't be fair to Franchot. I don't believe I'll ever marry again. Love demands so much . . . you want to give even more . . . but I'm afraid marriage makes lovers just people. They do all the romantic things until they attain each other."

Mayer co-starred Joan and Franchot in *Sadie McKee*. She was the maid. He was the "young master" of the house. This typical casting made it a popular movie, and rumors that the leading man and lady were in love were an asset.

Joan changed all the toilet seats in her Brentwood home and began to redecorate with the help of Billy Haines. "If Franchot's your man, Cranberry, there's much to be done here. The toys and dolls have to go. The kitchen should be remodeled, so why not build a wing for a new one and expand the dining room as well? You need space, dear heart. This isn't a dollhouse anymore. You're a sophisticated woman and an accomplished actress. Your home should reflect who you are."

"I never said Franchot is my man."

"I know you, Cranberry, and I can't help but think of him as I remodel this house."

"How well do you know him, Billy?"

He grinned. "I know he's never seen one of your movies."

"I know that."

"Did you know that Tallulah Bankhead does a howling imitation of you?" Joan glared at Haines. "No."

He laughed. "She does, and Franchot loved it."

"Did he?"

"When he pulled himself together, I remember he said, 'That woman must be impossible." So I asked him if he'd ever met you, and Franchot announced he had not and had no desire to meet you."

"And?"

"I told him that you were my dearest friend and not to say another thing about you. I also said when he did meet you, he'd fall in love."

Joan smiled. "He did."

"He's another Douglas, Cranberry."

"I'm not rushing into anything."

"You went to New York with him."

"To see a play, silly."

"You pulled it off."

"Franchot wants me to go into the theater. He almost has me convinced."

"Why don't you try being yourself for a while?"

"I'm strong, Billy, but not like you."

He took a deep breath. "I saw it coming when Mayer wanted me to get married. Can you imagine another Pola Negri fiasco? I can still see her at Valentino's funeral . . . crying over his coffin, but granting interviews about their phony engagement between sobs. I couldn't take that fake publicity shit, Cranberry. Mayer was trying to save my hide, but . . ."

"Yes, I know," she said, squeezing his hand. "Above all, you love Jimmy Shields."

"We plan to be married."

"I'm happy for you, Billy."

"And thanks to Carole Lombard, I got my big start as an interior decorator. She has guts."

"I understand you didn't send her a bill."

"And your dear friend, Marion Davies . . ."

"Why didn't you charge Lombard, Billy? She's richer than any of us."

"She gave me my first break. Did you know she planned a big party to show off my work, and when the guests arrived the house was empty. Wasn't that a grand gag?"

"Amusing."

"Carole doesn't give a damn what anyone thinks. By the way, she gave me a check for doing her house, but I tore it up."

"How can you afford to do that, Billy?"

"I needed the money, but no one else would give me a chance until she did. Now I have contracts to decorate for Jack Warner, Lionel Barrymore, Claudette Colbert, and a nightclub. Jimmy can't handle the inquiries, so I'm hiring an office staff."

"I'll stake you in the meantime, Billy," she said, "but this is between you and me."

"And Jimmy," he said.

"Yes, you dope! And your Jimmy. Be honest with me. Do you miss acting and all the fuss that goes with it?"

"No. When Mayer gave me a choice between my career and Jimmy, I didn't hesitate. I don't have to hide and lie any longer. Having my freedom means more to me than becoming a myth."

Joan lit a cigarette, leaned back on the couch, and looked up at the ceiling. "I had lunch with Uncle Douglas," she murmured.

"How *is* Don Juan?"

"Tired, old, hurt, but feisty. He's going to make British films."

"Maybe Mary will take up knitting with you on Sundays."

"She's retiring. Her last two pictures flopped."

"Robin Hood has been seeing a Lady Ashley. She's twenty years younger than he is, getting a divorce, and, from what I hear, will not give up until she gets Fairbanks."

"Uncle Douglas can't accept the fact he's over fifty," Joan sighed. "Maybe this silly romance will blow over. He's flattered, that's all."

Joan was deeply affected by the separation of Mary Pickford and Douglas Fairbanks, Sr. She bought *Why Not Try God,* Mary's new book, and read between the lines. America's Sweetheart had nowhere else to turn and had found solace in religion. Actor Buddy Rogers, who had been in love with Mary for years, had consoled her when the scandal erupted over Doug's affair with Lady Sylvia Ashley, whose husband accused her of adultery with Fairbanks. After three years of legal entanglements and disgraceful revelations, Uncle Douglas married Sylvia, and Mary married Buddy Rogers. Uncle Douglas died in 1939. Sylvia remarried, divorced, and then married Clark Gable, who divorced her so that she could become Princess Dimitri Djordjadze.

Buddy Rogers sold Pickfair to sports entrepreneur Jerry Buss after Mary's death in 1979. As Joan said, "An invitation to Pickfair was no less important than an invitation to the White House." But the popularity of Pickfair also signaled the birth of Beverly Hills as a residential area in the early twenties, when the first big stars had settled in downtown Los Angeles and Hollywood. Joan and Mary became lifelong friends.

"Long after Douglas and I parted," Joan said, "I continued meeting Mary at Hollywood social functions, and as time went by there was growing cordiality. She said, 'Billie, my darling, I am so proud of what you've done with your life. You not only set yourself a great goal, you've surpassed that goal!' I know now that Mary had a great capacity for friendship."

6

LIFE WITH THE QUEEN

Stanislas Pascal Franchot Tone was born in Niagara Falls, New York, on February 27, 1905. The son of the president of the Carborundum Company, he was educated in private schools, graduated from Cornell University, and planned to teach languages, but he became an actor instead. His first appearance onstage was in a stock company in Buffalo in 1928; later that year, he made his debut in New York City in *The Belt*. He worked successfully for the New Playwrights Company, the Theater Guild, and the Group Theater. He established himself in *The Age of Innocence* with Katharine Cornell.

Tone was a rebel. He had been dismissed from private school "for being a subtle influence for disorder throughout the fall term." Franchot dropped out of high school in his senior year but used his father's influence at Cornell University to be considered for admission. He passed the college entrance exams and graduated three years later with a Phi Beta Kappa key. He also spent a summer at the University of Rennes in France.

He was one of the founding members of the Group Theater and concentrated on its struggle for survival during the Depression. For this reason alone, he signed a five-year contract with M-G-M. "I had no intention of staying in Hollywood for more than a year," he said. "My goal was to finance the Group Theater." Tone considered movies beneath an actor's dignity.

At the time he had a reputable standing in New York theater circles. Stark Young attested, "Mr. Tone is one of the best of the young actors in the New York theater and the most promising in his chances of development. He does not have to go to Hollywood to get a good role; many roles in the theater are open to him. And for the same reason he doesn't have to stay in Hollywood when he gets there."

Tone's first M-G-M film was *Gabriel Over the White House* with Walter Huston and Karen Morley. His second was *Today We Live* with Joan Crawford. He knew all about the flapper with a red slash for a mouth and her fierce ambition as an actress and social climber.

"I would sometimes see him watching me on the set," Joan recalled, "his great thinking eyes so penetrating, a little crooked smile on his aesthetic face. He was biding his time. He was self-contained; he carried with him an aura of peace, as if he knew some safe harbor."

*   *   *

Franchot walked over to Joan and said, "Gee, you're a nice dame."

Joan was reading her script. She glanced at Tone, looked him over critically, and continued studying.

"Hurt your feelings?" he asked.

"Yes. The word 'dame' sounds rough."

"Well, it isn't. It's the nicest compliment a guy can pay a lady."

Joan said he invited her to have dinner with him and his roommate. She asked Franchot to come for tea at her home. "I served from a set of rare antique English silver," she recalled. "I wasn't attracted to him and surely not in love, but he was down-to-earth and fun. He wanted to know all about Hollywood. What was L. B. Mayer really like? And Selznick? How did they choose the themes for movies that influenced millions of people?"

Tone pursued her and she dated him, but Gable still played an important part in her life. "We lived with the situation," she said. "Clark and I grabbed every chance to be alone. We were scared shitless, but it was impossible to stay away from each other. No wonder our personal lives were all fucked up. How we looked forward to making *Chained* together!"

Gable was definite about leaving Ria. "She brought my father out here to make our little family a cozy one," he complained, "but I'll be damned if I'll let him call me a sissy every chance he gets. So, I bought him and his new bride a house of their own."

"You're supporting him, and he still thinks all actors are sissies?"

"Yeah. Maybe I should get Haines to decorate his house."

"Ria tells me her daughter is getting married in Houston." Joan smiled. "She hinted she might be staying in Texas for a while."

"That's right, babe, and that's when I make my move."

"Good!"

"But," he said, lighting a cigarette to avoid her eyes, "I'll never get married again. Never."

"I'm not so sure I want to either."

"Just wanted you to know that."

"You're many things, Clark, but you're not dishonest."

"I'm not?"

"Not in the true sense of the word. For example, did you call Mary for a date?"

"Mary who?"

"Mary Pickford."

"What about her?"

"Did you ask her out?"

"No, I did not."

"That's what I mean," Joan said. "You asked to see her at Pickfair."

"So?"

"On the servants' day off."

"I didn't want to impose."

Joan smirked. "And Carole Lombard?"

"She doesn't have any servants."

"As soon as you heard she was getting a divorce from Bill Powell—zoom!"

"Dames need consolation at a time like that. You said so yourself."

"Carole told you to shove it, right?"

He scowled. "Who told you?"

"She told Billy and . . ."

"And Haines told you."

Joan laughed. "I just wanted to hear it directly from you that two beautiful women actually turned you down."

"When they change their minds, I might not be interested."

"That's when I mean about you, Clark—not a dishonest bone in your body."

In an interview, Joan Crawford told writer Roy Newquist, "Few people understood my relationship with Gable. We taught each other how to laugh at ourselves and that, baby, is the first thing anybody in Hollywood tucks into the survival kit. Clark was a wonderful man. Very simple, actually, pretty much the way he's been painted. He was more of a womanizer than the studio wanted to admit, but any relationship he entered into was honest—no false hopes. He outgrew his first two wives, and he felt terribly sorry about the breakups. We both had a built-in bullshit alarm system, and we were surrounded by the stuff, but the only times we could really talk about it, and laugh at what went on, was when we were together."

Chained appealed to moviegoers. The *New York Times* said, "So long as Miss Crawford and Mr. Gable are in a picture, it is as inevitable as the coming of night that the characters they impersonate will not be disappointing in the end. Miss Crawford gives a facile performance, and Mr. Gable is as ingratiating as ever."

Mayer seemed satisfied that Joan and Clark were not planning any drastic moves despite Gable's crumbling marriage. He saw another Fairbanks in Tone and would give all concerned his professional support. Mayer paired Joan and Clark in *Forsaking All Others*, a light comedy. Neither was thrilled about it.

"Mayer's tryin' to catch up with *It Happened One Night*," Clark said. "He's just finding out people still know how to laugh, Depression or no Depression."

"Comedy is not my forte, either," she said. "Joe Mankiewicz was picked to read the script for me. Poor man was terrified, but he's an excellent writer, and I thought the dialogue was hilarious. Whoever sent Joe thought I'd throw him out, I guess. He's new around here and I kinda like him."

"Not a bad looking guy . . ."

"I didn't mean it that way," she said, "but there's something about him. Know what I mean?"

Gable frowned. "Do *you* know what you mean?"

Mankiewicz would be responsible for writing and producing many of Joan's films. They had an extraordinary rapport. He understood her moods better than any of her husbands did. "She woke up like a movie star," he said, "and she went to the john like a movie star. She had a special outfit for answering her fan mail and another for having lunch." During the next ten years Hollywood insiders took it for granted that he and Joan were lovers. L. B. Mayer confessed Mankiewicz was the only one who could handle Joan when she asked for roles unsuited to her. "Let Garbo and Shearer grab the plums," Joe told her. "You play to the middle class because they pay to see you. They identify with your characters and your clothes. The studio knows who makes money for them even if they won't admit it."

Mayer took Joan away from Gable and Mankiewicz for *No More Ladies* with Franchot Tone. M-G-M was trying to promote Tone's career as they had done with Fairbanks, but more important to Joan was the opportunity to work with director George Cukor, who took over when E. H. Griffith got pneumonia.

"I don't like dialogue directors," she complained. "They're perfectionists."

Tone beamed. "George is from the theater."

"You'll have to help me get through this."

"Remember what I told you, darling. Every word has meaning, and that's what George wants. He'll demand the same from me."

"I can't communicate with theater people," she pouted.

"Have you changed your mind about going on the stage, darling?"

"I have my doubts, that's all. I'm not certain if one who has been trained for motion pictures can feel comfortable in the theater. If I make a mistake when filming, I can do it over again. Onstage, one chance is all you get."

"In the meantime, you'll learn from Cukor. He's a brilliant director. Don't be offended by him. Promise?"

"Yes, my darling."

Joan said Cukor raked her over the coals. In the film, she had to make an emotional speech to Robert Montgomery. Tone helped her, and she knew it word-for-word. Cukor, however, said, "Very fine. Now could we please repeat? You've remembered the words, let's put some meaning into them."

Joan was anxious to learn and did what she was told. Cukor was tough and cold, but there were no outbursts. "Franchot was in *No More Ladies*," she recalled, "and it was illuminating to watch him work with George, both of them from the theater, speaking the same language. It was another mediocre part for him, but we were together, and this had come to mean everything to me. My friendship with Franchot, which had gone on for two years, slowly kindled into what I felt was the love of my life. How I respected this man! What poise and sanity he had. Yet I hesitated. Could two careers make for a happy marriage?"

A source very close to Joan thought it was her aloofness that had attracted

Tone. "Though she used the excuse that her divorce wasn't final," the friend said, "Joan was stung by failure. After all, she had married the most eligible bachelor in Hollywood. Doug was perfect for her, but he lived in the shadow of his famous father and the status of Pickfair. Here was a woman who had overcome more obstacles than most, and yet sat like a frightened kitten while her in-laws and her husband left her all alone. Why didn't she speak up as she had done many times in the past? If this perfect marriage that was so full of love fell apart while she watched helplessly, how could she possible contemplate another husband?

"Joan hated living alone. It had been two years since she had packed Doug's belongings. This is when her compulsion for cleanliness began— scrubbing floors, porches, bathrooms, and the kitchen. She found fault with hired help. One speck of dirt was the enemy. She cleaned underneath chairs and tables. God forbid if a guest bent over and saw some dust or a crumb! She embraced Christian Science but rarely talked about it. She swam and walked every day, loved tennis, and slept in a screened-in porch. Joan rarely drank but she was a heavy smoker. I don't think she inhaled, but her excuse for lighting up was the need to do something with her hands. Except for her nerves and deep depressions, she was in good health. I can't recall her complaining of stomach problems, headaches, or colds, although she would give in to any one of these ailments if it served her purpose. Joan also had claustrophobia, brought on when her brother Hal locked her in a closet as a child. She was terrified of airplanes, too, and never flew until she was over fifty years old."

If Tone was aware of Crawford's affair with Gable, he didn't allow it to bother him. Confident, smooth and gallant, he was persistent and patient. He moved from Santa Monica to Brentwood to be near Joan. She said he was a very romantic fellow with great charm and imagination. In her autobiography, Joan described the first night Franchot took her out dancing, but like so many stories she related in later years, Joan blended her movie experiences with those of real life. "I wore a collar of gardenias around my throat, and he a gardenia in his lapel. The fragrant blooms were my favorites. They meant luck and love. He always had the house and my studio dressing rooms filled with them. Photographers flashed a few pictures of us that first night we went dancing, but this man had a dignity that forbade intrusion."

The scene with the gardenias is right out of *Dancing Lady*. although Joan had gardenia-mania for a while. She handed them out to everyone on the set and carried one wherever she went. The house was indeed filled with the fragrant flowers—a nauseating smell for guests at the dinner table.

Although Joan said she fell in love instantly with Fairbanks and it took two years before she realized how much she loved Franchot, her longing for Gable was what prevented her from marrying anyone else. She knew he no longer wanted or needed Ria, who had pursued, supported, and spoiled him.

Winning the Oscar gave Clark the assurance he required to fight his own professional battles, and earning $3,000 a week gave him independence. But Joan understood Clark too well. After being married for ten years, he needed breathing room.

As the 1934 Christmas holidays approached, Joan was disappointed but not surprised to hear that Gable was romancing Loretta Young. In the state of Washington to film *Call of the Wild*, the cast found themselves snowed in for several weeks. The rumors were not taken seriously until director William Wellman complained that Clark was not himself.

"We had trouble on *Call of the Wild*, big trouble, on top of a mountain," Wellman wrote in *A Short Time for Insanity* (Hawthorne, 1974). "Gable wasn't tending to business, not the business of making pictures. He was paying a lot of attention to monkey business, and I called him on it, lost my easy-to-lose temper, and did it in front of the company, a bad mistake.

"He was a big man. I am not, but there was a big something in his favor, his face. He made his living with it, mine behind the camera. He might have beaten my brains out. I don't know, but I know that I could have made a character man out of him in the process."

Gable, who was always prompt, showed up late on the set and was not prepared with his lines. Reliable sources said Clark and Loretta Young were enjoying the long, cold nights alone together. Without identifying the stars, Hollywood gossip columnists hinted at the hot combination in the state of Washington that should have melted the snow and ice by now.

Ria was prepared to admit that her gravest fear was reality. Clark returned to Hollywood in one of his darkest moods. A few months later, Loretta announced that she was retiring from films for a year due to "health problems." The persistent rumor was that she was pregnant, and in 1935 this would have meant the end of Loretta's career. She simply disappeared and let reporters fight for reasons why she had left town.

Hollywood writer Anita Loos wrote forty years later that Clark had had an affair with a co-star during the filming of *Call of the Wild* that resulted in the birth of a baby girl. Director Wellman commented, "All I know is Loretta disappeared when the film was finished and showed up with a daughter who had big ears. She's grown into a lovely woman who resembles her beautiful mother." Miss Young, however, claimed that she adopted the child despite a California law forbidding single-parent adoptions. "I fell in love with her in a San Diego orphanage," Loretta said.

After *Mutiny on the Bounty* with Franchot Tone, Gable left for South America, stopping off first in New York, where he was seen having dinner with several lovely socialites. When he returned to Hollywood, he confirmed his separation from Ria but refused to answer questions about anything or anyone else.

His new address was the Beverly Wilshire Hotel.

*   *   *

Joan had nothing to say about the Gable-Young affair then or ever. She did, however, have a marvelous sense of humor about Loretta's devotion to Catholicism. During one of her parties, a friend was about to sit in a chair, and Joan grabbed him just in time. "Can't sit there," she said. "Loretta Young just got up, and it has the mark of the cross on the seat."

Miss Young's campaign to abolish swearing, pornography, and immoral literature was amusing to her peers in Hollywood. On every movie set she had a "swear box." Monies collected went to a home for unwed mothers. Some actors handed her a $10 bill and told her to lay off. Robert Mitchum, who didn't play little games, asked her how much she charged. "Five cents for every 'damn,' ten cents for 'hell,' and twenty-five cents for 'goddamn,' " she replied.

"How much for 'fuck'?" he asked.

She smiled. "That's free."

Joan never forgot the attention Loretta received at her tea parties. The stunning Miss Young had eloped when she was only nineteen. The marriage had been annulled the same year in a highly publicized court trial. But Loretta's big gray innocent eyes and virginal quality became a symbol of beauty. Although her ex-husband referred to her as "the Steel Butterfly" and skeptics said she was "Hollywood's Beautiful Hack," no amount of gossip could mar Loretta's class and refinement. Joan, on the other hand, was constantly being criticized for her mistakes, divorces, and affairs. "We were all typed," she said, "and it carried over into our personal lives. No one believed I went to church every morning because I projected a belief only in myself."

While Gable played, Joan concentrated on Franchot's career. He was making strides in *Lives of a Bengal Lancer* with Gary Cooper and *Mutiny on the Bounty* with Gable and Charles Laughton. In *Dangerous,* Tone co-starred with Bette Davis, who fell madly in love with him. "I knew he was crazy about Crawford," Betty said, "but I felt there was no harm in trying. I gave up when he came on the set every day after lunch with Joan's lipstick all over his face."

Still Joan procrastinated. "I'll never marry again as long as I live," she told a reporter. "There is no such thing as honesty or true love. If anyone ever catches me believing in anything, I hope they give me a good sock in the jaw."

She bought a lot behind her home and made plans with Franchot to build a little theater where a small group could actually produce the classics or rehearse their current film scripts. Franchot convinced her to study opera, also. "He didn't just have a voice," she said. "He had a hundred-piece orchestra inside that rib cage, and like a fine conductor, he had every nuance of the music, every instrument under complete control."

Unfortunately, Joan did not have the voice for opera, but no one told her. She took her operettas seriously, much to the dismay of dinner guests who were too stunned to react. David Niven said he didn't know whether he wanted to laugh or cry and did neither, of course.

Franchot's encouragement to play on radio broadcasts made Joan ill, however. When Bing Crosby invited her on this show, she went into a panic. "Play myself?" she gasped.

Tone laughed. "Yes, darling. What could be easier?"

"If I play another character and fall on my face, that's all right. But if I play Joan Crawford and act like a dope . . . no, I can't do it!"

Franchot convinced Joan somehow; consumed with fear, she was given a prop to lean on while her doctor stood nearby during the broadcast. Lux Radio Theater asked her often to repeat some of her movie roles on the air, but she turned them down. Franchot wanted her to accept. "Every major star's voice has been on that show," he said. "It's very important, darling. You got through 'The Crosby Show,' and while the feeling of accomplishment is still vivid, let's go to New York City and appear on Lux."

Joan said an evening spent with Alfred Lunt and Lynn Fontanne convinced her to marry Franchot. "They were inspiring people. In real life, as onstage, they presented each other in the most gracious light. Seeing how happy they were, I was ready to believe two careers could blend. Franchot and I became engaged."

Joan finished the radio reenactment of "I Live My Life" with Brian Aherne and planned to leave for New York to appear in "Paid" on Radio Theater. Tone was scheduled to do "East Meets West" for the Cavalcade of America. He rode in a different part of the train and got off at Harmon, New York. Nonetheless, trailed by fans and reporters, the couple did not escape unnoticed until October 11, 1935. They were married by Mayor Herbert W. Jenkins of Fort Lee, New Jersey, at his residence. Nick Schenck and Leo Friedman of M-G-M were witnesses. Joan wore a blue wool suit and hat and carried a bridal bouquet. That afternoon she rehearsed the radio show with her gloves on to hide her wedding ring.

They spent their honeymoon at the Waldorf-Astoria Hotel. Joan called Walter Winchell with the news but made him promise not to broadcast her marriage until Sunday night. "Franchot and I want the weekend alone together," she sighed. "By the time you go on the air, Walter, we'll be on the train. That's the least you can do for me since I'm giving you the exclusive."

Joan's wedding night was destroyed, however, when she received an anonymous phone call from someone who said he possessed a pornographic film made by her. She admitted to Franchot that she had gotten similar calls in the past, but this time she told the man to contact L. B. Mayer or J. Robert Rubin, the M-G-M attorney. The name of the film was *The Casting Couch*. The title explains the theme. Joan denied making any such films, but M-G-M, Mayer, and/or Joan paid a handsome sum of money to get the negatives. A former studio executive claims it was $100,000. Rumors persist to this day that one copy exists and that it is owned by an Austrian count who watches it daily in his Alpine castle.

Most likely the film in question is the risqué vignette Billie Cassin made in 1923 when she danced in the nude to earn train fare from Kansas City to Chicago. According to Joan, she was only fifteen at the time, but it has been proven that she was actually nineteen, living with the shady E. S. in Kansas City, and involved with his friends, who made their money selling dope, bootleg booze, and porno pictures.

Robert Slatzer, a newspaperman from Ohio, was invited to one of his first Hollywood parties in the late thirties. A friend pointed out Joan Crawford. Slatzer studied her carefully and casually mentioned he had seen her dancing in a nude film back in Ohio. "I was with a group of guys who got together at the lodge for a game of cards and a few drinks," he said. "They usually showed a 'girlie' film. There was nothing pornographic about the one Joan did. I thought it was common knowledge."

A few minutes later, Slatzer noticed the cocktail party guests separate "like the Red Sea" and Joan headed in his direction. "Are you the newspaperman from Ohio?" she hissed.

"Yes," he said, feeling a chill. She motioned for him to follow her out on the balcony, where they could be alone.

"You're the one spreading the story around about a film you saw in Ohio?" she asked.

He nodded.

"From now on keep your fuckin' mouth shut!" she said and walked away.

They ran into each other often after that. Joan always made an effort to say hello to Slatzer and to chat with him about his screenwriting career.

Joan and Franchot enjoyed the stops along the way on the train from New York to Los Angeles. Hundred of reporters waited to congratulate and photograph the newlyweds. The bride said, "Thank God I'm in love again. Now I can do it for love and not for my complexion."

They moved into Joan's Bristol Avenue house, which was being redecorated by Billy Haines. Franchot was the second husband to live there, but it made sense to him to move into Joan's house because his dream house would be in the Canadian woods or on an island far away from gaudy Hollywood. Tone had not given up his plan to return to the theater, but he loved Joan enough to wait until she was ready. During their first year of marriage she earned $250,000 and he made a mere $50,000.

While Franchot studied with his left-wingers from the Group Theater in the backyard studio, Joan tried to mingle. She preferred curling up in front of the fireplace with her husband and reciting the lines of Romeo and Juliet or Essex and Elizabeth. Subconsciously Joan and Franchot were not on the same path. She was terrified of the stage. "When I was a chorus girl, there was a whole line of us to bolster each other," Joan said, "but when I walk across an empty stage on my way to someone's dressing room, I feel faint. Once I stopped for a moment and said a few words, but my heart was pounding so, I could barely make it to the wings."

Franchot had been welcomed back to M-G-M with a part in a Crawford picture, *The Gorgeous Hussy*, with Robert Taylor. The reviews were terrible. The *New York Herald Tribune* noted, "Joan Crawford is handsome, although century-old costumes do not go well with the pronounced modernity of her personality." The *New York Times* wrote, "Miss Crawford's Peggy is a maligned Anne of Green Gables, a persecuted Pollyanna, and a dismayed Dolly Dimples."

Franchot Tone had only twenty-six lines in the film.

Joan admitted *Hussy* was a mistake, but she had wanted to do a costume picture. She had no idea that Franchot was signed for such a small role. Mayer explained, "We can't have a great cast like this, Joan, and then have you walk away into the sunset with some unknown actor. We have to have an important actor. That's why I signed Franchot. I didn't say anything because I knew you'd object. After all, no other actor would take so small a part."

"Humiliating," she emphasized.

"I can't do anything about it now," he said sympathetically.

"You know what people will say."

"Starring Mr. and Mrs. Joan Crawford?"

She nodded and began to cry.

"Let's face it," Mayer said. "There's only one major star to a family in Hollywood. Two is one too many."

"I don't believe that."

"In the meantime, I'm trying to keep Franchot's face on the screen."

"He's the greatest actor in the business."

"Whatever you say, Joan."

"Franchot will do *Hussy* if I ask him."

"Do me a favor," Mayer said with his usual hug. "Look after the new boy, James Stewart. He's shy but has promise. Be patient and supportive."

"What about Robert Taylor? Do I change his diapers, too?"

"All he has to do is show up."

"Like Franchot," she sniffled. "But you must keep in mind he's played with Katharine Cornell."

"And you've played with the Barrymores, Chaney, Beery, Garbo, Cooper, Montgomery, and . . ."

"Tim McCoy."

"I'm glad you brought that up," he said. "A real star can't be dimmed regardless of the role and that includes *Hussy*. You wanted it. Mankiewicz agreed. The cast will draw a big following, and your husband should be damn grateful."

"Franchot has great depth. He's not impressed with movie fame."

"Bullshit."

"The best part in a classical film would bore him," she exclaimed.

"In that case, his very brief role in *Hussy* won't be painful."

"Christ," she mumbled.

"I'll be damned if we're going to argue over Tone's ambition," Mayer said. "He'd better make a choice between Hollywood and Broadway because your marriage is nothing more than a taffy-pull. Besides, you have no respect for method actors."

"I've learned some valuable tips."

"Like how to impersonate an oak tree?"

Joan laughed with tears in her eyes. "That was a joke."

"Everything they teach is a joke," he bellowed. "I'm disappointed and saddened that you've been swayed. There's a naturalness about you and it shows on the screen. I advise you think twice about changing it."

According to Joan, *The Gorgeous Hussy* was the beginning of the end of her marriage to Tone although she didn't realize it at the time. While they were filming, he stayed by himself and talked with no one. At home he was silent. He was late reporting for work and stayed out all night. Joan could not accept his unprofessional behavior at the studio, and she feared he was seeing another woman. "I wanted to help," she said, "because I knew he was desperately unhappy in all phases of his life, bored with Hollywood, and leaning on his theater friends for consolation."

Mayer and Mankiewicz were not oblivious to the strain, and although *Hussy* was successful at the box office, Joan's fan mail proved she had paid a high price. M-G-M put her in *Love on the Run* with Gable and Tone. "We had a ball," Joan said. "Franchot walked off with the picture. I was relieved for him, but Clark and I were saddened by the death of John Gilbert. He was only forty years old and a victim of Hollywood. John drank himself to death from a broken heart. Garbo tried to help when she demanded he play her leading man in *Queen Christina,* but it was too late. The fickle public wasn't interested in the Garbo and Gilbert team anymore. Poor, poor John. There was a hush in town when he died. Clark and I talked about our careers; we were still two helpless lost souls. He had reconciled with Ria off and on even though the marriage was over. With all his women, Clark was lonely. He needed roots. We were trying to keep our sanity."

Franchot's solution to his problems was always the same—return to the theater. Clark was blunt and said he couldn't face an audience despite his previous stage experience.

"Why?" Tone asked.

"Because I'm Clark Gable, and people would come to see me in the flesh, which is what they would see after tearing my clothes off."

Joan asked him to join the Group Theater. Gable refused. "I don't go for their propaganda, and I'm not referring to acting."

"I refuse to discuss politics with them."

"They denounce capitalism, baby."

"And I refused to work when Mussolini's son visited M-G-M."

Gable scowled. "So, what do you have in common with the Group Theater?"

"Franchot."

"Listen, if you can tear yourself away from Stanislavsky, I want you to read a script."

"Which one?"

"*Parnell.*"

"You're mad! Who the hell's gonna believe you're the uncrowned king of Ireland? I won't do it!"

"Don't take your personal problems out on me, babe."

"Get Loretta."

"She's unavailable."

"You son of a bitch!"

Clark was livid and did not see Joan for a long time after that. Myrna Loy replaced her in *Parnell,* which was a flop. Gable put the blame on Joan, who refused to work with him in *Saratoga* because they weren't speaking.

If Gable was upset over *Parnell,* he soon perked up at the annual Mayfair Ball, where Carole Lombard caught his eye. She wasn't an easy catch, however. "Here's one dame who's not chasing you," this bouncy blonde announced. Carole agreed to go out with him but dated other men as well. When she moved to Bel Air, he rented a house nearby. It was no secret that she held the key to his heart and knew how to hang on to it. "God knows I love Clark," she said, "but he's a lousy lay." When reporters quoted Carole, Gable laughed. "Guess I'll have to do a lotta practicin'." She behaved herself at the ceremonies held to crown Gable the "King of Hollywood," but turned to friends and said in a loud whisper, "If Clark had an inch less he'd be 'Queen of Hollywood.' "

Joan thought nothing of the affair. Gable was still a married man and was seeing other women besides Carole. Ria had made no attempt to get a divorce, and there were no rumblings at M-G-M. While Carole amused herself by hanging *Parnell* stickers wherever Clark might see one, Joan had more important career matters to ponder. She was elated to be proclaimed the "First Queen of the Movies" in 1937. *Life* magazine said, "It is an axiom in Hollywood that movie favorites are usually created by women. Joan Crawford's public is predominantly female, predominantly lowbrow. A former shopgirl herself, she has risen to stardom as the Shopgirl's Dream." Joan had remained among the top ten in the *Motion Picture Herald*'s annual poll since 1932. It came as quite a surprise when Franchot Tone appeared on the list of Hollywood's ten most popular male stars.

He was unimpressed. Co-starring with his famous wife in seven films did little for his ego. Joan was forging ahead with her movie career, demanding better scripts and spending less time in the little backyard theater. Louella and Hedda criticized her for not cooperating. Joan tearfully tried to explain: "When I was married to Douglas we shared our life with the press and that's why our marriage failed. Lack of privacy. Franchot and I slipped off to New York for togetherness, and I don't regret keeping our wedding a secret because those few days were sheer joy. We danced until dawn, then stopped our taxi on Sixth Avenue and waltzed with an old man who was selling newspapers. He had no idea who we were.

"Franchot is a humble man and does not like interviews because he doesn't like to talk about himself. Yet I read in a fan magazine the other day that Hollywood must accept him for his fine work, his sincere portrayals, and credit his lack of the usual Hollywood social conscience to his determination to avoid hypocrisy—leaving him a stranger within the gates."

This statement was unfair, she stated. Furthermore, she attended premieres of her films openly despite M-G-M's preference that she sneak in a side door and out the back. "My fans put me where I am," she said. "If it wasn't for them I'd be back in Kansas City. Twice a year I go to New York specifically to see my fans. My schedule is no secret. They know where I plan to shop and where I'm having dinner. Frankly, I don't feel I have to go beyond that for any member of the press."

In her autobiography, Joan wrote that she had so many problems in 1937 and 1938 that she wasn't thinking clearly. Franchot's hopes to team with her on the stage were shattered.

"I was caught between the devil and the deep blue sea," he said. "The marriage went in reverse." Joan criticized him for his lack of ambition in Hollywood. He turned to the bottle and other women. His verbal battles with Joan became physical. Who struck the first blow wasn't important because no man had the right to beat his wife, and she had the bruises to prove it.

Joan told friends she had seven miscarriages during her marriage to Franchot. She blamed her inability to have children on allergies, strenuous work, or not seeing a doctor early enough in her pregnancies. She also claimed the studio did not want their major female stars having babies. It ruined their images.

After *The Last of Mrs. Cheyney* with Robert Montgomery and William Powell ("A very good film but I contributed nothing to it; my life was falling apart"), Joan starred with Franchot and Robert Young in *The Bride Wore Red*. The *New York Herald Tribune* raved: "Joan Crawford has a glamorous field day in *The Bride Wore Red*. With a new hairdo and more wide-eyed than ever, she plays at being a slattern, a fine lady, and a peasant with all of the well-known Crawford sorcery. It is not entirely her fault that she always remains herself." The *New York Times* referred to the picture as ". . . one of those seasonal rediscoveries of Cinderella." Crawford fans flocked to see the movie and left the theater with a warm feeling because Franchot won his wife at the end.

In real life he was losing her.

"With Douglas I tried too hard," she said. "With Franchot I didn't try hard enough."

More of a shock to Joan was being labeled "Box Office Poison" by *The Independent Film Journal* in 1938. "Among those players whose dramatic ability is unquestioned, but whose box-office draw is nil, can be numbered Mae West, Edward Arnold, Greta Garbo, Joan Crawford, Katharine Hepburn, Marlene Dietrich, and Fred Astaire."

Joan was devastated. Was it possible she had gone from queen to poison in only one year? She tried to convince herself she was in excellent company on that list, but how would Mayer approach her contract, which was up for renewal? She was in no mood for studio politics or fencing. Should she go to L. B. and cry it out? Play on his sympathy? Or stay away and pretend it didn't bother her? Be cagey and casual?

Nervous and impatient, she made up her mind to get it over with. The tension at home was taking its toll on her. Franchot was drinking heavily. He dreaded facing her at night, and Joan wasn't sure if she wanted him to come home at all. He told his friends, "Enough is enough. I don't mind apologizing to her, but she insists I get down on my knees."

Divorce was inevitable—another reason why Joan needed security at M-G-M. A second failed marriage and a Box Office Poison label meant bad publicity. She could handle Franchot for a little while, but being at the mercy of Mayer was frightening.

"Why should you care about a silly article?" Mayer asked.

"It's in every newspaper and magazine, L. B."

"Pay no attention."

"I'm deeply hurt."

"What you need is a good Crawford film."

"Shopgirl?"

"From rags to riches with Spencer Tracy."

She frowned. "Tracy?"

"Produced by Joe M."

"Wardrobe by Adrian?" she asked, her eyes filled with joyful tears.

"Absolutely."

"Tracy's a good actor when he's sober."

Mayer handed her the *Mannequin* script. "Look it over."

"Now?"

"Yes, now. Otherwise we can't discuss your new contract."

Joan thumbed through the pages . . . working girl married to small-time chiseler falls in love with shipping magnate (Tracy). Girl gets divorce and marries rich man, who faces financial disaster, but they confront the uncertain future together. "Like old times." She smiled nervously.

"Terms of the new one-year contract," Mayer stated matter-of-factly. "Three pictures, one hundred fifty thousand dollars each."

"One year?" she asked weakly.

"That's what I said, Joan."

"One year?"

"Yes."

"L. B., I'm part of M-G-M. For thirteen years I . . ."

"What did you have in mind?" Mayer interrupted.

"Five years."

He shook his head.

"Three?" she asked.

"If you'll settle for one hundred thousand dollars per picture."

"And you said that fuckin' Box Office Poison crap meant nothing! You're full of shit, L. B."

"You happen to be right this time, Joan, because I'm taking a big chance on a three-year deal with you."

He watched her take out a lace hankie, leaned back in his chair, and waited for the sobs of sacrifice, the tears of devotion, and the wails of supporting her mother and brother.

"Don't forget your husbands," he muttered.

She nodded.

"And the butler and chef and upstairs maid . . ."

"Damn you, L. B.! I live like a fuckin' star should. My fans sit on the curb where I live. I serve them all cookies and milk. They expect Joan Crawford to look like a million bucks when she steps out her back door to pick fresh flowers from the garden. I have to look glamorous when I leave for the studio before dawn and just as spiffy when I come home dead tired. I do it for Crawford, yes, but Metro-Goldwyn-Mayer reaps the harvest."

"Three years. One hundred thousand dollars per picture."

"I'll take it."

"Congratulations."

"If Irving were alive, he would not allow this humiliation."

"Thalberg never had power, Joan. He was a thinker."

"And a doer—a man with insight and generosity."

Mayer smirked. "He never spoke of you so kindly."

"To my knowledge Irving Thalberg never spoke about me at all," she said, walking to the door.

He smiled sadly. "I love you, Joan. I'll always think of you as a daughter."

She turned around and laughed. "Just the other day Robert Taylor came in here and said he needed more than thirty-five lousy bucks a week. When he walked out, Bob said, 'I didn't get a raise but I got a father.' The kid doesn't know what he has to look forward to."

"He'll get what he gives and that's respect, which is more than I can say for you and Gable, who've given me nothing but trouble. Irving bowed to talent. I use it."

Joan slammed the door behind her, smiled at Ida Koverman, Mayer's secretary, got into her car, and cried all the way home.

* * *

Spencer Tracy had an inborn talent and was considered the best actor in Hollywood by his peers. He had won an Oscar for his performance in *Captains Courageous* in 1937 and would go on to win another the next year for *Boys Town*. *Time* magazine referred to him as "cinema's no. 1 actor's actor." Tracy never tried to give a good performance. He approached each role effortlessly and could steal a scene by just standing still with no expression on his face. What was his secret? "Just know your lines and don't bump into any furniture."

At first Joan was anxious to work with Tracy because he had an honest and uncomplicated approach to acting. "He walked through a scene as he walked through life," she commented. Joan did not, however. She did the final take as it was rehearsed while Tracy was spontaneous. This threw her off. "Don't be so serious," he laughed. "Take it slow and easy."

"The part of Jesse calls for a serious approach," she argued.

He scowled. "Okay, but don't be so uptight about it."

Tracy clowned around on the set and took the stance of a boxer by rubbing his finger on his nose and teasing Joan until she laughed during take after take. "I think you're finally coming around," he said. She called him "Slug." As production of *Mannequin* progressed, Joan knew they would never finish until she learned to concentrate completely on her part and pay less attention to Tracy, who tried to throw her off by stepping on her toes during love scenes. She did not complain about his drinking because they were falling in love.

She knew he was a Catholic and a married man. She knew he and Loretta Young had fallen in love during filming of *A Man's Castle*. Tracy left his wife, but Loretta realized no love was great enough for her to turn her back on Catholicism. He claimed his wife would not divorce him because of their religious beliefs, but she was not a Catholic. So Loretta was forced to make the heartbreaking decision. Tracy had been very much in love with Loretta and took their parting very hard. Now, Hollywood watched the strange combination of Crawford and Tracy.

Joan had found Clark to be evasive and tough, but even he was a lamb compared with Spencer, who didn't give a damn about anything. He considered Joan's fears "a lotta bull" and had her in the palm of his hand. When he ate garlic before their torrid kisses, she managed to overlook the awful taste because he was trying to break her down. Her attraction to Tracy made the farce easy to take, but trying not to be distracted while remembering her lines made her ill, and she contracted pneumonia. During her recuperation Spencer invited her to the posh Riviera Club, where he played polo. The doctor permitted Joan to go on the outings for some much-needed fresh air.

"Slug was different off the set," she said. "We got to know each other better, and he helped me overcome my fear of horses. He taught me to play polo, and I bought two ponies of my own. Slug appeared to be very easygoing and I found myself leaning on him—wanting to be more like that. I was wound up too tight and was far too sensitive about every little thing. Nothing seemed to bother him. He made me laugh despite the fact that my marriage was breaking up and I didn't know which way to turn. What I failed to realize was—we are what we are.

"He was a very, very disturbed man. I understand he never took a drink until his son was born deaf. He blamed himself, even though his daughter was normal. After that first drink, he didn't stop, and Spence was a mean drunk. At first he was a clown and a prankster. He tried to put me at ease. I wanted to be like him. That was impossible. I wanted to lean on him. That was impossible, too. I was on the rebound, but from one drunk to another?"

Observers said it was the first time they had seen Joan laugh in quite some time. She played polo with Tracy and enjoyed the outdoors with him. She escaped from her woes for a little while.

When Joan and Spencer were asked to do *Mannequin* on Lux Radio Theater, Joan hesitated, but he accepted for both of them. At first she was cheerful about the show because Tracy had taken over. He thought nothing about it. Hell, she thought, he got me on a horse, I fell off and got right back on again. He had breezed through their film together.

Rehearsals for the radio program began. Joan was fine until Tracy noticed her hands were trembling. "What's the matter with you?" he asked gruffly.

"N-n-n-nothing," she sputtered. "N-nervous, I guess. Shall we try it again?"

"For Christ's sake, Joan, can't you read the lines?" he snarled. "I thought you were supposed to be a pro."

Crawford burst into tears, dropped the script, and ran from the studio to her car. Tracy made no effort to call her back or to follow. Twenty-five years later she was very blunt about her feelings for him. "Tracy was a bastard . . . an unmitigated son of a bitch."

Katharine Hepburn, who did not meet Tracy until 1942, said after his death, "Acting was easy for him. Life was the problem."

As for *Mannequin*, the *New York Times* said it restored Miss Joan Crawford to her throne as "Queen of the Working Girls."

Billy Haines joked about the prospect of redecorating the Bristol Avenue house again. "I whitewashed Douglas not long ago," he laughed. "Do I begin all over again when Master Tone leaves?"

"Don't be ridiculous! I'll change the toilet seats, that's all."

"Is there any reason why . . ."

"Billy," she interrupted, "I don't want to discuss such a delicate subject except to say that there is nothing more personal in one's home than . . ."

"A toilet sea. That's logical, Cranberry."

"I don't particularly enjoy the logical you," she remarked. "Any juicy tidbits?"

"Franchot had dinner with Loretta. I hear she's dating him just to annoy you."

"I have more important matters to ponder. Jeanette MacDonald and Nelson Eddy are fighting like mad. Nothing new, but this may be to my advantage. I've been studying with Rosa Ponselle's coach, Romano Romano," she said, putting on the phonograph.

"What is it?" Haines asked.

"*La Traviata.*"

"*Who* is it?"

"Me, silly. You'll love *Don Giovanni.*"

"Cranberry, you can't be serious about singing with Nelson Eddy."

"Very. And L. B. might reconsider that new contract he's drawing up for me."

Haines paled. "Might? I'm sure he will."

Joan finished *The Shining Hour* with Robert Young and Melvyn Douglas to mixed reviews. She spoke to Mayer about an operetta. He listened to her records and had nothing but praise. In shock, his only defense was to plead for her help: "I need you most desperately in *Ice Follies of 1939*," he said with misty eyes.

"I can't skate, L. B."

"I've hired the entire International Ice Follies, but I'll need your lovely legs and face to add class to this picture. Very big production, Joan, and you'll sing three songs."

"Who's going to hold me up?" she asked.

"Jimmy Stewart and Lew Ayres. They're praying you'll accept."

"I sing three songs?"

"Not Verdi, but you'll love the costumes. Spectacular. Gorgeous. Enchanting. Expensive."

"Don't forget the operetta, L. B."

"Jeanette and Nelson will work as a team or not at all."

Joan understood those words only too well, but she wasn't about to put on a pair of ice skates without getting something in return. "How about *Idiot's Delight?*"

"I'll think about it, Joan. *Gone With the Wind* takes up most of my time."

"I'd be perfect for the lead role of the phony Russian girl in *Idiot's Delight*, but the part of Scarlett is good, too."

"Joan, I'm stumbling over a thousand pairs of ice skates and the Civil War. Your timing is bad. Pick up your music for *Ice Follies* because I know how thrilled you are."

The Ice Follies of 1939 was refreshing entertainment. The story line was weak, and audiences wondered if Joan Crawford had accidentally walked on the wrong movie set. "It was trash," she said. "Jimmy, Lew, and I kept trying to figure out where we came in. I was supposed to be a singer in the picture, but my three songs ended up on the cutting room floor because they slowed up the skating numbers."

Disappointed and restless, Joan decided to attend the premiere of *Follies* in New York. "If any of my fans show up for this disaster," she laughed, "I owe it to them to be there."

Movie magazines were filled with articles hinting that her career was over: "Is Joan Crawford Slipping?" "Can Joan Crawford Hold On?" "Are Joan's Screen Days Numbered?"

Instead of being discouraged and depressed, Joan got angry at the publicity, hopping mad at writers and reporters who professed to be her friends, and furious that M-G-M hadn't used its usual influence with the fan magazines. She failed to realize that times had changed. The studios remained powerful but did not have complete control any longer.

In 1938, *Photoplay's* "Unmarried Husbands and Wives" forced Barbara Stanwyck and Robert Taylor to the altar. Paulette Goddard and Charlie Chaplin insisted they were married by the mayor of Catalina, even though the island of Catalina did not have a mayor. And M-G-M rushed Ria Gable to Reno for a quickie divorce.

Robert Taylor told Joan, "All I had to say about it was, 'I do.' I didn't know what happened." He reminded her that the press had hounded him with the "Pretty Boy" label because his roles were not manly. "When I filmed *A Yank at Oxford,* my picture was on the front page of every newspaper with the caption 'Taylor has hair on his chest.' Overnight I was a he-man, but I still break out in a sweat if anyone refers to me as 'Pretty Boy.' M-G-M did all it could. Something came out of it, though."

"What?" she asked. "Your marriage to Barbara?"

He hesitated, "Well, yes, but I was actually referring to the tough roles I'm assigned now . . . boxers, cowboys, gangsters . . . that sort of thing."

Joan was willing to live with an empty marriage until her career improved, but when she found Franchot making love to another woman in his dressing room she had no choice but to end it. Although she had closed her eyes to his dalliances, Joan felt obligated to ask why.

"To prove to myself I'm still a man," Franchot replied. "I love you so much I wish I liked you."

Joan insisted he leave the house immediately and, like Douglas, Franchot was gone without a trace a day later. She boarded a train for New York, and was greeted at Grand Central Station by hundreds of fans. M-G-M press agents and the police tried to protect her, but Joan's clothes were torn and ragged by the time she got to the hotel. Everyone in her entourage was relieved just to be alive, but Joan said joyfully, "Let's go back and do it all over again!"

One of Joan's dates in New York was Franchot. Her lawyers in Los Angeles were seeking an absentee divorce for her, but the judge declined since their client had been photographed dancing with Tone at a nightclub. She told friends he wanted to celebrate their divorce. "I thought it was a grand and sensible idea," she said.

Back in Los Angeles a month later, Joan went to court and told the judge, "I'm sorry we married. Marriage was a mistake for me. I'm not the marrying kind, and I want my divorce." She went on to explain that Franchot liked to go out every night, and she was tired after working all day. "He went out alone and came home very late and refused to tell me where he'd been."

The judge glowered at her. "Divorce is granted, but if your husband caused you so much anguish, how could you bear to go dancing with him?"

Joan glared back haughtily. "I hope I'm intelligent enough to be friendly with my husband!"

Tone had little to say about his ex-wife other than, "She's like that old joke about Philadelphia. First prize, four years with Joan; second prize, eight."

Douglas Fairbanks, Jr., married Mary Lee Hartford in 1939. They had three children.

7

A HOUSE IS NOT A HOME

Joan changed the toilet seats at 426 North Bristol Avenue again, but she was too preoccupied with getting a good movie role to fret over the divorce. M-G-M had three major films going into production: Robert Sherwood's *Idiot's Delight*, Clare Boothe's *The Women*, and Margaret Mitchell's *Gone With the Wind*, which would be produced by David Selznick, Mayer's son-in-law. Every actress in Tinseltown wanted to play Scarlett O'Hara, including Joan, who made a joke about it: "Suddenly every dame in Hollywood was talking with a Southern accent."

She and Gable were on speaking terms again. The sudden death of twenty-six-year-old Jean Harlow was so tragic that petty differences were put aside or forgotten. Production on *Saratoga* stopped. The stars and crew wept and held each other in silence. Jean had collapsed in Gable's arms on the *Saratoga* set. According to doctors, Jean's kidneys, which had been bruised when Paul Bern beat her with a cane on their wedding night, were not functioning, and as a result poisons from an infected gallbladder entered her bloodstream. Jean's mother, a follower of Christian Science, refused to admit her to a hospital until it was too late. Clark called every day and became suspicious. When Mayer refused to intercede, Gable demanded that Jean be given proper care in a hospital. "The Baby," as she was known on the M-G-M lot, was laid to rest at Forest Lawn Cemetery. Flowers at the funeral, estimated at more than $25,000, were worth more than Jean's estate.

Gable was overcome with grief; he completed *Saratoga* with a double substituting for Jean. Joan stopped by every so often to let him know she wanted to make peace. They became close friends again. When he began grumbling about studio policy, Joan knew he had accepted Jean's death. "Life is strange," she said. "Remember how everyone ogled when you and Lombard double-dated with Harlow and Bill Powell at the Oscar banquet?"

"Yeah."

"I'm no hypocrite, but seeing Jean and Bill so much in love was a treat. Why the hell did they hesitate about getting married until it was too late?"

Clark shook his head.

"Was he still in love with Carole?"

"They're dear friends, and I'm not in the mood to discuss it."

"He'll need someone to console him, God knows. By the way, I hear you've been chosen for Harry the hoofer in *Idiot's Delight*."

"I'm learning the dance routines now."

"Need any help?"

"Carole's been coachin' me."

Joan winked. "Put a good word in for me."

"I don't follow."

"*Idiot's Delight*—the part of Irene."

"Sorry to disappoint you, my dear, but Norma . . ."

"No!!"

"I thought everybody knew."

"I begged L. B. I pleaded."

"There's an explanation . . . I think."

"Let's have it."

"Norma was being considered for Scarlett and . . ."

"Scarlett?!"

"Yeah, but she thinks she's wrong for the part and bowed out so Mayer rewarded her with the part of Irene."

"Who ever heard of a cross-eyed Scarlett?"

"Joanie, I know how you feel about Norma and I'd help if I could, but I've got problems of my own."

"Since when is *Gone With the Wind* a problem?" she snapped.

"Christ, I can't get through the book. It's long as hell. Besides, I'm only playin' Rhett if Carole gets Scarlett."

She smiled. "L. B. *wants* you to believe that. "M-G-M, in exchange for half-interest in the film, will loan Selznick one million dollars and you if *I* play Scarlett."

"When you draw an honest breath, let me know. I've never seen anyone choke to death."

Joan laughed. "I know there are tons of rumors—the Bette Davis and Errol Flynn deal and gossip that Gary Cooper turned down the part of Rhett, but the public wants Gable and Crawford."

"I'll take your word for it. No one else spends as much time in the mail room as you do."

"I deserve one of those roles, damn it! Are you sure about Norma and *Idiot's Delight?*"

He nodded and handed her his handkerchief.

"I never . . . and I mean never, wanted anything so much in my whole life," she sobbed. "Never, never, never."

"I'm sorry, babe."

"Then insist I play Scarlett!"

"Carole wants . . ."

"Fuck her!"

"I'm up to my neck in divorce proceedings, trying to buy a house in the

Valley with money I don't have, dancing in a chorus line with six dames, and tryin' to finish a book about the Civil War. I got Carole on my back, Ria on my back, Mayer on my back, and Selznick on my back. Why don't you ask your fans to picket M-G-M with 'Joan for Scarlett' banners?"

"I need a good picture, Clark. Otherwise, I'm finished. Here's your hankie. Thanks."

"Keep it. Carole might notice the mascara and lipstick."

"Sure, it's something I can use in the bathroom. Thanks for nothing."

He kissed her and she melted. "It's still there," Joan whispered.

He grinned. "Did you think it wasn't?"

"No. I can hope for a lotta things, but not that."

Joan might have gotten the part of Scarlett if it hadn't been for her affair with Gable. M-G-M knew how Lombard felt about Clark's lady friends. During production of *Idiot's Delight* she caught a pretty chorus girl flirting with him and screamed, "Get that whore out of here!" Jealous of Lana Turner and Clark, Carole threatened to have her fired from *Honky Tonk* and was banned from the set.

The search for Scarlett continued and Joan campaigned. Her biggest disappointment was losing *Idiot's Delight*. In candid interviews years later she did not change her mind about this heartbreak and said that Norma Shearer had no chemistry with Gable on the screen. As for Scarlett, she agreed with Clark about British talent invading Hollywood. "He hated Vivien," Joan said, "but treated her with great respect. Director Vic Fleming told her to shove the script right up her royal British ass."

Joan next set her sights on the part of Crystal in *The Women*. Mayer roared louder than Leo the lion. "Are you out of your mind? It's a small part."

"But a juicy one."

"Crystal's the heavy."

"She's a hard-boiled perfume salesgirl who steals another woman's husband against all odds."

"Norma's husband," Mayer argued.

Joan smirked. "Are you afraid to put me in a film with her?"

"I'll leave that up to George Cukor. He's directing the picture."

"Oh, Christ."

"And a few Hail Marys. Gable had him fired from *Gone With the Wind*."

"Clark did not appreciate Cukor calling him 'Dear' on the set."

"George is a genius, but not a happy one right now."

"I'll take my chances, L. B."

"All Scarlett rejects are in *The Women*."

"Who the hell cares? The script and cast are excellent. That makes for a great picture and I want it."

Everyone at M-G-M was surprised, but George Cukor finally relented.

He wasn't sure if Joan was the type, but as she said, "He had faith in himself and what else mattered?"

Plenty. Joan and Norma had not been on the same set since Lucille LeSueur doubled for Miss Shearer more than a decade ago. The running joke was whether an ambulance was waiting at the studio gate when production began. Cukor was a woman's director, but could he handle this time bomb?

Fortunately Joan and Norma had only one scene together—the confrontation of wife and mistress in a gown-fitting room. The rehearsal and final take went well, surprisingly. Cukor pretended to be calm, but the color returned to his face as they prepared for close-ups.

Since Miss Shearer had higher star status than Miss Crawford, Joan sat next to the camera with her knitting and began delivering lines to Norma. Cukor was sorry he didn't insist someone else recite the dialogue because trouble erupted in seconds.

Norma looked at him and said politely, "Mr. Cukor, the knitting needles . . ."

He glared at Joan.

Knit, purl. Knit, purl.

"Mr. Cukor," Norma hissed. "I cannot concentrate."

Knit, purl. Knit, purl.

Miss Shearer trembled. "Mr. Cukor, would you kindly feed Miss Crawford's lines to me?"

He looked at Joan and said quietly, "You're excused for the day." She took her time leaving while Norma's maid powdered her nose from a silver tray of cosmetics and mirrors.

"I will not tolerate such behavior," Cukor said, holding Joan by the shoulders as if prepared to shake some sense into her. "Tomorrow you will apologize to Miss Shearer."

"I will not."

"I'm ashamed of you."

"I'll send her a telegram."

"And you will come in tomorrow with a polite and professional attitude."

Joan sent a telegram. No one knows what it said, but she indicated there were years of frustration and anger in the message. The following day she did not look at Norma as she read her lines, hugged Cukor, and shook hands with the crew before leaving the set of *The Women* for the last time.

But the speechless confrontation was not over between the two reigning queens trying to squeeze onto one throne. According to John Kobal's *People Will Talk* (Knopf, 1986), photographer Laszlo Willinger was assigned to take publicity pictures of Norma, Joan, and Rosalind Russell at ten in the morning. Rosalind finally arrived at eleven and apologized for being late. Willinger knew Joan's dressing room was across the street. He looked outside and saw Norma's limousine pass his door and then Joan's, round and round. Willinger called publicity. Howard Strickling laughed. "Miss Shearer won't go in until Miss

Crawford does and Joan won't go in first." Strickling waved down both cars and delivered the ladies. Norma walked through the door first while Strickling held Joan from trying to squeeze in, too.

Rosalind wore the highest heels and tallest feathers on her head, much to Norma's distress. Joan maintained silence because all she had to do was stand in the middle. Norma claimed Rosalind was overdressed. Rosalind, who didn't give a damn, said, "Maybe so, but I sure as hell am going to wear it!"

He posed the three women on stairs, turned his back for a few seconds, looked through the camera lens and saw only legs. As one moved up, the others followed. Willingers took as many shots as possible, but with the ladies shifting for the number-one position, he got only three prints.

Norma was impatient. Finally she asked Willinger, "Don't you think it's about time you started working with the stars and sent Miss Russell home?"

Joan was in heaven.

Willinger photographed Joan often and thought her face was perfectly proportioned. She was willing to pose all day and change clothes and hairdos gladly. The problem was getting her to the photo sessions. "If her limousine did not show up, neither did Joan," Willinger said. He asked her if there was anything wrong with walking across the street. She replied, "It's in my contract that I have a limousine." Her chauffeur was immaculately uniformed, complete with puttees.

The Women had an all-star cast that included Mary Boland, Paulette Goddard, Phyllis Povah, Joan Fontaine, Lucile Watson, and Marjorie Main; it is a classic. Although Joan loses her stolen husband and new lover at the end of the picture, in character as Crystal she turns to the group of catty women and says, "There's a name for you ladies, but it's not used outside a kennel."

Gable married Carole Lombard during production of *Gone With the Wind*. They settled in a small house in Encino. Vivien Leigh and the movie won Oscars, but Clark did not. He told Joan, "Only you could understand how I feel. I deserved the award for playing Rhett. I did not deserve it for *It Happened One Night*. I'm mad, I'm sick, and I'm depressed."

"The premiere in Atlanta was far superior to the Academy dinner," she said. "Besides, you gave away your Oscar to a little boy. Did you want the kid to have another?"

"I never worked harder in my life," he grumbled.

"Buck up! You left every goddamn night at six while Vivien was still in her hoop skirt and corset. You refused to speak with a Southern accent. You refused to cry when Scarlett had a miscarriage. You insisted on a whole new wardrobe and that ain't cheap, baby. You got George Cukor fired. This all takes balls."

"If I've got 'em, you shake 'em!" Gable said. "I hear you use elephant tusks for knitting needles, and it took you over two hours by limo to get across the street for a ten-minute photo session."

She smiled. "Well, we won't have to worry about those petty annoyances in *Strange Cargo*. We'll be wearing dirty, tattered clothes, and I don't have to worry about makeup."

He grinned. "How will I know you?"

"Don't worry about me. Just be sure to bring your teeth."

"If they're not in my mouth, you'll find them in my back pocket biting my ass."

"Don't be bitter about the Oscar, my love. It's an honor just to be nominated."

"Would you buy that?" he asked.

"No, damn it. That proves we're still suckers—two hicks who can't take it, and what frightens me is maybe we never will."

Strange Cargo was one of their best joint ventures. As the dirty escaped prisoner, Gable sported a shaggy beard and tangled hair; Joan, playing his runaway girlfriend, had pale lips and eyebrows. Both characters stood in harsh contrast to their previous roles as Rhett and Crystal.

Film Daily wrote that *Strange Cargo* was a good, raw, stark melodrama that held suspense from the start: "Clark Gable fits his role admirably, but the acting is high grade with Joan Crawford giving her best performance to date." *Variety* said, "Miss Crawford is provided with a particularly meaty role as the hardened dance-hall gal who falls hard for the tough convict. This role is a departure from those handed her during the past several years by her studio and reminiscent of her earlier work that carried her to popularity originally. The Crawford characterization will give studio executives ideas of proper casting of her talents for the future."

Joan was elated. "For *The Women* I had a forty-thousand-dollar wardrobe. For *Strange Cargo* I had three dresses worth less than forty dollars altogether. The last one was soaked in sea water, dragged through the mud, and deliberately ripped every morning before filming."

Her luck was changing, but her values were, too. She recalled what F. Scott Fitzgerald had noted about her a few years earlier when he was assigned to write a script for her: "Why do her lips have to be glistening wet? Don't like her smiling to herself or such hammy gestures that most actresses get away with . . . Cynical accepting smile has gotten a little tired. Bad acting to following the stage direction 'as an afterthought.' She cannot fake her bluff or pretend to. Her smile is brighter in outdoor situation than in drawing rooms. Hearty laughter rather good. A sad smile not bad, but the serious expression best. Absolutely necessary that she feel her lines. Must be serious from first. So much better when she is serious. Must have direct, consuming purpose in mind at all points of the story—never anything vague or blurred. Must be driven."

Had Fitzgerald seen beyond the flapper when he jotted down these notes? She was in transition at the time but understood what the writer had done when he viewed her early films. Despite her degrading M-G-M contract, Haines thought Joan was progressing nicely on a new course.

"We are going from the Depression into a war," he said. "The shopgirl is now a young woman who wants desperately to hang on to what she's got. Maybe she's fighting to keep her job or her husband or her place in society, but she'll never go backward. That's Joan Crawford, vintage 1940."

"I'm changing a lotta things about myself, Billy. I'm not proud anymore. I wanted *Susan and God* with Fredric March even though M-G-M bought the script for beady-eyed Norma. They never bought a fuckin' story for me! Anyway, the widow Thalberg turned *Susan* down. Believe it?"

"Because she didn't want to play the mother of a fourteen-year-old girl?"

Joan laughed and kissed him. "You bet! So I went for it, and Mayer was shocked. I told him I'd play Wallace Beery's mother if it were a good part."

"What did he say?"

"Mayer wanted to know if I could face George Cukor after my display of nerves in *The Women*."

"Display of nerves?" Billy laughed. "Those knitting needles sounded like an amplified Morse code."

"George wants to work with me. We're both perfectionists. Maybe we fight, but we both get what we want. We talk the same language."

Joan considered Haines her confidant. There were few secrets they didn't share. She gave parties for Billy's gay crowd and relied on his homosexual friends to escort her to dinner. Joan thought nothing about undressing in front of Haines and his "wife," Jimmy. She was unquestionably loyal to them and proved it by always discussing Billy in glowing terms. Joan helped Haines "beat the system" when his homosexuality became front-page news. Not only did she befriend him, she backed him in business—it was her way of getting even with Mayer, who did not try to protect Billy's career.

She would always be indebted to George Cukor, who was a discreet gay, and refused to discuss the turmoil over his being fired from *Gone With the Wind*. If Gable had been "serviced" by Haines in return for a bit part in films, that was their business. George and Billy were good friends, but they did not mingle openly in the same crowd.

The subject was brought up a few years before Joan's death, and she was amused. The Gable-Haines incident was "skirted." She nodded and had a good laugh. "I can't blame Clark for having a fit when George called him 'Dear' on the set," Joan said. "It was fairly obvious what that meant. If Clark had been in a better frame of mind, he might have laughed it off, but he wasn't going to take direction from a man who looked right through him with knowledge of an indiscretion that would have destroyed his reputation with Hollywood insiders. Clark thought I knew the truth and it's possible Lombard did, too, because she was very friendly with Billy.

"Carole was very good for Clark, who wasn't a happy man. She was funny and raw and loved to put him down. She made him laugh. He was more fortunate that I was because my husbands, for the most part, were not amusing. Billy was the only one who could dry my tears and put a smile on my face. He was the first to tell me when I was wrong, but he knew how to get away with it. If we disagreed over decorating, he won. Billy had a delightful crowd of friends."

Joan had seen Gertrude Lawrence on Broadway in *Susan and God*, the story of a woman who sacrifices her husband and daughter when she becomes a religious fanatic. Joan overdramatized her concept of Susan and tearfully admitted the dilemma to Cukor. "You're taking the part too seriously," he explained. "Susan is zany. She's a nut. She means well, but she has no idea what honest religious belief means." Joan had difficulty blending the real and imaginary, but with Cukor's help, she conquered the role. Critics once again criticized M-G-M for overlooking Joan's dramatic talent. *Variety* said, "There's still a tinge of the glamour girl in Miss Crawford but the role provides the studio with the key to future assignments for its star, which might bring her back considerably as a box-office personality."

Armed with renewed strength and enthusiasm, Joan told Mayer she wanted to do *A Woman's Face*. "I had seen Ingrid Bergman in the Swedish version," Joan recalled. "It was the story of a scarred woman who hates the world. L. B. said I was crazy. How could I appear with one side of my face disfigured? Playing Anna Holm might destroy my career. Maybe that's why L. B. didn't argue with me, but he emphasized that the public might not pay to see a beautiful actress with a hideous scar on her face. I sensed he was more concerned about the box-office profits than my career. I spoke to George Cukor, who went ahead with the screenplay and cast of players."

"Mayer wants no publicity pictures of the disfigurement," Cukor told Joan. "He's afraid it might discourage people from seeing the movie."

"I agree," Joan said, "but not for the same reason. I want them to be shocked and disgusted, and by that time I guarantee no one will leave the theater."

Cukor warned her about "prop-reliance." "Anytime an actor has a cane or a wheelchair or a scar or a limp, he automatically considers it part of his character and doesn't project as much into the role. He fails to realize that his personality and outlook are warped. He does not have the enthusiasm or optimism. He doesn't have drive. He hates the world."

"I'm too emotional, is that it?" she asked.

"That's what concerns me," Cukor admitted. "As Anna Holm, you're exhausted, sick of life, tired of it all. She's a woman who speaks in a monotone voice laced with hopelessness and hate."

"I can do it."

"When the film's done, you'll feel that scar on the right side of your face for a long time, Joan. Remember that you are the scar, not the other way around."

Joan said Cukor drilled her for hours. "He rehearsed the very life out of me. He made me recite the multiplication table by twos until all emotion was drained and I was totally exhausted."

Critics applauded her with words of praise. "I say a prayer for Mr. Cukor every time I think of what *A Woman's Face* did for my career. It fortified me with a measure of self-confidence I'd never had—the *succès d'estime* I'd longed for—what critics called 'the best picture to emerge from Hollywood in a long, long time' and what others called 'the best picture of the year.' "

Regardless of the acclaim, Mayer did not seek another good picture for Joan. She asked for *Random Harvest* and *Madame Curie*. Greer Garson, Mayer's favorite in the early forties, starred in both. He had seen her perform on the London stage, persuaded her to return to Hollywood with him, properly chaperoned by her mother, and made her a number-one star. "He felt this way about Jeanette MacDonald, too," Joan said. "She was Mayer's pet. He was attracted to ladies, not in a physical sense, however. L. B. put them on a pedestal with his mother. God forbid if anybody said anything about one's mother or wife! They were God's chosen people. He cleaned up every script, too, and would shed tears watching a scene about a poor mother in a shabby kitchen cooking stew on an old stove while her rich children dropped by for a brief visit.

"Jeanette MacDonald was on her way out when she refused to co-star with Nelson Eddy. Guess she wanted her own identity. Clark almost quit when he was signed to do *San Francisco* with her. She was not his type at all! He and Tracy went on a few binges makin' that one. Meanwhile, Greer Garson got the royal treatment and the rest of us, including Garbo, were finished. They didn't chop our heads off . . . just a little bit at a time."

Joan's competition bowed out gracefully. Norma Shearer realized too late that it had been a mistake to turn down *Mrs. Miniver* and *Gone With the Wind.* Instead, she chose to do three flops and retired in 1942, shortly after remarrying.

M-G-M, in an attempt to change Greta Garbo's aloofness, put her in *Two-Faced Woman* with Melvyn Douglas. Audiences were disenchanted. Garbo decided to resume her movie career in Europe after the war, but she felt she was too old.

Joan was trying to hang on. "I didn't have a husband like Shearer or a lot of well-invested money like Garbo," she said. "I needed and wanted to work."

M-G-M gave birth to Lana Turner, Judy Garland, Elizabeth Taylor, Laraine Day, Ava Gardner, Kathryn Grayson, Deborah Kerr, Hedy Lamarr, Ann Sothern, and Esther Williams. Meanwhile, Joan Crawford read dozens of trashy scripts suited to an old-timer and tried to salvage a project to keep her going.

When Ladies Meet was a good story, but the film was badly done. The combination of Joan, Greer Garson, and Robert Taylor flashing on the marquees in 1941 attracted moviegoers. Oddly, it was miscast. Joan, in love with a married man (Herbert Marshall), spends a weekend with his wife (Garson) not knowing her true identity. Finding out her lover is a philanderer, Joan returns to Taylor. With all due respect to Marshall, the male roles should have been reversed because Taylor came across as the playboy. The plot fell flat.

Joan made only two films in 1941—*A Woman's Face* and *When Ladies Meet*. "You're only as good as your last picture," she said.

Following a successful war-bond drive, Carole Lombard boarded a plane for Los Angeles on January 16, 1942. After a brief stop in Las Vegas, the plane took off and hit Table Rock Mountain. All passengers were killed instantly.

"Clark came to me that night," Joan recalled. "He was drunk and he cried. There was nothing I could say. Nothing meant anything to him anymore. Clark Gable walked through my door and never returned, except in body, maybe. He was never the same again. Clark was a walking corpse. He had every right to drink that night, and he never stopped. He was in another world and never came back to us whole."

Joan volunteered to take Carole's assigned role in *They All Kissed the Bride* for Columbia Pictures. She donated her salary of $125,000 to the Red Cross. The film, with Melvyn Douglas, had a nice flair (shrewish businesswoman finds love) and was a pleasant surprise for Joan, who, insiders guessed, got a vicarious thrill stepping into Lombard's shoes regardless of the tragic circumstances.

Socially, Joan dated Glenn Ford, Jean-Pierre Aumont, and Cesar Romero. Clark came to the Bristol Avenue house for dinner several nights a week. "He could drink a quart of booze before dinner," she recalled. "I tried to tell him to cut down, and he knew it was all wrong. Then he'd cry. There were times he stayed until dawn, but I often tried to distract him from the bedroom. It was automatic for him to make a sexual advance but talking was better therapy, and I was willing to listen. He didn't want to be alone."

Although Gable reminisced about Carole incessantly, he and Joan discussed their frustrations at the studio. Mayer had been very kind to Clark during the dark days following the tragedy, but Gable made up his mind to join the Air Force and said he had no intention of coming back. Joan asked if he was frightened. "Yes," he replied, "that I won't get through basic training." Joan knew he was escaping from M-G-M and the empty ranch in the Valley.

There were many farewell parties at the studios for the men who had enlisted—Robert Montgomery, Jimmy Stewart, and Robert Taylor. Douglas Fairbanks, Jr., came by to see Joan before going into the Navy. She stood in the doorway of her dressing room looking for a familiar face. An invasion of new and younger actresses pranced around. Joan could not get excited over the crop of leading men, either—Van Johnson, John Carroll, John Hodiak, Peter Lawford, Frank Sinatra, and Mickey Rooney.

Approaching her fortieth birthday, Joan couldn't help feeling old. She chatted with Mayer about a good role. He said the world was at war and the public wanted musicals. "It's our job to build up the morale of moviegoers," he said. "Battle films promote the sale of war bonds. Your grudge against the studio is untimely, Joan."

"Your red-headed English goddess is getting all the plum roles."

"I assume you're referring to Greer Garson, who won an Oscar for her splendid performance in *Mrs. Miniver*."

"I can't win. You offered the part to Norma Shearer, and she turned it down. Don't I have any seniority around here?"

Mayer sighed. "Must we always go round and round, Joan? I have a fine script for you. Did you think I'd let you down?"

"What is it, L. B.?" she asked, leaning forward in her chair.

"*Reunion in France*," he replied, handing her a box of Kleenex.

"I'd rather die!"

"With John Wayne."

She wailed. "I'll kill myself."

Mayer winked. "Handsome, virile guy."

"Yeah, on a horse," she sniffled.

"Joan, M-G-M's leading men are on the battlefields fighting for our country, and you have the audacity to complain?"

"Jesus Christ, I'm as patriotic as the next person, but give me someone else. Wayne will probably wear his spurs."

"I'm sorry you feel that way."

"Meaning that's it."

He laughed. "Unless you'd like to audition for an Andy Hardy movie."

Joan didn't storm out of Mayer's office. She sensed this was the end. Her contract was up for renewal, which, in a way, meant her pride was up for renewal, too.

Maybe Joan resented appearing on the screen with John Wayne, but that did not stop her from trying to seduce him. She called him often. He wasn't interested then or later. "Hell, she's been trying for years," Wayne said casually in his dressing room one day. "I don't take her calls, that's all."

She tried to brighten up her social life with Haines and his friends. Other acquaintances introduced her to eligible bachelors, one of whom was actor Phillip Terry. She refused to give him her telephone number, but he got it anyway and called her for a date. Knowing he wouldn't take no for an answer, she had dinner with him.

Three years younger than Joan, Terry had been brought up in the oil fields of Texas and Oklahoma before enrolling at Stanford University. He had studied acting in England and was trying to establish himself in Hollywood complete with a British accent. They laughed about his bit part in *Mannequin*, but at that time Joan only had eyes for Spencer, a subject that was not brought up in her conversation with Terry. Though he'd been in Hollywood for only five years and was just holding his own at Paramount, he understood the ups and downs, the pitfalls and terror of being a popular star facing decline.

Joan poured out her heart to Phillip about *Reunion in France.* "He thought I should keep going," she recalled. "Had I forgotten how important it was to keep my face on the screen? He reminded me that my fans were busy with the war effort and not as concerned about my makeup or hairstyles. They wanted to see Joan Crawford in anything. I reacted to Phillip. He made me feel alive and willing to take on a dull assignment."

It's possible Joan mistook peace of mind for love, but the previous few years had been distressing for her. Desperate for company, she had tried to spend time with her mother, who did little more than plead for Hal, who had become an alcoholic and drug addict. Joan said the studio helped her to keep his escapades out of the newspapers, but eventually she had him committed to a sanitarium for a few years. Mother and daughter were further apart than ever, but Anna was at Joan's mercy and was not permitted to visit the Bristol Avenue house, although she was seen delivering homemade pies and relishes at the back door. Joan was ashamed of the way Anna dressed. "She still wore old scuff slippers as if I hadn't bought her decent shoes. Her housedresses were drab, too. She lived a comfortable life, grew her own vegetables, and enjoyed gardening."

Anna was no consolation to Joan, who was dating Charles McCabe, a married man from New York—a romantic but hopeless interlude. He introduced her to the world of business and public affairs. "We went hunting, fishing, and camping together," she said. "I even carried my own gun and waded through streams in the vanguard." These carefree days were filled with love and laughter, but returning to Hollywood put Joan in frequent black moods and depressions. While she craved a man who belonged to someone else, and "the King of Hollywood," who grieved for someone else, she spent lonely nights reading or writing poetry (from A *Portrait of Joan,* Doubleday, 1962).

Where are you?
My heart cries out in agony,
In my extended hands
I give my heart with
All its cries—its songs—its love,
But it's too late.
You are not here to see its sorrow
Or hear its throbbing of your name
Perhaps it's better that way
You who love laughter
Did you ever know I love laughter too?
Oh my beloved
Where are you?

Unlike Doug and Franchot, Phillip Terry was uncomplicated, reserved, and comfortable. Joan was truthful about her feelings. She loved Terry but was not "in love" with him. As for his prospects as an actor, he had had little more than supporting roles. But, as Mayer said, the world was changing and the thoughts, wishes, and ambitions of the people would consequently change, too. Joan didn't care whether Phillip was ambitious. She craved love, companionship, and a warm body lying next to her at night. Her life empty and uncertain, Joan prepared herself for the worst at M-G-M, and she could not bear going through it alone.

Six weeks after Joan met Phillip Terry, they applied for a marriage license in Ventura, California, under their legal names, Lucille Tone and Frederick Kormann. On July 21, 1942, they became man and wife at the home of her attorney, Neil McCarthy, in Hidden Hills, California. They waited until one minute after midnight to qualify for the three-day waiting period, and at nine that same morning the bride reported on the set of *Reunion in France*.

John Wayne wasn't thrilled about the film either, and when he saw his co-star make her entrance, he wisecracked, "I knew what kind of a marriage it was going to be right away. First came Joan, then her secretary, then her makeup man, then her wardrobe woman, and finally Phil Terry, carrying the dog."

No one at M-G-M knew who Phillip Terry was. A few remembered his face, but reporters were dumbfounded. They quickly dug up any information they could on the third Mr. Crawford. He was six feet one and weighed 170 pounds. He had played on Stanford's football team, had attended the Royal Academy of Dramatic Arts, and had appeared in four movies.

While writers typed frantically to make the evening editions, the cast and crew gave the newlyweds a party on the set. Stories abound from Joan's friends about her third marriage and how impulsive she was and how foolish it was for her to pick up "excess baggage" when the road ahead would be a long and bumpy one. Terry could not possibly afford Joan. Nor could he compete with her ambition, her drive, and her demands.

Haines wondered if Phillip would be a better secretary.

"What on earth do you mean?" Joan snapped.

"I called you once, and Franchot said you were scrubbing toilets and couldn't come to the phone. He said the same thing to Louella."

When Roy Newquist asked her about *Reunion in France*, Joan moaned, "Oh, God. If there is an afterlife, and I am to be punished for my sins, this is one of the pictures they'll make me see over and over again. Get John Wayne out of the saddle and you've got trouble."

Joan played a spoiled and rich Parisian career woman in love with a Nazi informer (Philip Dorn). While France falls to the Germans, she becomes involved with an American flyer (John Wayne) who is hunted by the Gestapo. In the end, Joan finds out Dorn is a double agent and they are reunited. Critics said the plot was bad beyond description.

Above Suspicion with Fred MacMurray was Joan's last movie for M-G-M under the contract system. She admitted wartime melodramas were not for her, but there was nothing better in the offering. Joan and Fred were good friends. "He had one of the few happy and well-adjusted marriages in Hollywood," she said. "His wife did not approve of swearing, but their parties were divine. I remember Carole Lombard was so frustrated one night she jumped into the swimming pool wearing an expensive white chiffon dress. For the rest of the evening she wore Fred's pajamas, but she didn't utter a blue word."

In *Above Suspicion*, Joan and Fred were newlyweds in England prior to the outbreak of World War II. They became involved in a Secret Service plot. The *New York Herald Tribune* said, "There are so many spies in *Above Suspicion*, it is hard to keep track of them. Unfortunately, neither Joan Crawford nor Fred MacMurray looks quite bright enough to unravel the tangled skeins."

Again and again Joan asked Mayer for *Madame Curie* or *Random Harvest*, but Greer Garson was the chosen one. If Crawford had accepted the younger generation taking over Hollywood, seeing them in action made it more painful for her. Betty Grable was "the Pin-Up Girl," Lana Turner was "the Sweater Girl," Ann Sheridan was "the Oomph Girl," Dorothy Lamour was "the Sarong Girl," and Marie McDonald was "the Body." Myrna Loy was very successful in the *Thin Man* series. Barbara Stanwyck had held up very well and was the highest-paid actress during the war. Joan admired Barbara, who as an independent refused to be bound by contracts. "I'd been with M-G-M for almost eighteen years," Joan said. "It was like a one-sided marriage. What the hell did I get out of it in the end?"

Mayer did not fight Joan when she asked to be released from her contract. "You've been here almost as long as I have," he said. "What are your plans?"

"I'm going to concentrate on my marriage for a change."

"I wish you all the best, Joan, and I want you to think of me always as your father—the one man you can talk to and lean on, the one man who . . ."

". . . let me down," she exclaimed, extending her gloved right hand. He smiled and shook it with both of his. She turned and walked regally to the door and left it wide open.

Joan had begun adoption proceedings when she knew her marriage to Franchot was crumbling. After the divorce, she had petitioned the thirteen states that permitted single-parent adoptions. A blond, blue-eyed baby girl born on June 11, 1939, came home to 426 Bristol Avenue ten days later. The real mother was a student and the father was a sailor. The chubby little girl was named Joan Crawford, Jr., but the final adoption papers listed her name as Christina Crawford.

A year later, Joan adopted a boy and her family was complete until the baby's mother claimed him. Legal battles loomed. Joan was shattered; she gave the boy back only to find out that his mother had sold him at a higher price to someone else.

Christina became Joan's world. "I don't remember so much happiness coming into my life in one small bundle," she told the press.

Shortly after her marriage to Terry, they adopted another Scandinavian blue-eyed blond infant boy, who they named Phillip Terry, Jr.

Joan's interviews were filled with a new and more vital motivation—her home and family. "It was a miracle," she said. "What a shame that career women are envied when it is the housewife and mother who lives a full life. Glamour cannot replace a loving husband and the laughter of children," she beamed.

No one doubted her joy, but Joan Crawford was still a renowned actress. Whether M-G-M squeezed her out or she volunteered to leave wasn't news. Who would take a chance on Box Office Poison? A washed-up flapper? Jack Warner did, only two days after Joan drove out of the gates of M-G-M. She was signed for two pictures a year at one-third the salary she had received at M-G-M. Why?

"I want good scripts, and I don't want to be typecast," she told Warner. He agreed and put her on salary. Unfortunately, he had nothing for her yet. Billy Haines told Joan, "This is Jack Warner's way of keeping Bette Davis in line."

"He doesn't need me for that."

"You're both suited to the same roles, Cranberry."

"She's one of the best. I know the press will build up a big feud—Crawford and Davis at the same studio crap—but I'm prepared for that."

Bette Davis gave little thought to M-G-M's Grande Dame moving into a newly decorated dressing room on Warner's lot. She had serious problems and was struggling for survival. Bette's second husband had died suddenly from a head wound. Reliable sources said he was killed accidentally by a friend who caught him in bed with his wife. She had put aside the ugly gossip when her demented sister suddenly rebelled and had to be put into a mental institution. Davis was deeply troubled and in debt. Joan told friends she sympathized, "but after all, her first husband caught her in bed with Howard Hughes. According to her, Hughes had a problem 'getting it up' and she offered to help. God knows how many times I turned him down."

Bette Davis made no effort to welcome Joan to Warner Brothers. She felt that if she made an occasion of it, the press would turn the meeting into a circus—every glance and gesture would be analyzed and the outcome twisted into an exaggeration of mutual jealousy.

While Joan waited for a script, she fawned over Phillip, who signed a contract with RKO. Louella Parsons wrote in her column, "Terry is going to amount to something soon. The studio thinks he's a combination of Clark Gable and Cary Grant." Joan accompanied him almost every day and remained in his dressing room until it was time to go home. Depending on her moods, she might stay home with the children or lounge around the pool. When the war was at its peak, she closed down some of her twenty-seven rooms. The nurses, chef, and other household help were needed in the defense factories. Phillip's option at RKO was dropped. He got a job at one of the aircraft factories. For more than two years Joan stayed home, cleaned, cooked, cared for her children, sent her husband off each morning with his lunch pail, and planted a victory garden.

Once a week she worked at the Hollywood Canteen, serving sandwiches at the snack bar and writing postcards to families of GIs, signed "Joan Crawford." She volunteered for the Red Cross and joined the American Women's Voluntary Services, helping to organize a day school for children whose mothers worked in war plants. "Can you imagine a woman leaving her kids in a car all day?" Joan exclaimed. "It was inhumane!"

Bette Davis, meanwhile, starred in *Old Acquaintance* and *Mr. Skeffington*—two excellent films that Joan had wanted very much to do. She soon realized Warner was sending her Davis rejects. "It's hard to believe that I'm getting worse scripts to read here than I got at Metro," she complained.

"Finally, I was asked to make a guest appearance in the movie *Hollywood Canteen*. Everyone was in it, including Roy Rogers' horse, Trigger. I danced with Sergeant Dane Clark. Swell. It seemed to me that players were more in awe of their own graciousness and hospitality instead of being concerned with entertaining the troops. Most upsetting was that I hadn't been in a film for over two years."

Following this brief appearance in *Hollywood Canteen,* Joan's life at home became routine—seeing Phillip off to the war plant early in the morning, caring for the children, cleaning, scrubbing, cooking, and gardening. In the evening she was waiting at the door for her husband. Phillip was an expert bartender and took great pride in his mixed drinks. Until now Joan had never had more than two or three glasses of champagne, but Terry's cocktail hour became a pleasant and mellow pastime at the end of a boring day.

At the age of forty, Joan began drinking hard liquor, and only she knows when she started abusing it. The dark cloud casting a shadow over her life had been forming for a while, and she thought she was prepared for it. But Billie Cassin and Lucille LeSueur had been waiting for a long time to surface if ever Mother Crawford failed to cope.

Joan's alcoholism was blamed for her neuroses, and not long after she became accustomed to an innocent cocktail or two before dinner, her relapse into the confused, rebellious, uncouth, and envious Billie was beginning. The change occurred slowly and, at first, within the confines of her home; to outsiders a more determined, level-headed, and brave woman seemed to emerge.

Jack Warner, who expected Joan to be interested in one of the several hundred scripts he sent for her perusal, avoided a personal confrontation. Instead, he sent a letter intimating her lack of cooperation considering the huge salary she was earning. Joan called him for a showdown but was told he wasn't available. Joan told Warner's secretary, "Don't bother sending me another check until I can find a decent picture!"

Tired of fighting her own battles, she approached the biggest booking agency in the country, Music Corporation of America, and spoke with its mogul, Lew Wasserman. "I'm not being difficult," she told him. "After so many years at Metro I know a good script from a bad one, and Mr. Warner hasn't given me one that can be salvaged. If I'm all through, say so."

"We'll find something."

"If it isn't Garson, it's Davis. They get the plums. I get shit."

"Warner has a point and you do, too. He wants you on the screen, and I know how much you want another fine film. I know it will turn out very well for all concerned."

When Warner Brothers bought the rights to *Mildred Pierce*, the censors turned down several script revisions. The amount of time, money, and effort put into the screenplay was for the benefit of Bette Davis, who ultimately turned it down. It's unlikely that Joan knew about this. Lew Wasserman approached her and waited for the explosion. There was none. "Jerry Wald would like to produce *Mildred*," he said. "And Ranald MacDougall will write the finished script. Wald's a guy who started at the bottom and worked his way to the top. He's also seen all of your films."

Joan liked Wasserman's approach, but she wanted to read the script first. "Forgive me," she said nervously, "but I don't trust anyone anymore. You understand."

He smiled. "I don't think you'll be disappointed this time."

Joan read every word of dialogue and without hesitation called Jerry Wald during the night. "I'll do it! I love it!" she cheered over the telephone. He listened while Joan discussed other details. "Ideas are popping in my head like firecrackers," she said. "I hope you don't mind."

They talked about *Mildred Pierce* for more than an hour and in the middle of the conversation, Joan laughed. "I forgot to ask who's going to direct."

"Mr. Warner insists on Michael Curtiz," Wald said.

"He's excellent—*Casablanca* and *Yankee Doodle Dandy*."

"And many more." Wald hesitated.

"What's the matter, Jerry? Is something wrong?"

"Of course not. I'll call you tomorrow."

"Me direct that temperamental bitch!" Michael Curtiz bellowed at Wald. "Not on your goddamn life! She comes over here with her high-hat airs and her goddamn shoulder pads! I won't work with her! She's through. Washed up! Why should I waste my time directing a has-been?"

Wald explained to Joan that Curtiz was a temperamental Hungarian. "He's reluctant to direct you" was the explanation.

"No problem," she spoke up. "I'll make a test for him."

Wald was stunned. "You're a star."

She frowned. "I thought so, too. But make arrangements for the test and make sure Mr. Curtiz is there to direct it!"

The test went very well. Joan had all the confidence she needed without flaunting it. She wanted *Mildred Pierce* and she wanted Curtiz. She got both and was so relieved that she offered to appear in screen tests with other members of the cast. "I wanted to show everyone at Warner Brothers that I was cooperative," Joan recalled. "And I needed to look around, get acquainted with the technicians, and see how different they were from the crew at M-G-M." Joan took sixteen-year-old Ann Blyth under her wing. Curtiz thought Ann was a goody-goody and would not be right for Mildred's bitchy daughter, but Joan's coaching helped Ann get into the role of Veda. Bruce Bennett was cast as Mildred's weak husband, and Zachary Scott played the penniless aristocrat who romances mother and daughter. Eve Arden played Mildred's loyal wisecracking friend, and Jack Carson was cast as the overly ambitious cad.

Crawford found out during production that if Curtiz couldn't get Bette Davis for *Mildred Pierce,* he wanted Barbara Stanwyck. Jerry Wald had fought for Joan and won. Curtiz, however, was not convinced. The first day on the set was horrendous. He glanced at her and yelled, "What is this lipstick mess? And the fancy hairdo?" Joan left the set without a word and returned wearing one of the dresses chosen by the wardrobe designer. Curtiz raged, "You and your goddamn Adrian shoulder pads. I warned you!" Joan turned around calmly, changed the dress, and returned to the irate director, who again cursed bitterly about the shoulder pads. Joan looked up at Curtiz, who was sitting on a camera boom. "I bought this dress this morning for $2.98 at Sears, and there are no shoulder pads."

"I don't believe you!" he shouted.

Joan ran to her dressing room in tears. One of the crew convinced her that Curtiz was difficult under the best of circumstances and to ignore his nastiness. "He called Miss Davis a bum."

Joan blew her nose and forced a smile. "Did he really?"

"She was supposed to struggle with Eddie Robinson and Curtiz yelled, 'That's not the way to fight him, you goddamn bum!' "

"What did she do?"

"She screamed back, 'You show me what you want me to do and I'll do it!' Miss Davis and Mr. Curtiz became good friends. He does a very funny imitation of her, the hips rolling and the nostrils filtering cigarette smoke. She laughs the loudest when he does it."

Joan knew she had to prove herself not only to Curtiz but also to everyone at Warner Brothers. There was a rivalry between the studios, and M-G-M was noted for pampering its contract players. If anyone fit into that category, it was Joan Crawford, but she did not display a haughty attitude, complain, or ask for special favors. She spoke to everyone—producers, stars, technicians, security guards, the cleaning lady, and the extras. She remembered names and birthdays and showed an interest in everyone at Warner Brothers.

Two years off the screen had changed Joan's aura. As Mildred Pierce she was in command. She connected. Without a glamorous wardrobe and hairdo, Joan was flawless. She was believable and all-consuming.

Jerry Wald knew she was the best, but he was in awe watching her during production of *Mildred Pierce*. He began to campaign for Joan to win an Oscar. Louella Parsons thought it was a joke, but she hinted in her column that Joan's performance as Mildred was Oscar material. One bit of gossip led to another, and by the time the picture was finished, Hollywood was almost convinced.

Director Michael Curtiz said he'd expected Joan to be difficult, but he would be the boss. "She took it," he said, "and she is one swell actress. I love her."

Mildred Pierce was Joan Crawford. The dialogue intertwined their determination to be loved and admired:

VEDA: Why do you think I want money so badly?

MILDRED: Why?

VEDA: With this money I can get away from you—from you and your chickens and your pies and your kitchens and everything else that smells of grease. I can get away from this shack with its cheap furniture. You think just because you made a little you can get a new hairdo and some expensive clothes and turn yourself into a lady. But you can't. You'll never be anything but a common frump whose father lived over a grocery store and whose mother took in washing!

Mildred's second husband, played by Zachary Scott, sells her his mortgaged mansion and spends his days at the racetrack. She confronts him: "You look down on me because I work for a living. You always have. I cook food and sell it for money, which, I might add, you're not too proud to share with me."

He looks her in the eye and says, "Yes, I take money from you, Mildred, but not enough to make me like kitchens or cooks. They smell of grease."

Joan summed up her attraction to the role: "*Mildred Pierce* was a blending of many roles I had played and of my own personal experiences, which can be eerie . . ."

Joan and Phillip attended the premiere of *Mildred Pierce* in October 1945 in New York. Hundreds of her fans and admirers were waiting. She heard their cheers several blocks away. She waved as her heart pounded. The police lined the streets as the star of *Mildred Pierce* emerged from the limousine. She clung to Phillip, and, for a few seconds, bathed in the glowing admiration of so many people. As she approached the theater, Joan felt nauseous. In a panic, she turned white and told Phillip, "I'm going to puke!" Quickly she ran into the theater and down to the ladies' room while half of New York followed. Leaning over the toilet, an eager fan asked Joan for an autograph while a few dozen others gathered around to watch Mildred Pierce regurgitate.

Crawford returned triumphantly to Hollywood. Beside her was an innocent bystander—her husband. When Joan resumed her career, she assigned the running of the household to Phillip. Although her servants had a daily schedule, it was up to him to make sure her orders were carried out. Before Joan left for the studio, she wrote memos to the nurses. The schedules were jotted in fifteen-minute intervals—wake-up time, potty time, lunchtime, and so on. Potty time indicated exactly how the children were to "perform."

Terry claimed Joan's schedule extended to their personal life. "I had to check my allotted hour for sex," he said. Another one of his duties was to punish the children when they misbehaved. Phillip was strict but tender. What sickened him was Joan's tying up and locking up the children. He'd try to prevent it or would let them go. Terry adored Christina and Phillip Jr. and they were extremely fond of him. When the marriage was nearly over, he became a disciplinarian in an attempt to save the situation. The children knew it was just a matter of time before their mother would ask him to leave. Joan's friends felt the same way. Louella Parsons was given the exclusive divorce announcement, but she already had the copy prepared. One day after Phillip Terry left the Bristol Avenue house there was not a trace of him left anywhere inside. All three of Joan's marriages had lasted four years.

On April 25, 1946, Joan testified in Los Angeles Supreme Court. "For the first year and a half of our marriage I was never allowed to entertain or to go out of the house at night. Consequently, I lost many valuable contacts in the motion picture field. He would tell me I was wrong about a script many times when I felt I was right. I turned down script after script because of his criticisms."

Reporters were waiting when she left the courtroom. She volunteered, "I'll never go through that again."

"Does that mean you'll never listen to 'The Wedding March' again, Miss Crawford?"

She smirked. "Maybe that's the trouble. I never had any music at my weddings."

To close friends she said, "I owe Phillip an apology for marrying him."

PART THREE

8

OSCAR, AND OTHER
STRANGE BEDFELLOWS

Joan Crawford was nominated for an Oscar for her performance in *Mildred Pierce*. She was the delight of the fan magazines again. Newspaper columnists clamored for interviews. Scripts were delivered to her every day, and her door was open. No one gave Phillip Terry much thought. It was as if he'd never been Mr. Joan Crawford. Christina and Phillip Jr. (his name was changed immediately to Christopher after the divorce) were terrified without Terry's protectiveness. The press was invited to the children's birthday parties, lavish affairs complete with merry-go-rounds, clowns, trained animals, magicians, and a circus arena. The little guests wore party dresses and suits and ties appropriate for an evening at Pickfair.

The Joan Crawford Club News was mailed to her fans monthly with a personal letter from their idol and information about her. "Yes, she still loves chewing gum, but has the habit under control. Her favorite perfume is Jungle Gardenia and her favorite color is green. She can't resist bags and shoes (size four) and she adores salads."

Joan coughed. "I'm not going tonight."

"You must!" Jerry Wald pleaded. "Do it for everyone who worked so hard in *Mildred Pierce*."

"That's the point," she wept. "I know I'm going to lose."

"Isn't that silly? You're the girl who showed this town how to fight back. I have a gut feeling you're going to win."

"And what if I do? That means getting up in front of all those people and giving a speech. You know I'll make a fool of myself."

Joan was so terrified she called her doctor, who claimed she had a temperature of 104 degrees. The word got around that Joan could not appear at the Academy Awards because she had a mild case of pneumonia.

Another version was that she had had a dispute with the Academy in the thirties. Their policy was to rotate the awards so that no studio won two years in succession. She lost the fight, walked out, and swore if she were ever nominated she would not be there to accept the award.

The real reason Joan did not attend the Academy Awards ceremonies was sheer fright—such terror, in fact, that she was forced to stay in bed. Her doctor made excuses for Joan. It was fairly obvious she could not go out with a high temperature.

Early that evening press agents from Warner Brothers arrived at her home on Bristol Avenue. Newspaper photographers and fan magazine writers were also welcome. By coincidence Joan's makeup man and hairdresser offered to keep her company. Finally, her lawyer and business manager managed to crowd around the radio, too. The doctor warned Joan not to get excited. "Try to remain calm," he said. "We don't want to aggravate your weakened condition."

The great moment arrived when Charles Boyer faced Joan's peers and said, "The nominees for Best Performance by an actress in 1945 are: Ingrid Bergman, *The Bells of St. Mary's*; Joan Crawford, *Mildred Pierce*; Greer Garson, *The Valley of Decision*; Jennifer Jones, *Love Letters*; Gene Tierney, *Leave Her to Heaven*; and the winner is . . . Joan Crawford in *Mildred Pierce!*"

Joan jumped out of bed, stepped into the shower, put on an exquisite negligee, and sat in a chair to have her makeup applied and her hair styled. Looking healthier and more beautiful than she had in years, Joan sipped a glass of champagne. Michael Curtiz arrived with her Oscar, and there was more celebrating. Dozens of Joan's fans stood on her front lawn cheering. Could she step outside for just a moment? "All right," the doctor said, "but only for a minute."

Joan waved weakly, blew a kiss, and said, "God bless you."

The famous picture in the newspapers the next morning showed Joan asleep in bed with Oscar, Kleenex, nose spray, and telephone.

"I knew winning an Oscar meant the beginning of the end," Joan said. "It opened doors to the upper crust in Hollywood. I don't think I was ever truly accepted until I was voted Best Actress. I was 'in,' if you know what I mean. But I had mixed emotions. It might have been nice if I'd gotten an Oscar at M-G-M, but they made damn sure I didn't. So, what the hell. I knew my performance in *Mildred Pierce* was *one* of my best, but I deserved it for *A Woman's Face* and maybe for *Strange Cargo*. As happy as I was holding that beautiful Oscar, I couldn't help fearing the future. Did I have to live up to winning that thing every time I appeared on the screen?"

Joan did, however, enjoy her freedom. She had almost drowned from three failed marriages, rejection from M-G-M, and financial problems (she had to mortgage her house), but she emerged with grace and pride. She had beaten Greer Garson out of an Oscar, too. Poor L. B. The old goat deserved it!

She felt at home at Warner Brothers, but she had yet to meet Bette Davis. This was neither earth-shattering nor unusual. Joan never would have met Greta Garbo if she hadn't deliberately planned the stairwell encounter, but similar efforts failed with the star of *Jezebel*. The circumstances were different, too, because Joan Crawford was in love with Bette Davis. The one-sided courtship began with little gifts—perfume, flowers, letters, and invitations to dinner. According to Charles Higham in his book *Bette* (Macmillan, 1981): "Crawford had for years nourished a secret desire for Bette. This greatest of suffering female stars admired this greatest of actresses sexually as well as professionally. There is something odd, unsettling and grotesque about this over the years. Davis has confided this to friends."

It's possible Joan heard the same rumor Elizabeth Taylor blurted out to Bette: "I've heard it said that you and Mary Astor had an affair years ago. Is it true?"

Bette shrieked, "Every son of a bitch in the world's been asking me that for twenty years. Shit! Everybody *knows* I adore men! I married four of them for Christ's sake!" (B. D. Hyman, *My Mother's Keeper*, Morrow, 1985.)

Although Bette would have plenty to say about Joan during the years ahead, she was clever about it. She could bury Joan without a shovel. Joan had to dig and throw dirt in all directions. There would be a showdown, and although Joan would never seduce Bette, she would get revenge—her way.

Christina Crawford said in *Mommie Dearest* that her mother tried to sleep with a hired nurse. Joan was drinking heavily and persisted until the woman was forced to leave. "I knew about my mother's lesbian proclivities," Christina said, "and this only added to what I had already figured out for myself."

Louise Brooks in an interview with John Kobal (*People Will Talk*, Knopf, 1986) said her autobiography was too explosive for publication. A Paramount starlet who was the rage in Europe, Brooks said that Greta Garbo made a pass at her. As for Joan Crawford, Brooks told Kobal: "I never liked her. Never. I hate fakes. She's 'one of the girls,' incidentally, who went back and forth. And, of course, a terrible drunk. She was an awful fake. A wash woman's daughter."

Joan had several approaches, but the one she used most often was not obvious. A woman author (Miss A.) who prefers to remain anonymous met with Joan on two occasions to discuss a book about the Golden Era. On the second visit Joan said they could continue the conversation while she dressed for dinner. Miss A. had not expected Joan to be quite so casual. "I was under the impression she was always impeccable," the author said. "There was no reason for me to stay, but she enjoyed talking about the good old days. When the subject of clothes came up, she made a remark about my dress not being the right color for me. She looked through her closet and told me to try on several outfits that she never wore. I felt strange, but didn't want to be rude, so I thanked her and said a friend was picking me up and there was no time."

"These are designer dresses!" she snapped.

"I don't feel right about it."

"I'm giving them to you. Try them on, goddamn it! This pink one will be perfect with your coloring."

Miss A. smiled, looked at her watch, and said she was late already. "I had the feeling she wanted to see me undressed. There was something about her eyes. I wasn't upset or embarrassed or shocked. I just knew I had to get out of her apartment. She called a few days later and was very nice. Would I like to continue our discussion about Hollywood? And, by the way, she had put the two lovely frocks aside because she wanted me to have them. We chatted for a few minutes, and I told her I would call when I returned from California. I never got around to it."

Marilyn Monroe found herself in a similar situation with Joan when they met at a cocktail party in 1948. Joan tried to give Marilyn tips on how to dress properly. It was an honor for Marilyn when Joan laid out several expensive dresses on her bed and said, "They're yours if they fit." Marilyn was taller and heavier. "I wouldn't even attempt to try them on," she smiled, "but thank you."

At a cocktail party Joan was slightly drunk and made a sexual pass at Marilyn; their friendship abruptly ended. Joan would bide her time and get revenge . . . her way.

Joan's friends saw her going through a transition they didn't like. Louella Parsons said it began when M-G-M let her go: "The people at the studio became her family. She was the first contract player groomed for stardom at M-G-M. Joan and Clark had the biggest dressing rooms on the lot at one time. Suddenly she found herself working with new directors and stagehands. Joan was a pro, but she was afraid people wouldn't like her if she was demanding. She earned less and less money. Franchot and Phillip didn't support her. She had to mortgage the house. The articles about her being washed up hurt her terribly. With no one to help her, she found solace in a few cocktails at first, and then began hitting the bottle after work. The Oscar, she said, was her farewell to Hollywood. I thought that was an odd remark, and yet I understood what she meant.

"At M-G-M she believed she *was* Joan Crawford. When her creators let her down, I think she slipped backward. She was like a madwoman, scrubbing and cleaning. She was Billie Cassin or maybe Lucille LeSueur, but it wasn't Joan Crawford. I don't know why she adopted children, but in the beginning Joan adored Christina and took her everywhere. I think she had problems with Christopher. Bed-wetting, perhaps. When her marriage to Phillip was over, she went to pieces inside. Sadly, she took out her frustrations on the children as if Billie Cassin were getting even with the world."

One can only imagine how shocked Hollywood insiders were to find out Joan had adopted two more girls, Cathy and Cynthia. She referred to them as "the twins," although the babies were not related. Having witnessed Joan's cruel treatment of Christina and Christopher, friends said it was inconceivable that she would want more children, or, for that matter, that she would be permitted to adopt them. There was no investigation as to her capabilities as a mother, and Hollywood protects its own. It wasn't until after *Mommie Dearest* that Joan's celebrity friends related what they had seen. Many were so appalled they deliberately put the incidents out of their minds. They all agreed, however, that Joan's mind was twisted.

June Allyson and her new husband Dick Powell moved to Brentwood shortly after they were married. Joan sent roses to welcome her new neighbors and invited the terrified June for lunch. Powell said, "You must go. It's ridiculous for you to turn down the opportunity to meet Joan Crawford and get to know her. You can learn from her."

"What will I say?" June asked.

"You don't have to say anything. Listen."

Allyson needn't have worried about talking. From the moment Joan greeted her at the door she monopolized the conversation. "Miss Crawford demanded to know how tall I was," June wrote in her book, *June Allyson* (Putnam, 1982). "I said I was 5'4½". She laughed. 'I'm only 5'1½", but I hold my head as a queen would.' " Allyson noticed Crawford was wearing high heels like stilts.

Christina curtsied, sat down, and then didn't stir. This made Allyson very nervous. She tried to liven up the dreary luncheon by mentioning *Dancing Lady*.

"I helped Fred Astaire get started in movies," Joan exclaimed. "I was his first dancing partner. Nobody remembers that. Only Ginger, Ginger, Ginger. I gave him the glamour he needed." Allyson listened to Joan's life story in the movies while Christina sat across the table in silence. After lunch Crawford said, "Christina is getting the silent treatment. She knows what she did, don't you, Christina? Go upstairs and find the box that's all wrapped up and bring it here."

Allyson said when the little girl returned she was told to sit on a bench. "You know that is the birthday present you are supposed to take to the party this afternoon. And for punishment for what you did you will sit on that bench holding that box until the party is over."

Crawford obviously wanted a witness to this humiliation. Allyson said the episode still haunts her.

Dorothy Manners, a long-time friend of Joan's, said, "Joan was generous and kind, but her one blind spot was her children. She dressed the poor boy in velvet and made all of the children bow and scrape. She felt in her heart that she was doing the right thing. Her reasoning was that she got where she was by being a disciplined person. Therefore she tried to discipline her children. She believed that undisciplined people were unhappy."

Helen Hayes commented, "Joan tried to be all things to all people. I just wish she hadn't tried to be a mother."

Adela Rogers St. John was probably right when she remarked, "I don't think Joan liked children. Some women don't, you know."

Joan obviously liked to see Christina suffer. The little girl hated artichokes but was forced to eat them anyway. When she threw them up, she was told to eat the disgorged matter. Christina was also told to eat her hot cereal sprinkled with dead bugs. "Don't worry about it," Joan told her daughter. "The bugs are cooked."

Household help was hard to find and more difficult to keep. The truth was so outrageous few servants wanted to talk about it. One maid said, "Who would have believed it, anyway, but I can say for a fact that *Mommie Dearest* didn't tell the half of it."

Christopher's famous bed harness wasn't hidden from view. He was tied to the bedposts at night to prevent him from kicking off the blanket and sucking his thumb. When Betty Grable and her daughter, Jessie, were invited to Joan's home, they were looking around and walked into Christopher's bedroom. Jessie froze when she saw the contraption. Betty wasn't fazed. "Forget it," she said casually. According to Spero Pastos (*Pin-Up: The Tragedy of Betty Grable,* Putnam, 1986), "Grable and Crawford shared a peculiar and distorted view of sex. They seemed to find sex unwholesome and repugnant despite the fact both women spent their lifetime in secret and not-so-secret premarital and extramarital affairs. Both Joan and Betty had been psychologically abused by their parents and in turn victimized their children."

Dan Dailey was a married homosexual, but he and Betty fell in love and had a blazing affair. When he was photographed in drag, Betty came to his defense and saved his career. Her husband, Harry James, found Betty and Dan together in her dressing room. Dailey ran for his life while Harry beat up Betty. Grable's unhappy marriage lingered just as Joan had allowed hers to drag on and on. Both women were fighting a younger generation, financial difficulties, divorce, and alcoholism. Jessie would suffer from her mother's wrath, also, but Grable had the sense of humor that Joan lacked. Marilyn Monroe, her co-star in *How to Marry a Millionaire,* had practiced for years to be like Betty. During production Marilyn was late; the cast and crew fumed while Grable laughed. "So what? It's her time." The two beautiful blondes attended the premiere of *Millionaire* together because neither had a date!

Clark Gable was one of the very few people who paid little attention to Joan's erratic behavior. He wouldn't take any nonsense from her. His surprise marriage to Lady Sylvia Ashley came as quite a shock. "I was drunk," he told Joan.

"Just think," she said. "If I were still married to Doug, you might have been my father-in-law."

It took Gable only a few weeks to realize his marriage was finished before it began, but he didn't lock Sylvia out until three years later. Joan's friends hoped she would not be as foolish but knew her only salvation was love. She dated Billy's gay friends, enjoyed going out dancing with Cesar Romero, and frequently agreed to be seen with young actors who needed the publicity. She stayed out all night with Rock Hudson and dated his best buddy, George Nader. Yul Brynner said he came to the house to pick her up and was ushered into the bedroom. Cocktails were served upstairs while Joan decided what to wear. This routine became a habit—Joan greeting her dates wearing only sheer undergarments. "I was a highly sexed woman," Joan admitted a few years before she died.

There were many social occasions, however, that Joan chose to attend alone. During dinner she had time to look over the eligible gentlemen and would ask one of them to escort her home. The chosen man would either return to the party very late or not return at all. Joan's routine was the same. The gent had to get out of the car to open the door for her. Then she invited him in for a quick drink, and, as one man said, "Next thing I knew, I was following her upstairs."

William W., a former real estate broker, now lives with his son in Los Angeles. He's an attractive man with a deep tan and white hair. His trim physique belies his age—nearly eighty years old. "I met Joan Crawford at a dinner party," he recalled. "I was separated from my wife and accepted the invitation from one of my wealthier clients, a society matron whose name I don't remember. I'm going back forty years or so. Miss Crawford sat across the table and caught my eye several times. I don't recall thinking anything about it, and I knew nothing about her personal life other than that she'd been a prostitute in New York. Maybe a dance hall girl would be more appropriate because that's what she was. Still, Joan Crawford was, without a doubt, the one Hollywood celebrity who personified the term 'star.' She was lovely, and the night we met, I admired her gown, jewelry, and furs because she knew how to wear them.

"I had just been served coffee when she asked my date if it would be all right if I drove her home early. It was a thrill for me to be the chosen one! In the car she wanted to know all about me. I think she made a crack about my date being a phony. By the time we got to her house we were laughing, and she asked me to have a brandy with her. It was early, and I saw no reason not to have a nightcap with Joan Crawford.

"She asked me to get the drinks and excused herself. I sat in the living room for quite a while until she appeared in a dressing gown. During my second drink I realized how fascinating she was. She teased and flirted but was very sophisticated. When I felt her hand on my knee, I was hooked."

William laughed and shook his head back and forth. "I don't know many men who would turn down an opportunity with a woman, but even fewer who were almost hypnotized. She took me by the hand and led me upstairs into the bedroom. Later . . . much later I found my tie and belt on the stairs!"

William said Joan was in complete command. "She was a small woman," he said. "Her shoulders were broad, but she had trim hips. She wasn't busty, but there was nothing flabby about her. I had never been with any woman like Crawford. I forgot about the dinner party, who I was, who she was, and where I was. I'd been around, but never met anyone who thoroughly enjoyed making love as much as she did.

"When it was over a few hours later, she asked me to go downstairs and get her another drink. I knew she had kids, so I got dressed and we sat together on the bed for a while talking about real estate, of all things. When she finished her brandy, Crawford turned her back to me and went to sleep. But that's when I woke up! What the devil was I going to tell my date, who had obviously gotten a ride home from the dinner party? And what about the others who were there? Also, I was only separated from my wife and she could use this as ammunition.

"When I got home I was torn between some pretty passionate memories and some pretty frightening consequences. Fortunately, nothing was said. No one asked me any questions. I ran into Joan at parties once or twice after that, but she merely nodded. From what I understand she always found out about the men she chose, and I wonder what might have happened if I hadn't been married. She was cautious about that though she was involved in several divorce suits. My wife and I reconciled and I loved her very much . . . but not enough to give up that one night with Joan. Amazing woman!"

Joan's other habit was widely accepted at dinner parties. "Joan wanted to make a grand appearance alone," a friend said, "but had no intention of staying. She just wanted a few drinks and lots of attention. She always managed to sit near a telephone. Suddenly, she would pick it up and gasp, 'Oh, God. I have to leave right away!' Naturally everyone would want to know what was wrong. 'I'm too upset now,' she'd say. Then Joan would leave and drive herself home. The next day the hostess would receive a long apologetic telegram. And what was the emergency? 'Nothing important,' she would laugh. Joan staged this show often. Guests who didn't know the routine came out with the inevitable, 'I didn't hear the telephone ring.' Another silly act Joan staged was visiting a friend's dressing room and, in the middle of a chat, calling out, 'I'll be right there!' The third time Joan would say she just had to run because 'they' were calling for her. She was the only one who ever heard the voices. This was her way of being needed, being wanted, and being indispensable."

One of Joan's on-again, off-again affairs was with the handsome attorney Greg Bautzer, who was quite a ladies' man. Tall, tanned, and available, he was sought after by many beautiful women who still wonder how Dana Wynter caught him. Gable tried to figure out how he remained single past forty.

Lana Turner met and fell in love with thirty-year-old Bautzer, her first lover. She attended dinner parties with him at Joan's house in 1939. The romantic and innocent seventeen-year-old Lana accepted a small diamond from Greg and heard wedding bells until she received a telephone call from Crawford (Lana Turner, *Lana*, Dutton, 1982).

Joan invited Lana to the house. "I'd like to talk to you about something very important."

When Lana arrived, Joan fussed over making her comfortable and, with a friendly smile, said, "Now, darling, you know I'm a bit older than you, and so I may know some things you haven't learned yet."

"Like what?" Lana asked, thinking that Joan was *quite* a bit older.

"Well, dear, when you're young you see things a certain way, but that's not always how they are." Joan went on and on about the complexities of life until Lana asked her to get to the point. Joan was very dramatic—her hand to her forehead, then to her heart—and after inhaling deeply from a cigarette, she said, "Well, darling, I feel it's only right to tell you that Greg doesn't love you anymore—that he hasn't for a long time. I couldn't let you go on believing. What Greg and I have is real. It's me he truly loves. But . . . he hasn't figured out how to get rid of you."

Lana said she didn't believe it. Joan didn't give her a chance to say much of anything. "So, Lana dear, why don't you be a good little girl and tell him you're finished—that you know the truth now, and it's over . . . make it easier on yourself. He doesn't want to hurt you."

Greg denied it, but his affair with Lana faded. She married Artie Shaw on the rebound.

For ten years Bautzer and Joan were torrid lovers. Billy Haines said, "To be Joan Crawford's boyfriend, a man must be a combination bull and butler." Hollywood thought Joan and Greg were a perfect match.

Rosalind Russell said, "He treated her like a star. When they entered a room he remained a few steps behinds her. He often carried her dog or her knitting bag—she was always knitting—and at the dinner table Greg did everything but feed her. Joan expected her escort to place her napkin in her lap, light her cigarettes, and open doors for her. Not many men would put up with it. Greg did all these things without losing his masculinity. He made it seem as if it were the natural thing to do. They were nuts about each other."

Gable and Bautzer were both seeing Joan at the same time. The two men had suites at the Bel Air Hotel and often had a drink together. When Greg found out he was competing with a friend, he bowed out until Gable's sudden elopement.

One of Bautzer's habits was climbing up a rose trellis to Joan's bedroom in the middle of the night. Either they had had an argument and she refused to take his calls, or he had a sudden urge to be with Joan and did not want to wake up the children. She confided to a friend it was very romantic when Greg forced his way into her bedroom. "I hate him and love him at the same time," she cooed. Their battles were loud enough to be heard by the neighbors, who recall seeing Joan climbing up on the roof while Greg scrambled off the balcony after her. She threatened to call the police, and he escaped through the front door.

Perhaps their bitter and almost amusing fights led to a stronger and sexier bond each time they reunited. According to Joan, the great romance ended when Greg danced with another woman at a party. Joan was very sweet about it and offered to drive home. "You must be tired, darling," she said lovingly. In the middle of nowhere Joan stopped the car. "I think we might have a flat," she said. "Do you mind getting out to take a look?"

He did, and she drove off, leaving Greg three miles out of town. Was that the night he climbed up her rose trellis, fell, and broke his leg?

Humoresque with John Garfield was Joan's second major film for Warner Brothers. She specifically asked for the part of the destructive rich bitch and insisted that Adrian design her gowns. Joan wasn't pleased with Garfield's casual approach to her. She thought he was perfect for the part of the struggling musician, but off-camera he had little respect for her. "I thought I was doing well," Joan said, "but I should have known what it would be like to work with a method actor again. They do it their way. Production went along very well, but I was still accustomed to the perfectionists at M-G-M, and this time around I called the shots."

Humoresque was a popular film and a good follow-up for *Mildred Pierce*. Jack Warner offered Joan a seven-year contract, paying her $200,000 per picture, and she accepted. Joan was nominated for an Oscar as Best Actress for her performance in *Possessed* (no connection to the film she made with Clark Gable in 1931). Her co-stars were Van Heflin and Raymond Massey. Joan, who portrayed a psychotic, spent time in psychiatric wards at hospitals in Santa Monica and at UCLA. She consulted psychiatrists, script in hand, and asked them how she should interpret the psychosis of the woman in *Possessed*. "I never worked so hard in any film," she said. "Every actress will tell you how draining and depressing it is to portray a madwoman. I did well because the Academy nominated me for another award, an honor in itself."

Joan agreed to do *Daisy Kenyon* at Twentieth Century Fox if she could have Henry Fonda and Dana Andrews as co-stars. Neither actor was eager to work with her, but they were bound contractually. Daisy, a successful career woman, almost gives up one man (Fonda) for a married man (Andrews); she is caught between the two men, who pursue her until she makes her choice. Joan was attracted to Fonda and flirted with him throughout the filming. An observer said, "She was trying to seduce Henry, and he wasn't tuned in. Joan made a jock strap of rhinestones, gold sequins, and red beads, gift-wrapped it, and gave the box to Henry. He looked at the jock strap and turned it over a few times until he figured out that it *was* a jock strap. In the next scene he had to carry Joan up the stairs, and she whispered in his ear, 'How about modeling it for me later?' Henry stopped dead in his tracks and almost dropped her. Crawford wasn't known for her sense of humor, but she was attracted to

Henry's implied innocence. His kind of shyness brought out the motherly instinct in his leading ladies who fell in love with him. Joan was quite open about wanting Fonda—if for only one night—but he was oblivious to her."

Joan's new contract gave her the right to control the temperature on the set—a chilly fifty-eight degrees. Her co-stars could complain, but they were told to wear heavy sweaters or coats. She bought Fonda long underwear. He laughed nervously and said, "I might just wear them."

Joan smiled. "And I might just help you take them off."

Joan did not make a habit of going out with her co-stars or socializing with many of them, but she had a reputation for affairs with her directors—Ranald MacDougall, Vincent Sherman, Robert Aldrich, and David Miller, to name a few. There were rumors about Jerry Wald, too. Joan was named in several divorce suits, but there were no major scandals.

The children were told to call Mommy's boyfriends "Uncle so-and-so." The only one who protested was Bautzer, who disliked "Uncle Greg." Joan said she made the rules, they argued, and he gave in. She demanded an apology. "I'm sorry," he said. "I was wrong." She insisted he get down on his knees. Bautzer thought it was a joke. "Franchot did," she said. Years later Greg had a chance to find out firsthand. Tone wasn't ashamed to admit he did it many times. "I didn't mind getting down on my knees," he smiled.

Don "Red" Barry was a popular star of Republic westerns in the forties. In 1942, the *Motion Picture Herald* Fame Poll voted him one of the top ten money-making western stars. He was rather short in stature and had an inferiority complex about his height. Somehow he always managed to show up at a party with a beautiful young starlet on his arm—the flashier the better. Barry was moderately successful, although Republic did not have the prestige of an M-G-M or RKO. This complex Barry kept carefully hidden; he was usually the jolly, red-headed, well-dressed, peppy fellow who was, or tried to be, the center of attention.

Hollywood was aghast when Barry was seen escorting Joan around town. She often told the technicians that supporting actors were sexier than the leading men. "Maybe they don't get top billing," she laughed, "but they get the highest marks in the bedroom."

Barry knew that Joan had stopped dating Brian Donlevy because he was not her equal. He also knew Joan was a champion in bed, a legend on the screen, and a press agent's delight. When she received a white mink coat, a diamond necklace, and a jeweled vanity case from Barry, Joan was overwhelmed. How could he afford to spend a year's salary on her?

She found out soon enough when the furrier and jeweler claimed the gifts had not been paid for, unless, of course, she wanted to pay for them.

Joan never saw "Red" Barry again.

In 1980, after an argument with his wife, actress Peggy Steward, Don Barry shot and killed himself. He was sixty-eight years old.

*   *   *

Billy Haines, always a favorite of Joan's, accepted her as she was—a victim of Hollywood who wasn't six feet under. They loved to gossip and tell dirty jokes. Once, after Joan had recently attended a party for L. B. Mayer, she discussed it with Haines, who was itching to find out all about it.

"He misses me," Joan said proudly. "And he shows *Mildred Pierce* and *Possessed* after all his dinner parties."

"Do you believe that shit, Cranberry?"

"He likes to take credit for my renewed success."

"How did you happen to pick Bill Dozier for your date?" he asked.

"He's producing one of my films. We're dear friends."

"It's all over town."

"What is?" she asked.

"You walked out on him because he danced with another woman."

"Bill knows how sensitive I am."

"Cranberry, you were on the dance floor first. He was just being polite."

"When a gentleman escorts me somewhere I expect him to . . ."

"Sit like a lump and watch you dance with another guy? Or maybe all three of you could do the fox-trot together."

Joan mixed a drink and lit another cigarette. "I don't know what came over me," she said nervously. "It was embarrassing when I got back to the table and he wasn't there. I was alone."

"You were jealous, Cranberry."

"Of Barbara Stanwyck? She's one of my dearest friends!"

"Why did you disappear then?"

"I like Bill very much, and if he wants to see me again, it's time he found out what I expect him *not* to do in my company."

"Yeah, you really let him know who's the boss," Billy laughed. "I hear his office was filled with flowers the next day—compliments of a frightened little girl, Joan Crawford."

"Bill would never tell a living soul!"

"The whole studio knew it before he did. Honestly, Cranberry, I wish you'd try to be a little more tolerant."

"You only hear the bad things, Billy. I'm very tolerant—to a point—and patient, too. Why, just the other day the studio sent a new photographer to my dressing room so we could become acquainted. He was very shy, and I was in a hurry. While he took notes, I changed clothes and I could see him in the full-length mirror looking me over. I must have been naked for at least five minutes and he said nothing."

"Nothing?"

"Nothing."

"What did you expect the kid to do?"

"Say *something* about my body, for Christ's sake!"

"Did you have him fired?"

"Of course not! He's supposed to be a photographer and to capture the real me. He should know what's underneath."

"Maybe he's gay. What's his name?"

Joan shook her head and, with a husky laugh, said, "You don't think I'm going to waste my time on children, do you? I want a man! A real man!"

"I liked Greg, you know."

"He was at the party," Joan said, making another drink, ". . . with Ginger Rogers."

Haines snickered. "So, *that's* why you left!"

"Greg and I thought it best not to see each other again. Our parting was mutual."

"Seeing him with another woman—especially Ginger—must have driven you home to apply an extra mud pack."

Joan's fights with her boyfriends occasionally involved the children, especially Christina, who said she had to "save" her mother from being hurt. Joan did not take these battles seriously because she allowed the "brutes" back into her life the next day. Christina was frightened by the threats and noise and physical abuse. When Christina was ten years old, Joan sent her away to school. After several attempts at running away, Christopher was also put in a private school. Joan complained bitterly that she could not handle her two oldest children. Close friends hoped that Joan might pull herself together with only the "twins" at home. She rarely—if ever—complained about Cathy and Cynthia.

Christina said she and her brother were sent away because their mother wanted more privacy to entertain her boyfriends. A former servant said, "There was a steady flow of men. They came and went at all hours. If she had a date, I used to see her take him by the hand at the end of the evening and lead him upstairs. I don't know if she was sexy in a playful way or playful in a sexy way, but Miss Crawford always succeeded, and, as I recall, a few gentlemen were a bit reluctant."

Warner Brothers was a madhouse the day Bette Davis clashed with director King Vidor on the set of *Beyond the Forest* in 1948. Jack Warner and his staff rushed to the scene, but the battle raged until Davis said, "Jack, if you don't get another director, I want to be released from my contract. It's him or me!"

"Okay, Bette, it's you," Warner exclaimed.

Davis was stunned. "Draw up the papers," she bellowed.

"We can do that right here on the set in fifteen minutes," Jack replied. That's precisely what happened to Bette Davis after thirteen years with Warner Brothers.

Joan was the reigning queen at Warner Brothers after Bette's departure, but her scripts did not improve. The lurid *Flamingo Road* with Zachary Scott, David Brian, and Sydney Greenstreet had potential, but Joan was not pleased with the outcome. It was a heavy drama directed by the tough Michael Curtiz, who appeared to have lost his stern control over Joan. It was assumed that she slept with all her directors, and even though Curtiz was never mentioned as a lover, she had tamed him.

It's a Great Feeling with the Warner players—Doris Day, Dennis Morgan, Danny Kaye, Errol Flynn, Ronald Reagan, Jane Wyman, and Eleanor Parker—was great fun for Joan, who did a spoof of her usual sophisticated screen personality and women-of-the-world roles. "The critics said I was a great comedienne," Joan emphasized. "It was a wonderful relief to do something frivolous on camera. Having fun eased the tension."

In 1950, Joan teamed with David Brian, Steve Cochran, and Kent Smith in *The Damned Don't Cry*. This was a Joan Crawford film from beginning to end. In a conversation with the mild-mannered Kent Smith, she could have written the dialogue herself: "Don't talk to me about self-respect! That's something you tell yourself you've got when you got nothing else. The only thing that counts is that stuff you take to the bank. That filthy buck that everyone sneers at but slugs to get. You gotta kick and punch and belt your way up because no one's gonna give you a lift. You gotta do it yourself because nobody cares about us but ourselves."

She spoke those lines for Billie Cassin and Lucille LeSueur.

Joan summed up her philosophy in *The Damned Don't Cry*: "A woman has only a short time when life can be exciting for her. When she can enjoy being a woman. Well, I want that time desperately. I'm going to drain everything out of those years. I'm gonna squeeze them dry. I can't help myself."

Joan was loaned to Columbia Pictures for *Harriet Craig,* produced by William Dozier and directed by Vincent Sherman, an excellent follow-up to *The Damned Don't Cry* for her, according to catty friends, because she was playing herself again. She portrayed a domineering shrew whose only concern was her meticulously kept and richly appointed house with remarkable ease. Harriet Craig, a neurotic perfectionist and a stickler for absolute cleanliness, *was* Joan. At the end of the picture, Harriet's husband (played by Wendell Corey) smashes her favorite vase and walks out. The *New York Herald Tribune* wrote, "In every mannerism of speech or gesture, Miss Crawford suggests that she is a queen in the country of cinema, playing a dominant woman whose unkindly rule of her home has psychotic origins."

Although the quality of Joan's films was not the best, she remained in character—the strong-willed, gutsy bitch, broad, or dame who refuses to take one step backward. Joan took advantage of her good reviews and concentrated on publicity. Fans gathered at her house and stuffed envelopes. Each photo was signed personally. "There's only one Joan Crawford," she said. Every letter received a reply. (Form letters were taboo.) Press agents made sure her name was mentioned in the right columns. Fan magazines had merely to call, and she was available for an interview.

She confided in *Modern Screen:* "This is a man's world, and a girl has to fight for everything she wants. Men taught me how to fight. They taught me how to live. But I've been described as love-starved, man-crazy, husband-hungry, altogether unhappy, and a domineering hermit who lived only for her career. Thanks to Douglas I've learned to live graciously. Franchot helped me channel brain power into a better understanding of the arts. If you read somewhere that Joan Crawford is not in the market for marriage, that's she's had her fill of it, that she's been reported as saying, 'No more husbands for me!'—it's pure poppycock. I know a little more about life and men and the birds and the bees and if I walk down the aisle again it will be for keeps. Chances are I won't marry an actor. They don't make very good husbands."

To Louella Parsons she said, "I get letters from people who are basically intelligent. They like the fact that I worked my way from rags to riches. They liked stories about the way I dressed and when I went out, my silver service, my china, my parties, my husbands, my escorts. To me it became such an obligation to appear glamorous that I went a few steps beyond M-G-M expectations. Goddamn it, if they wanted to see Joan Crawford the star, they were going to see Joan Crawford the star, not a character actress in blue jeans. They paid their money and they were going to get their money's worth. I kept hearing all I would do were drab roles. All I want are acting roles, Louella, and if they are old ladies, okay, or if they are good girls or bad girls, I don't care, so long as they have character."

Playing a congresswoman who returns to the college that expelled her years before, Joan renews an old romance with "Professor" Robert Young in *Goodbye, My Fancy*. Janice Rule made her film debut and was overly anxious and nervous. Joan felt the cast and crew paid too much attention to the pretty young newcomer and groaned every time Janice made a mistake, making matters worse. Finally, Joan commented, "Miss Rule, you'd better enjoy making films while you can. I doubt that you'll be with us long!"

Vincent Sherman knew Joan well enough by now to placate her without offending anyone. She credited him with the success of *Goodbye, My Fancy*. Unfortunately, she did not have Sherman to save *This Woman Is Dangerous*. "Trash," Joan recalled. "Utter trash! The worst. Jack Warner expected Dennis Morgan and me to refuse to do it so that he could get rid of us. Dennis was reluctant but agreed, and so did I. It was a mistake. I was having financial problems, I was disgusted with Hollywood and my children. I was restless. I was depressed, and why not? M-G-M . . . and now Warner Brothers was about to give me the boot. I told my agents to break my contract."

This Woman Is Dangerous was a disgrace. The astonished critics tried to express their reactions to the film. The *New York Times* review is representative: "The incredibly durable star, whose theatrical personality has now reached the ossified stage, appears as a woman criminal. There is only one possible explanation for such fictitious junk as this, which is willfully delivered in the name of dramatic fare. That is as pure contrivance for the display of Miss Crawford's stony charm. Those who admire the actress may be most tenderly moved by the evidence of the suffering she undergoes. And to these the arrant posturing of Miss Crawford may seem the quintessence of acting art. But for people of mild discrimination and even moderate reasonableness, the suffering of Miss Crawford will be dangerously matched by their own in the face of *This Woman Is Dangerous.*"

"Darling, where have you been?"

"In Nevada tryin' to get unhitched," Clark replied.

"Poor Lady Ashley. It'll take her a year to dig up all those rosebushes she planted on your ranch."

"What do you want, Joanie?"

"I want you for my comeback film, *Sudden Fear,* at RKO."

"How many comeback films have you made, anyway?"

"Almost as many as you have."

"Sorry, babe. I'm goin' to Africa for *Mogambo.*"

She laughed. "The remake of *Red Dust?* Jesus!"

"I'd rather face the wild animals in Nairobi than the ones here in Hollywood. *Mogambo*'s about my last one for M-G-M, Joanie."

"Clark, we'll plan *Sudden Fear* around your schedule."

"Afraid not."

"Why?"

"Do you want the truth or a lotta bullshit?"

"I'm listening."

"You can't afford me," Gable blurted out.

"Fuck you."

"Let's face it, Joanie, no one can afford either one of us these days. Besides, I need *Mogambo.*"

"And I need *Sudden Fear.*"

"Well, I'd offer you the part of a Watusi, but you won't fly."

"Damn it, Clark. They're trying to ram Jack Palance down my throat."

"Have you seen *Panic in the Streets?* Jack's very good."

"But hardly suitable for my leading man."

Clark laughed. "They're giving me a green kid who's done only two films—Grace Kelly. Ever hear of her?"

"With Coop in *High Noon?*" Joan sighed.

"Yeah."

"Darling, please reconsider *Sudden Fear.*"

"I'll call you as soon as I get home," he said.

"When will that be?"

"Oh, I figure about two years."

"Two years?!"

"Yeah . . . well . . . I have two films in Europe to avoid taxes—one with Gene Tierney and the other with Lana."

"You son of a bitch!"

*   *   *

Director David Miller explained to Joan that "in your last pictures you played not only the female lead but the male lead as well. That won't work in *Sudden Fear*. Your husband marries you with only murder on his mind. Also, Joan, it's time you worked with an unknown."

"Another goddamn method actor!"

"I don't expect you to get along with Palance, Joan. He's a new breed of actor, but ideal for the part."

Miller's patience and charm finally got an okay out of Joan, but her relationship with Palance was strained. She doesn't mention him as her co-star in her autobiography, despite her third Oscar nomination. She lost to Shirley Booth, who starred in *Come Back, Little Sheba*.

Jack Palance said that Joan complimented him on a good performance. "But," he said, "I know for a fact that she made it known she would never work with me again. She accused me of copying Marlon Brando and told me so in the middle of a scene. Every morning she'd walk in with her entourage and every morning she greeted everyone—everyone except me."

Miller must be given credit for directing Joan through several mediocre pictures, taking her guff, and waiting for her to compromise. He saw in Joan a great star from the Golden Era, and he understood her. She loved him for it and, in turn, his admiration for her was intense.

In *Sudden Fear* Joan refused to appear in bed with a bare shoulder. Miller had wanted to give an illusion of nudity.

"I want to wear a nightgown," she insisted.

He smiled. "The audience will see only a shoulder strap."

"I want to test all eight nightgowns."

"All eight?" he yelped.

"That's what I want," she said loud and clear.

Late that night she called Miller. "You want to say to me, 'Go fuck yourself,' right?"

"Right."

"I'm sorry. I apologize. It'll never happen again."

9

HELL HATH NO FURY . . .

The year: 1953
The place: The Crystal Room at the Beverly Hills Hotel
The occasion: The *Photoplay* Awards Dinner
The outcome: Revenge

Joan Crawford was in her glory at this annual event. Her friends, peers, and the press had praised her excellent performance in *Sudden Fear*. Radiant, beautiful, and gracious, she held court at her table.

Halfway through dinner the crowd of three hundred was drawn to a commotion in the outer lobby. There was laughter and flashbulbs were popping. Obviously someone very important had arrived late and was about to make a grand entrance.

Twenty-seven-year-old Marilyn Monroe, dressed in a very low-cut gold-lamé pleated gown with paper-thin lining hand-stitched to her nude curves, inched her way to the Twentieth Century Fox table. Master of Ceremonies Jerry Lewis stood up on a chair, trying to get a better look at her cleavage, although it was clearly visible from any angle. The whole room roared and screamed. It got worse when Marilyn walked to the dais to receive the award for "Fastest-Rising Star of 1952."

Joan was outraged by the wolf calls, howls, and whistles. She was furious at Monroe, who had been so shy and lonesome a few years ago and who had turned away when Joan offered a "close" relationship.

Sheilah Graham wrote, "The crush of photographers and reporters has never been equalled before or after. Not even Elizabeth Taylor. I realized then from the shoving and the hysteria that a new star had risen in Hollywood and that she could make any demands and she would get them. Once they are sure you are a star, every door opens, everyone is rushing to kiss your rear end and how Marilyn flaunted her rear end! In her public-appearance gown you could see every crevasse. I was shocked. I had never seen anything like it in public. She was the living end."

Marilyn's rejection of Joan was one thing, but turning a respectable Hollywood banquet into a burlesque was unforgivable. Joan's jaws were clenched. While the gentlemen tried to catch a glimpse of the girl "who was blond all over," the ladies chatted about *anything* else until the gala was over.

Joan told her friends she was embarrassed for Hollywood. "I had to work damn hard before I got that much attention," she hissed. "Today an artificial chin, a nose job, and a bottle of peroxide's more important than talent and class."

According to writer Bob Thomas, he met Joan and her publicist for cocktails the next day. The subject of Marilyn Monroe came up. Joan's eyes shone fiercely. "It was the most shocking display of bad taste I have ever seen," she said. "Look, there's nothing wrong with my tits, but I don't go around throwing them into people's faces." She vented her anger and before departing told Thomas, "I know you've got a good story, but when you quote me, for God's sake, go easy."

Thomas wrote the following article.

Hollywood, March 2, 1953 (AP)—Joan Crawford today aimed this curt message to Marilyn Monroe: Stop believing your own publicity . . .

"It was like a burlesque show," said the horrified Miss Crawford, who was present at the affair. "The audience yelled and shouted, and Jerry Lewis got up on the table and whistled. But those of us in the industry just shuddered.

"Certainly her picture isn't doing business, and I'll tell you why. Sex plays a tremendously important part in every person's life. People are interested in it, intrigued with it. But they don't like to see it flaunted in their faces.

"Kids don't like her. Sex plays a growingly important part in their lives, too; and they don't like to see it exploited.

"And don't forget the women. They're the ones who pick out the movie entertainment for the family. They won't pick anything that won't be suitable for their husbands and children.

"The publicity has gone too far, and apparently Miss Monroe is making the mistake of believing her publicity. Someone should make her see the light. She should be told that the public likes provocative feminine personalities; but it also likes to know that underneath it all the actresses are ladies . . ."

Marilyn told Louella Parsons, "I cried all night. I've always admired Miss Crawford for being such a wonderful mother—for taking four children and giving them a fine home. Who better than I knows what that means to homeless little ones?"

The news media considered the Crawford versus Monroe story a sensation, and there were items in gossip columns every day. Marilyn refused to comment, but told Louella she was hurt by the crowd's reaction at the awards dinner. "I walked like a lady. And they all jumped on me. Why?"

Hollywood took sides. Joan attacked poor Marilyn without knowing her; Marilyn shouldn't have worn a see-through costume to the event; Joan was jealous of the beautiful newcomer as she grew older and her career waned; Marilyn was innocent and Joan's past was tainted; Marilyn had sincere respect for "the lady with four adopted children," but made no mention of Joan's success as an actress.

The public identified with Joan's tradition. She had campaigned against movie players appearing on television, calling those who did traitors. She expressed her fear that Hollywood was doomed if the stars overexposed themselves in America's living rooms. Smearing a sexy blonde with big boobs did not cost Joan any fans.

Marilyn alone was responsible for choosing the dress despite stern objections from others. The evening had been humiliating enough without a star of Joan's magnitude expressing disgust and disgrace. Marilyn was reluctant to attend public functions after the *Photoplay* Awards dinner and toned down her wardrobe. When she was scheduled for a premiere, those responsible for getting her ready reminded each other—and Marilyn—that they *must* avoid another Crawford episode.

Joan was offered the role of the army officer's faithless wife in *From Here to Eternity*. Thrilled à la Crawford, she expressed her dismay at the wardrobe and insisted she use her own designer. Harry Cohn, head of Columbia, couldn't be bothered. "Tell her to fuck herself!" he said. Deborah Kerr was chosen instead.

As if destiny had played a part in it, *Lisbon* at Paramount was abandoned, and a script from M-G-M was sent to Joan for her consideration. *Torch Song*, the story of a selfish and ambitious musical comedy star who falls in love with a blind pianist, was ideal for Joan. Not wanting to blow the deal as she had with Cohn, Joan requested Charles Walters, a fine choreographer who had directed *Lili*, and held her breath. Without negotiating, he was available and looking forward to working with Joan, who wanted more than anything else in the world to return "home."

Above the gate at M-G-M flew a huge banner—"WELCOME BACK, JOAN." A red carpet was laid from the street to Joan's dressing room, which was actually three in one. It was filled with flowers. Gable sent a market basket full of chocolate from Italy, Fred Astaire sent roses, and the technicians gave her orchids and violets. Telegrams arrived from all over the world, but she treasured most the ones from her peers in Hollywood. This was one of the happiest occasions in Joan's life, but there was a price. "I hadn't danced in fourteen years," she said, "and *Torch Song* was my first technicolor picture. It was thrilling, and it was grueling. I decided to live at the studio until I was finished." Joan would continue this practice. With only the twins at home, she had nothing to worry about.

Relying on Charles Walters for support, she frequently drove to his beach house for dialogue rehearsals. For these visits, Joan dressed casually. One evening she arrived wearing an elaborate robe that she opened, standing in front of him. "I think you should see what you have to work with," she said. Walters looked over the forty-nine-year-old actress and nodded approvingly. "Very, very nice, Joan." He stared. "Very nice . . ."

Fade to a sunset resting on the ocean as frothy waves massage a peaceful beach . . .

Joan's nerves were shattered before production began. "It's the dancing," she told Walters. "I'll never get through it."

"We could film the musical sequences first," he suggested, ". . . get them over."

"Oh, Chuck, if only we could!"

Walters rearranged the schedule, and on the first day of shooting he went to Joan's dressing room. She was wearing black leotards and appeared ten years younger. He smiled and offered his arm. "Shall we?"

"I'm paralyzed," she trembled. "I can't do it. I can't move."

"You can do these dance numbers in your sleep, Joan."

"Chuck, have a drink with me."

It was early in the morning, but Walters knew this was the only way to get Joan on the set. "I'll pour," she said, filling up two glasses with straight vodka. After several drinks they tottered onto the set. Walters danced with her in the intricate sequences, and by early evening they were finished. Joan was so relieved she blessed and kissed everyone. Instead of waiting until the last day, she gave presents to the cast and crew. Walters got a potted rubber plant laden with vitamin pills, steaks, and a cashmere sweater for those days on the set when the temperature was only fifty-eight degrees. She pointed to the food and winked. "We have to build you up. You're much too thin."

Walters blushed.

Torch Song was a sentimental experience for Joan . . . the M-G-M sound stages, the friendly faces, the commissary, and so many beautiful memories of an era that belonged to her as much as to anyone . . . maybe more. At night she walked her dog and chatted with the watchman and guards.

Douglas Fairbanks, Jr., told Gregory Speck (*Interview* magazine, August 1987): "All Joan cared about was her own job at M-G-M. When we went abroad, which was her first time out of the country, she absolutely hated every minute and couldn't wait to get back to Culver City (M-G-M). It was like going back to the womb, the only place where she felt secure and confident in herself. It was where all her hopes and ambitions were centered."

Fairbanks said Joan was so much a perfectionist she had very little interest in broadening herself; however, this dedication created the legend she became. He was more adventurous, considered acting a job he liked, but preferred traveling, meeting interesting people, and spending more time in Europe.

Returning to M-G-M for *Torch Song* was bittersweet for Joan, however. L. B. Mayer had been replaced by RKO's Dore Schary. Gable was filming his last Metro picture in Europe and told the studio what they could do with his contract.

Spencer Tracy was about to begin *Tribute to a Bad Man* in Colorado, but he disappeared after a bitter argument with director Robert Wise. Tracy refused to shoot a single scene and supposedly locked himself in a hotel room. He might have slipped out of Colorado to consult with Katharine Hepburn, but the bottom line was he wanted another director. M-G-M executives flew to Colorado and tried to reason with Tracy, who refused to budge. To his astonishment, Spencer was fired on the spot. He sat down, covered his face, and sobbed.

One of the only major contract players left at M-G-M was Robert Taylor, who became the fifties' "Knight in Shining Armor" in *Quo Vadis* and *Ivanhoe*.

Joan's co-star in *Torch Song* was Elizabeth Taylor's second husband, Michael Wilding, a mild-mannered Englishman who left London to be with his famous wife. Elizabeth came on the set frequently and paid little attention, if any, to Joan, who was hurt and insulted by the twenty-one-year-old beauty. After one snub too many Joan told Wilding, "You'd better teach that little bitch some manners. Next time I expect her to acknowledge my presence!" It's unlikely the meek Wilding said anything to his wife. She was the moneymaker in the family. Michael had turned down Rex Harrison's role in the national company of *My Fair Lady* and ignored *The Swan* with Grace Kelly because he wasn't interested in hard work. Wilding had never met anyone like Joan in his life. He had no idea such people existed. "My God!" he exclaimed. "That woman actually lives at the studio. Such dedication is incredible. If I didn't see it for myself, I'd never believe it."

Joan said little about Wilding other than that he was on time and always knew his lines. As for Elizabeth Taylor, Joan remarked, "She has potential if she ever gets around to using it."

The *New York Herald Tribune*'s review of *Torch Song* was excellent: "Joan Crawford has another of her star-sized roles . . . playing a musical comedy actress in the throes of rehearsal and in love with a blind pianist, she is vivid and irritable, volcanic and feminine. She dances, she pretends to sing: she graciously permits her wide mouth and snappish eyes to be photographed in technicolor. Here is Joan Crawford all over the screen, in command, in love and in color, a real movie star in what amounts to be a carefully produced one-woman show. Miss Crawford's acting is sheer and colorful as a painted arrow, aimed straight at the sensibilities of her particular fans."

Technicolor removed the veil from Joan Crawford's famous cheekbones, strong jawline, and lavish eyes. Moviegoers felt they were seeing her for the first time. *Torch Song* was well received, but Hollywood insiders knew she couldn't pay her bills doing only one film a year.

She did not want a party for her forty-sixth birthday (it was really her fiftieth) and asked Billy Haines, "What's there to celebrate?"

"You can still kick as high as any chorus girl, Cranberry."

"It nearly put me in traction, but once a dancer, always a dancer."

"Let's have that birthday party!" he pleaded.

"No. It reminds me that I'm getting older."

"I know, Cranberry, but whether we celebrate or not, no one can turn back the clock."

She closed her eyes and tears of mascara streaked her freckled face.

Joan was nipping vodka day and night. Finding her passed out was nothing unusual for the household staff. During her nights alone she'd seethe about something or someone, make a drunken phone call, and forget what she'd said. Telegrams had been her style, but the liquor changed her personality. With friends she was usually a fun drinker, but by herself her thoughts, worries, and frustrations ballooned until they singed the telephone wires.

Owing two years' tuition at Chadwick School for both Christina and Christopher, Joan accepted a Republic western, *Johnny Guitar* with Mercedes McCambridge, Sterling Hayden, Scott Brady, and Ward Bond. Joan was cast as Vienna, an ambitious operator of a gambling saloon. McCambridge was Emma, a bitter, sexually frustrated cattle queen who wanted Vienna's land. Throughout the story the two women hate each other until they shoot it out at the end. The relationship between Joan and Mercedes was the same as that of the characters they played—each harbored jealousy, gossip, lies, and insults.

In britches, gun belt, and boots, Joan posed for the lighting director as if she were filming *The Women*. She kept her dressing room door open while answering piles of fan mail to prove, obviously, that she was a star of great magnitude. Joan's attempt at "hanging out" with the male cast members worked because she had an abundance of booze. Mercedes wasn't invited. A crew member saw Joan staggering around in the middle of the night. When she finally went to her room, he found costumes belonging to Mercedes scattered across the highway.

There were many stories about Joan's odd behavior. Friends suspected the surfacing of her lesbian tendencies. Was there something about Mercedes that attracted Joan? Was Joan aware of her feelings? Was it merely a clash of personalities or was Joan flaunting her star status? The feud attracted reporters, who managed interviews with both women, playing one against the other. The *Los Angeles Herald Examiner* quoted Joan: "I wouldn't trust McCambridge as far as I could throw her."

Mercedes said, "Some days we're friends and some days we're not. I tried to talk to Joan—to reason with her, but she turned her back on me."

Joan said, "It's just one of those silly things. Mercedes is doing a terrific job in the picture."

Mercedes retorted, "I'm paid a very handsome salary to do such things."

Co-star Sterling Hayden said, "There is not enough money in Hollywood to lure me into making another picture with Joan Crawford. And I like money. Her treatment of Mercedes was a shameful thing. There is one thing about Crawford you must admire: her ability to create a myth, a legend about herself."

In her autobiography, Joan did not mention Mercedes McCambridge by name, referring to her only as "an actress who hadn't worked in ten years, an excellent actress but a rabble-rouser." Joan said Mercedes was perfectly cast in the picture, but she played her part offstage as well. Her delight was to create friction. "Did you hear what *he* said about *you?*"

Joan said making the picture was a nightmare. "She would finish a scene, walk to the phone on the set, and call one of the columnists to report my 'incivilities.' I was as civil as I knew how to be. As if that weren't enough, she also had a friend in camp, an actor with an equally dubious reputation.

"Shortly after *Johnny Guitar,* the *Los Angeles Mirror* ran a series of scathing articles about me. I was deeply hurt." Joan contradicted Jack Palance, who had heard reports of the conflict, came to Mercedes's defense. "He said my 'Good Mornings' were a performance—so artificial it turned his stomach. Well, I meant those 'Good Mornings,' every one of them. Coming on the set each day is a homecoming for me. It's where I'm part of a team. What a pity Mr. Palance has never experienced being part of a team."

At the premiere party for *Johnny Guitar,* Mercedes and Joan chatted and posed for pictures, but the press forged ahead with the feud until the public tired of it. *Variety* suggested that Joan leave saddles and levis to someone else and stick to city lights for a background in her films.

Mrs. Sterling Hayden was the last to have her say. "Joan Crawford hates all women, except those who can help her. If I ever see her again, I'll probably strike her in the face!"

Safely back in Brentwood, Joan expressed her feelings in an interview: "Too many actresses today are little more than tramps and tarts. Half of them have to go to a psychiatrist before they can get on a movie set. What they really need is a kick in the pants. I keep hearing how it is their unhappy childhood that is at fault. Who grew up happy? How can you be two hours late on a set and blame it on your childhood? We're living in the present, not the past."

Unfortunately, she criticized the younger actresses who were taking her place. They had no manners, no class, no consideration, and no concept of hard work—all tits and no brains. "They didn't know how to curtsy to the Queen at the Command Performance!"

Joan failed to realize that a lady might have to curtsy only once in a lifetime, if at all. Christina, of course, curtsied a dozen times a day. God help her if she failed to say "Good night" to one of her mother's friends and not curtsy properly. Christopher was expected to bow.

"I tried to discipline them with threats, disappointments, hard work, and, as a last resort, a slap across the face." She never regretted adopting the "twins," but Christina and her brother were labeled as defiant. "Maybe they inherited rebellious attitudes," she told Billy Haines, who thought Joan should "take it easy."

"What the fuck do *you* know about children?" she snapped.

Cesar Romero also asked Joan gently to "ease up" on the kids. "If anyone else said that to me," she harped, "I'd throw them out of my house! No one knows what they've put me through."

The fan magazines were filled with pictures of Joan and her four children swimming; camping; opening Christmas presents; arranging the long dining room table for a birthday party with balloons, hats, and noisemakers; jumping rope; playing tag; hugging; and always laughing.

"Christina is a serious child," Joan explained. "She has a will of her own. It is not easy to discipline her, but I am forced to when she insists on doing things her way. I find punishing her by hurting her dignity is very effective. Christopher is happy. He'd much rather leave things behind and coax everyone to wait on him. It's hard not to spoil him, but that's one thing I'm determined not to do."

Christopher would attempt to run away at least six times. On one occasion he was missing for a week. Reporters were on hand when the boy returned home from one of his disappearances. Joan asked Chris why he ran away. "Because I couldn't have any chocolate syrup on my ice cream," he replied.

"Chocolate syrup, indeed!" Joan replied. "You're lucky to have ice cream!" She told him to go upstairs. "I'm going to tan his hide," she said to the reporters. "He won't be able to sit down for a week. Chocolate syrup, indeed!"

Nurses and housekeepers complained about Joan's treatment of her children. Some said her schedule was too rigid. Others feared her bouts with the bottle. Joan was tough, Joan was strict, and Joan had a drinking problem, but her friends and enemies agreed that *Mommie Dearest* was grossly exaggerated. How can two servants who worked for Crawford at the same time disagree totally? The public will never know to what extent Christopher and Christina misbehaved.

The children of celebrities were protected by the studio and the press the same way their parents were. As they grew into young adults, they represented the gods and goddesses of Hollywood. Who is to blame ultimately?

Christina admitted she was with a boy for the first time at the age of eleven. The word got around Chadwick, and Joan rushed to the school. Although Christina was still a virgin (as related in her book) she had been seen making love with a boy and enjoying it. Christina defends herself in *Mommie Dearest*. "My mother's reaction hurt me very much," she said. "Of all the people I thought she'd understand. She had so many boyfriends, told so many dirty jokes about sex, got dressed in front of half the world. I didn't understand why she was so mean to me, calling me a whore and refusing to listen when I tried to explain."

A nurse who was fired because she did not adhere to Joan's daily schedule said, "There aren't many secrets in Hollywood, especially among servants who go from job to job. I had no complaints, except living by a set of rules that rivaled the military's made me a nervous wreck. I mean, kids don't piddle just because it's written down in blood that it's time. Dogs, maybe. Not children. What really shocked me was that Christina wasn't afraid of her mother finding out she'd been with a boy. It made no sense to me at all. In the most loving homes, this matter is a major crisis. All that bunk about Miss Crawford having boyfriends had absolutely nothing to do with her eleven-year-old daughter. It didn't make any sense to me that Christina would want to volunteer anything to her mother."

The boy who was involved with Christina was expelled from school. Her punishment was one hundred hours of hard work, and she was not allowed to go home during the semester break.

The "night raids" depicted in the movie *Mommie Dearest* left nothing to the imagination: Joan's finding a wire hanger in Christina's closet and beating her with it; the tile-scrubbing at four in the morning; the chopping down of the orange tree and beautiful rosebushes in the garden until the yard was bare under the gaze of a full moon.

Although Christina admits her mother was fighting for survival in all phases of her life, she doesn't reveal what incidents might have caused Joan's flare-ups. Joan was consistent with her obsession for cleanliness. She showered several times a day, washed her hands repeatedly, and brushed her teeth every few hours, fearing germs and dirt much like the late Howard Hughes. Bette Davis said it was her understanding that Joan's children were required to wear white gloves around the house. Again, we have no clue as to when or why.

The final page of Joan's last will and testament reads as follows: "It is my intention to make no provision herein for my son Christopher and my daughter Christina for reasons which are well known to them." The document was dated six months before her death. She had stopped drinking two years before.

A year later *Mommie Dearest* became a best seller and made more than a million dollars for the disinherited Christina.

The press dug out every bit of material in their files that pertained to interviews with the actress about her children. "If anyone thinks it's easy getting up at five o'clock in the morning, working all day at the studio, and dragging yourself home late five or six days a week, they should try it," Joan said. "Frankly, I don't think actors and actresses can do justice to marriage or children. I wanted a family. I wanted to love and be loved. Maybe I tried too hard, but I wasn't the only parent who found out the hard way that Hollywood is no place to bring up children.

"Barbara Stanwyck sent her adopted son to military school when he was five years old because she didn't want him to be a Hollywood brat. He got into trouble anyway, and she refuses to discuss it. Robert Taylor wouldn't allow his stepchildren to set foot on his ranch. His stepson died of an accidental drug overdose while Bob was dying of cancer. His wife, Ursula, went through sheer hell. I could go on and on, but it's no one's business although the truth will come out. Always does. We try to convince ourselves these kids have a chance, so we protect them with the help of the studio, pay off the police, and demand respect from the press. We didn't have the time or the patience. The little time I had with my children was spent organizing our lives, and that takes discipline. Good household help was hard to find, so I had to spend what free time I had being firm."

Bette Davis attributed Joan's conduct to her drinking. "The book was actually about a child's lifelong effort to win the love of her mother, which she never did," said Bette, whose daughter, B. D. Hyman, wrote *My Mother's Keeper* ". . . to prepare the way and make straight your path." Hyman's book was a fairy tale compared with Christina's. Davis, who enjoyed her cocktails, too, comes across like Margo Channing in *All About Eve* and the reader says, "So what?" Bette followed up with *This 'n That,* ending the book with "Shut up, B. D.!"

Forty-nine-year-old Christina suffered a mild stroke after her book tour and today lives in Los Angeles. It's said around Hollywood: "It was almost as if Joan put a hex on her." Talking frankly with old-timers who knew Joan casually or very well is a repetitious task because she remains as much of a legend as Mary Pickford. Regardless of nude films, cheap films, frostbite on her movie sets, and finally a scathing indictment by her daughter, Joan Crawford remains one of the strongest links that keep Hollywood memories alive while the "tramps and tarts" come and go.

Joan's secretary for thirty-five years, Betty Barker, said Christina wrote the book for money. She saw or heard none of the incidents described in *Mommie Dearest.* She preferred not to discuss the "other side of the story," but hinted Joan had her hands full. Barker was blunt about what she claims is a book full of lies written for the money. She said nothing about revenge. Her anger stemmed from the horrid publicity and false accusations. Fairbanks said (*Interview* magazine, August 1987): "I'm not sure that what the daughter had to say was so accurate. But I didn't know Joan well at that point in her life. I do know that her secretary [Barker] doesn't remember ever seeing anything like that at all. When I knew Joan, she didn't drink—not even a sip of wine. I don't recall even seeing her in a temper. We had disagreements, but they were civilized ones."

At the Hollywood memorial for Joan, Christina was one of the last to arrive. Myrna Loy, one of Joan's oldest friends, got up and left the room. Why? (*Mommie Dearest* hadn't been written yet.)

Nine actresses turned down the part of "Mommie" for fear of offending Joan's powerful Hollywood friends. Ironically, Faye Dunaway, whom Joan admired most, played the role.

One of Joan's favorite directors (and a lover) who requests anonymity agrees with Bette Davis. "Joan was an alcoholic. She had a lifetime to drown in alcohol. She was wrong, I admit, but how can anyone possibly understand her tortured life? There was a saying around M-G-M—Shearer got the productions, Garbo supplied the art, and Joan Crawford made the money to pay for both. Joan was forever struggling. She was never satisfied with herself, and she was, therefore, never satisfied with her children. There is no one reason why she adopted them. For love and companionship in the beginning. The publicity paid off, and she ate it up, but at a time when money was tight and Hollywood didn't need Joan Crawford. She was on a pedestal, yes, like a statue of an ancient myth. If it hadn't been for her fan mail, Joan would have had nothing to look forward to.

"As for the children, they might be compared to cuddly and playful puppies. Then they grow up and aren't what you expected. The fun's over and, speaking of puppies, Joan's dogs could mess on her white rug, and she'd clean it up, pet the dog, and that was it. I worked with Joan, socialized with her, made love to her, and spent weekends with her and the children. Joan learned and worked hard. Whatever her kids were, she expected them to conform as she had. They had all the advantages she never had.

"Eventually they got in her way, and she drank more. Her only solution was to send the oldest kids away to school, but long-distance problems made it more aggravating for Joan—running back and forth, trying to make a living, and always, always, always reaching out to be liked and admired. *Through it all,* I sympathized with Joan."

One of Joan's boyfriends in 1954 was Milton Rackmil, president of Universal Studios. Although Joan eluded his marriage proposals, he offered her the lead in *Female on the Beach.* "I played the bitch whose eternal hobby is destroying men," she said. Rackmil gave her both a royal welcome at Universal and the co-star she requested, Jeff Chandler, who was described by Joan as "a very bright and handsome actor." Joan portrayed a rich widow who falls in love with a beach bum. It took ninety-seven minutes of film for her to find out he did not marry her for money. Joan was haughty as she lost her heart to a man who preferred bathing suits to tuxedos but became a member of the human race at the end.

Rackmil provided Joan with the largest dressing room on the lot, and she moved in for the duration of *Female on the Beach.* Production continued through the holidays, but she settled down with her vodka and caviar and fan mail by herself on New Year's Eve. Her friend Earl Blackwell called from Las Vegas. "Happy New Year, Joan!"

"And many more to you, darling." she cooed.

"I'm calling from a very gay and intimate party. Everyone wants to wish you well."

Later on the phone rang again.

"This is Alfred Steele, Joan. Where are you? What party?"

"I'm in my dressing room alone."

"Why?" he asked.

"I'm in the middle of a film. Besides, I'm not fond of New Year's Eve parties."

"Nobody will believe that Joan Crawford doesn't have a date tonight and is at the studio by herself."

She laughed. "My fans would adore it."

"I should be in Los Angeles on business soon. Perhaps we can get together."

"I'd like that," she said.

Joan had met Alfred Steele, president of Pepsi-Cola, four years before at a New York dinner party. He was five years older than Joan, had two children, and was in the process of divorcing his second wife. Joan liked Alfred. "He was a most attractive, rugged, and distinguished gentleman," she said. "He had salt-and-pepper hair, soft blue eyes, a sense of humor, and was well informed about everything. He was exciting."

Steele was a man of power, money, and prestige, too.

Joan thought about him that night and began 1955 knowing Steele was thinking about her, too. They had been attracted to one another from the start, but he was a married man living on the East Coast, and she was a movie actress living on the West Coast.

Crawford was preparing for *Queen Bee* at Columbia when Steele invited her to a small dinner party. She was flustered. "He said six-thirty and I wanted to say that was too early on a working day, but I was only five minutes late. I wore a white chiffon dress and white mink stole. Waiting at the door, Alfred took my hand and never let it go. He'd been around the world and I'd never flown. Alfred ignored my fears. He had to leave Los Angeles on business, but would stop in Los Angeles for twenty-four hours just to see me and then return to New York. I thought that was ridiculous. All that flying out of his way just to be with me for such a short time. Very romantic. He flew seven thousand miles and spent the day on the set of *Queen Bee*. That night he said, 'I'm going to marry you, Joan.' No proposal. That was it. I knew my answer and so did he."

After Steele returned to New York, Joan struggled through *Queen Bee* with Barry Sullivan and John Ireland. "I hated myself in that role," she admitted. "I was so happy about Alfred, it was difficult playing a woman that two men and the entire audience wanted to kill." She joked about the words used to describe her—evil, depraved, and dominating. But *Queen Bee* is one film that is identified with Joan. Christina said it was "typecast." The *New York Times* said: "When Miss Crawford is killed at the end, as she should be, it is a genuine pleasure and relief." The *New York Herald Tribune* noted: "Miss Crawford plays her role with such silky villainy that we long to see her dispatched."

*   *   *

The wedding date was set for May 24, 1955, at the New Jersey home of Sonny Werblin, then an executive at MCA, who had introduced Joan to Alfred.

"I'm planning a very special reception for you here in Hollywood," Billy Haines rejoiced.

"You're a treasure."

"And you're a naughty girl, buying a trousseau all in white."

"I feel like a bride."

"That's what you said two years ago, Cranberry. I *do* hope you won't do *that* again. I was a wreck."

She pondered. "Two years ago?"

"God! Have you forgotten?"

"Oh, that," she giggled.

"You wanted to marry Milton Rackmil, didn't you?"

"I thought it was a good idea at the time."

"And one silly spat on the way to the wedding—poof! Guests waiting in Las Vegas and . . . oh, Cranberry, I cried, but I don't think you shed a tear."

"I loved Milton and still do, but . . ."

Haines sighed. "You're like Garbo . . . running away at the last minute."

Joan looked at him coldly. "No one has the right to tell me what to do, when to do it, or how to do it, except during working hours. And no one makes a damn fool out of me then, either."

"My pet, can't you give in once in a while?"

She picked up her knitting, and the muscles in her jaws clenched. "Milton Rackmil, as head of Universal Studios, could have benefited my career enormously, but he wanted his own way. Alfred is stubborn, but I rather like it. With him, I'm not afraid of people or life. He understands my fears. My God, Billy, I thought *I* had energy, but Alfred really has it. When the rest of us are half-asleep, he's patting everyone on the back and buying another round of drinks."

"I'll have the party when you come back from your honeymoon, Cranberry. By the way, are we redecorating again?"

"No," she smiled, throwing her knitting yarn at him. "Alfred and I will be living in New York, too."

"I thought you signed with Columbia for two more pictures?"

"No problem."

"I can tell now that Alfred the Great fell in love with Joan Crawford, the Star."

"He insists I continue my career and maintain my image."

"You're right, Cranberry. Alfred is a very, very wise soul."

Five hundred guests were invited to the garden wedding scheduled for May 24. Joan planned to wear a white satin gown and coat trimmed with silver beads. Her European honeymoon wardrobe filled four custom-built trunks. Shoes, hats, and cosmetics were packed separately. (The stock value of white tissue paper probably tripled. Joan used thousands of sheets on an average trip.)

In the meantime, Alfred spent what little spare time he had in California getting acquainted with the eight-year-old twins.

On the evening of May 9, they were at Romanoff's restaurant. In the middle of dinner Steele leaned over to Joan and said, "Let's fly to Las Vegas and be married right now."

"Fly?" she gasped.

"The Pepsi Lodestar's at my disposal. I'll call Luke."

"Luke?"

"My pilot. Say yes, Joan."

"The only time I ever flew was to Catalina Island in a single-engine plane. I was as green as that asparagus . . . terrified and sick."

He laughed. "That was twenty years ago. C'mon, let's fly to Las Vegas and get married."

"But I have to go home and pack!"

"We're going straight to the airport before you change your mind."

On the smooth flight to Las Vegas, Alfred held Joan in his arms and described the mountains and clouds and landmarks. Shortly after 2:00 A.M. on May 10, they were married by a municipal judge in the penthouse suite at the Flamingo Hotel.

Christina Crawford heard the news on the radio. "Alfred who?" she asked her brother.

On May 26, the Steeles sailed on the SS *United States* from New York to Europe. The other passengers were thrilled to see her. She maintained dignity and privacy but could not refuse giving autographs or chatting with her admirers. Passengers in nearby staterooms were taken aback by the bitter fights between the newlyweds, which were nightly occurrences. Physical battles were evident—a slap and a thud, a glass broken, or an object smashed against a wall. One voyager said, "I figured the marriage was over or get ready for a funeral. They really went at it. I found it frightening."

Joan referred to the sailing as a royal battle. She said Alfred wanted her to know right from the start who was boss. When she made a suggestion, he had something else on his mind and that was it. Alfred had cleverly waited until they were on the high seas before showing her what he expected from the current Mrs. Steele, and she wondered if his first two wives had been put through the same indoctrination.

They stayed at the Hôtel Place Athénée in Paris. Alfred's daughter, Sally, touring Europe with college friends, stopped by to meet her new stepmother. It was a "blasted intrusion" as far as Joan was concerned. She was annoyed by Steele's monopolizing their trip and was in no mood "to have a kid hanging around." Joan was drinking, of course, and found the silly juvenile chatter an utter bore. Sally described her tour and told her elegantly dressed stepmother, "The Mètro is great fun. You should try it sometime."

Joan turned to Sally with a blasé expression and piped, "Listen, kid, you live your life and I'll live mine" (Bob Thomas, *Joan Crawford*, Bantam, 1978).

Joan had been courted and wooed with tenderness and adoration. Then the impulsive elopement and his beautifully satisfying lovemaking—all too good to be true. What Joan hoped would be a romantic honeymoon turned into one of Alfred's business trips for Pepsi. Three for dinner ended up to be forty-five. She had married a man who was as dedicated to his job as she was to hers. Wherever he went, Steele felt obligated to entertain business associates and clients. He reminded his publicity-minded wife she was no different. But the fights continued. "I'm not in the mood to entertain a mob on my honeymoon!" she yelled. "You'll do it!" he shouted.

Joan said they laughed about it later, but at the time it was a bloody war. "It was his will against mine, and when two strong-willed people collide, it's hell."

After the honeymoon, Alfred returned to his New York apartment at 36 Sutton Place and Joan went on to Hollywood to do *Autumn Leaves* with Cliff Robertson, who had had only a small part in *Picnic*. Joan played the part of a spinster who falls in love with a young psychotic. Robert Aldrich was the director. He became annoyed at the long drawn-out lighting procedures Joan demanded. Despite their disagreements, the two became very close friends before production ended, and Aldrich would play an important part later in Joan's life when she needed help. Joan said *Autumn Leaves* was one of her favorites. She raved sincerely about Robertson and kept in touch with him until her death.

Motion Picture Herald wrote: "Miss Crawford brings to her latest role all the acting resources she has cultivated so successfully in 31 years of picture making." The *New York Herald Tribune* agreed: "Miss Crawford is as attractive as ever and she brings the whole spectrum of emotions to her role."

Alfred Steele said, "You get your goddamn ass home when you finish work!"

"I prefer living at the studio," Joan countered. "You knew that before you married me, darling. Remember New Year's Eve? You were having a wonderful time at a party, and I was all alone in my dressing room."

"You're married now."

"That has nothing to do with my career. How I go about it is my business!"

Was there a struggle, or did Alfred just haul off and hit her? No matter. She went home that night and called in sick the next day. Makeup could not conceal the bruise on her face.

Meanwhile Christina finally reached her mother. Joan asked why it took so long for her daughter to congratulate her. "The instant I heard her voice," Christina said in *Mommie Dearest*, "I could have strangled her. She was arrogant, pompous, condescending, and every inch the consummate bitch!" Joan said calmly, "All you had to do was call Las Vegas. The whole world knows where *I* am. Obviously you didn't try very hard."

Billy Haines kept his promise and had an elegant party for the Steeles at Romanoff's. Alfred had urgent business in New York and could not attend. Reporters asked about the "discontented" rumors. Joan smiled. "I've never been happier. My husband is a very busy man."

But she told Billy in confidence that Alfred was furious. "I thought he understood the pressure I'm under these days."

They discussed Franchot's problems, too. Joan had stuck by him when his name appeared in some very unpleasant headlines over a romance with starlet Barbara Payton in 1951. Franchot had been beaten senseless by ex-boxer Tom Neal, who claimed Payton was engaged to both of them. Extensive plastic surgery was required on Franchot's face, but gallantly he married Barbara. They were divorced a year later. Joan said she was happy he was appearing on the stage occasionally. "He always calls to tell me if he's on television, doing a film or play," she said.

Clark Gable was happily married to Kay Spreckles. "I think this marriage will last," Joan sighed.

"Did Kay's ex-husband really beat her with a high-heeled shoe?" Billy asked.

"It's in the divorce testimony, but he settled millions on her. That's a hell of a lot more than I ever got!"

"Cheer up, Cranberry. Alfred's buying you a new apartment in Manhattan, and I'm going to decorate it. What more could you want?"

"Always a classic film, Billy . . . always a juicy role."

Alfred paid Joan's past-due bills and offered to take her and the four children to Switzerland for Christmas. Christina and Christopher hadn't seen their mother in a year and a half. "Daddy" wasn't exactly what they expected. Steele was overweight, slightly hard of hearing, and wore glasses. He wasn't the "Uncle" type at all, but the children liked him right away. Joan told them he had played football at Northwestern University and that he had graduated in 1923.

"He tried advertising before being hired as vice president for marketing at Coca-Cola. When he found out Pepsi was going out of business, Steele asked his best friend, D. Mitchell Cox, 'Do you think we could run Pepsi?' They gambled. First they reduced the sugar content to save money and emphasized fewer calories. They modernized the containers and went on a personal selling campaign. Pepsi sales tripled. Alfred's brilliant. He's genuine, kind, and generous. This will be a wonderful chance to get acquainted and to have a good time. You children are very fortunate to be vacationing in Europe. When I was your age I was working in a laundry seven days a week!"

Until now Joan had neglected her daughter's wardrobe, but on the train trip and in New York, Christina was treated like a queen. She was too shocked to question the drastic change.

Alfred was anxious for publicity and arranged photo sessions and press conferences. They were for Joan's benefit, too. The Steele family's every move was covered by reporters. They sailed on the *Queen Mary*, and then took a luxury overnight train from Paris to the Palace Hotel in St. Moritz.

The children skied and skated. They saw very little of Joan, who strayed from the hotel only to pose for pictures in her winter sport wardrobe. Alfred was low-key and tried to be attentive to the children without excluding his bored wife. Their family dinners were strained and quiet. Only the twins were immune to the red-haired volcano whose flasks of vodka were covered with material to match all her outfits.

Behind closed doors, Joan and Alfred fought bitterly. She blamed their fights on the altitude. "We were tired," she said, but their physical brawls were the talk of the hotel. Joan told friends in later years that the torrid arguments often came to an abrupt end with a stinging slap across her face that rattled her brain.

Christina related another incident that happened on the voyage home aboard the *Andrea Doria*, although few people who knew Joan believe it. After dinner one evening, mother and daughter gave each other a good-night kiss. As Christina was leaving, Alfred entered the stateroom, and she kissed him on the cheek. Joan grabbed Christina and slapped her repeatedly. "I got my man, now you damn well go out and get your own!" Joan shoved her to the door. Christina claims that after this experience Joan never allowed her husband and her oldest daughter to be alone together. But after the other children had been sent home, Christina remained in New York with Mommie and Daddy and accompanied them to nightclubs, to the theater, to dinner parties, and to magazine interviews. Christina admitted Joan bought her more clothes. "If I'd gone to a party every night for a month, I couldn't have used them all," she said.

Joan filmed *The Story of Esther Costello* in London. She was delighted with her co-star Rossano Brazzi and relieved to have David Miller as producer and director. Joan arrived with her husband and thirty-seven pieces of luggage. This was the first movie she made abroad. The *London Daily Mail* referred to Joan as durable and amazing. "She arrived in the almost forgotten manner of the great stars. She brought 28 suitcases, 48 film costumes, one trunk of furs, and a millionaire husband."

Joan Crawford was also presented to Queen Elizabeth and the Royal Family. "They are more beautiful than their pictures," she said.

Alfred attended to business matters in Spain, Italy, and other European countries while Joan worked. She said it was the last fine film offered to her. "I played a wealthy American woman who takes a deaf and blind girl out of Irish squalor and launches a fund drive for help only to find her efforts thwarted by the Italian philanderer she married. Heather Sears, a very talented English actress, played the girl. She was eager to learn, and I made every effort to help her."

Joan told Alfred *The Story of Esther Costello* might be a new beginning for her. "Everything was perfect," she explained. "The cast, the story, and the pace. I feel like a million."

Joan said this film was the last of her top pictures. "In fact," she announced, "I deserved an Oscar for it."

The *New York Times* wrote: "It must be said here that Miss Crawford, whose role repeatedly shifts from stage center, is tackling her most becoming assignment in several seasons. Miss Crawford, Mr. Brazzi, Mr. Patterson, and all the minor players are professional throughout."

The *New York Herald Tribune* said it wouldn't be a Joan Crawford picture without plenty of anguish. "And her fans will have their usual good time smiling through their tears. The plot enables Miss Crawford to run a full-course dinner of dramatic moods, from loneliness to mother love, from pride to passion with her husband and finally to smoldering rage. This may not be your kind of movie, but it is many women's kind of movie and our Joan is queen of the art form."

Unfortunately it would be three years before Joan would make another film. She could have accepted a good role, but she sent back all scripts. This gave her time to plan and decorate a new penthouse apartment in New York and to travel with Alfred. The bitterness and disagreements dissipated as Joan became more involved in her husband's business. Although it terrified her to make personal appearances as an actress, she was at ease sitting next to Steele on the dais. He was proud of Joan Crawford's presence, of course, and told her the crowds were gathering to catch a glimpse of a great movie star. Alfred Steele did not walk several paces behind her, however. As the months passed, and Joan became acquainted with the president of Pepsi-Cola, her love and respect for him grew stronger. She liked the idea of being a business-woman and began to sit in on Alfred's board meetings. He was surprised that she actually understood many of the intricate matters discussed at the conferences.

It was Alfred who flew to the United States when Christopher ran away again. Joan was busy filming *The Story of Esther Costello*. Alfred agreed that the boy needed special attention and psychiatric care. "I can't handle him any longer," Joan said wearily. "I've done all I can."

Alfred told his wife, "I thought you were hard on him at times, but now I believe you weren't strict enough."

Joan was venturing into a new world with almost as much enthusiasm as she had had as an M-G-M newcomer. Within less than two years she'd flown more than one hundred thousand miles to sell Pepsi-Cola in Europe, the Middle East, Central America, and Asia. Thousands turned out to meet their plane in Mozambique, East Africa. "Well, look at that," Joan exclaimed. "You'd think they'd never seen an airplane."

Alfred smiled. "That's not the reason. They came to see a movie star."

She laughed. "Always teasing." But when she appeared in the open doorway, the crowd of natives chanted, "Joan Crawford! Joan Crawford! Joan Crawford!"

She looked at Alfred with tears in her eyes.

Her appearances at business meetings and conferences had an influence on the wives of Pepsi's executives. If Mrs. Steele attended, maybe they should show an interest, too.

Joan referred to Pepsi-Cola as "our child." She became concerned about profits and marketing. It was unforgivable to miss an opening of a new plant. Heads of state invited the Pepsi entourage to formal dinners because Joan's presence lent prestige to all occasions. Had she given up her career? "No," she replied. "It has been years since I've been able to travel, and with my husband it's a delight. The twins are away at school. Christina's in college and there's less and less to do at home. Alfred and I are refurbishing a penthouse apartment in New York. It should be ready for us to move in very soon."

When asked about her home in Los Angeles, she replied, "I have auctioned my antiques and other items of value. It's difficult selling the house on Bristol Avenue after living there for so many years, but I'm thinking very seriously of doing it in the near future."

Billy Haines flew to New York and into an interior decorator's dream—two apartments on two floors converted into one, eighteen rooms transformed into eight, at Two East Seventieth Street, an exclusive address just off Fifth Avenue.

Alfred was shocked to learn that Pepsi had merely loaned him the $400,000 construction costs. Joan was livid. "We intended to use the apartment for visiting clients. That was the whole idea." Pepsi pointed out that the Steeles were out of town more days than they were in New York and indicated they had no intention of paying his expenses at home and away from home at the same time. Alfred didn't smile at the 6 percent interest Pepsi charged him on the "loan."

Anna Bell LeSueur Cassin died in 1958 after a series of strokes. Joan attended her mother's funeral and wept regardless of her distant relationship with Anna over the years. Was Joan crying over what might have been? She talked very little about Anna and bluntly said she had no guilt. "I took care of her financially to the end," she exclaimed.

Hal was working as a clerk at the Parkway Motel when he died of syphilis in 1963. He was buried at Forest Lawn, but Joan was not on hand to bid farewell to her brother.

Their deaths represented the end of Billie Cassin, but Joan's family had not dragged her down with them. When Gable called to console her over Anna's death, he said, "My father followed me to Hollywood and never changed his mind about actors being sissies. I built him a house and supported him and his third wife, and he called me a sissy."

With few ties left in Hollywood and few good roles available for older women, Joan concentrated on her new apartment. The tour of the penthouse was enthralling. Overlooking Central Park, it had a free-flying staircase, skylight, raised fireplaces in the drawing room and bedroom, a working fountain in the two-level bedroom, tall ceilings, a double-decker dressing room, highly polished (and slippery) floors, and white carpeting. Her closets were models of elegance and organization: Each dress was categorized and labeled. Nolan Miller, one of Joan's costume designers, said people thought Crawford was difficult, ". . . but it's more that she was definite. She cursed me only once because I hadn't packed enough tissue paper with her new dresses, and they arrived a bit wrinkled."

Joan was at her peak of happiness now. "I never dreamed when I danced my way into pictures that one day I'd be a lady executive. As a director of a large corporation, I'm having as much fun now as I ever had in those crazy Black Bottom and Charleston days when Scott Fitzgerald called me 'the best example of the flapper.'

"Alfred and I have separate dressing rooms but share one bed. Once a man is convinced that his creature comforts—and his sex life—are going to be taken care of, he'll start thinking happily. He'll be proud of you and you'll come alive!

"It was a very rough start for Alfred and me, but my years with him have been the best—the happiest of my life. He's been the strong one, and I learned to lean as well as comfort and protect. We share a common bond and I work as hard to promote Pepsi as I did on any picture."

Alfred was chairman of the board now and determined to "beat the shit" out of Coke. Before taking Joan on their eight-week tour of the country, the most strenuous of his career, they flew to Half Moon Bay in Jamaica for a rest. "It's heaven to find love and be loved," Joan said. "We were content with only each other, the breeze, the turquoise water, and holding hands. There are things you learn in a good marriage. I learned that you don't use sex. You give it."

She often told the story of her coming out of the ocean with dripping hair and no makeup. Alfred watched her walking toward him, took her in his arms, and whispered, "This is how I like you best."

The tour was a seven-day-a-week project. Joan's energy and well-organized thought patterns helped Alfred get through the long, grueling days and nights. She took his place whenever possible, but he was expected to give the "pep" speeches—"Give 'em hell until Pepsi's number one!" They wound up the tour in Washington, D.C. Alfred was exhausted. "I don't know what to say tomorrow, darling," he said. "I'm so tired."

"Go to bed," she urged. "I'll go over your speech, make notes, and list the important people you'll be expected to know. Also, I've made up my mind that from now on we'll go on the road for a month and take off a week."

"Maybe you're right," he sighed.

In the morning he was up early and appeared rested, but Joan saw him slowing down before lunch. They had a snack together before presenting the Multiple Sclerosis Society Citation to Senator John F. Kennedy. Alfred gave a speech that concluded with ". . . and I want to thank you, my darling wife, for your untiring dedication to me as a man and to Pepsi. You've helped me so. Everyone who's ever met you knows how much."

Joan wept.

Joan and Alfred returned to the penthouse and looked forward to relaxing in Jamaica again before the board and stockholders of Pepsi awarded Steele a lifetime contract and an option on 75,000 shares of stock.

Joan prepared a simple dinner on their first night home and insisted they retire early. Alfred suggested a game of gin rummy and fell asleep holding the cards in his hand. She put him to bed. The next morning she found him on the floor, covered him with blankets, called the doctor, and assured Alfred he would be all right. The doctor told Joan her husband had died instantly of a heart attack. Pepsi executives rushed to the penthouse; Joan called the twins, who came to New York on the first plane.

Two days after Steele's death in April 1959, Joan was elected by stockholders of the corporation to the board of Pepsi-Cola—"a calculated business deal."

Stunned and downhearted over Alfred's sudden death, Joan was consoled by the twins, who refused to leave her side during the sedate funeral and burial. Christina was living and working in England when she heard the news; she phoned her mother but did not return for the funeral. Joan kept her head high and her eyes focused straight ahead. Her only consolation was knowing Alfred did not suffer or cry out her name for help. She knew, also, that one of her marriages was successful and they had loved each other to the end. His needing her meant the world to Joan.

Being elected to the board of Pepsi-Cola was not only an honor but also a source of steady income. Incredible as it may sound, Steele was broke when he died. His estate was valued at around $600,000, but after taxes and debts Joan was left with nothing. She had loaned him $100,000 without a note shortly before his death. They had essentially "wiped out" each other.

*   *   *

Whether Joan's old friend Jerry Wald called her from Hollywood or she called him, Joan accepted a small role in *The Best of Everything*. Louella Parsons considered this good therapy until she heard the Bristol Avenue house was up for sale, too. Joan was candid with Parsons. "I'm flat broke," she confessed. "Alfred expected to be reimbursed for the half-million dollars we spent on our apartment."

"Does that mean you're resuming your career?" Louella asked.

"I'm obligated to Pepsi, of course, and they're paying me a yearly income, but paying off our debts will take a long time. The Brentwood house is too big, and I can't afford to keep it up." (Donald O'Connor became the new owner.)

Louella Parsons published her scoop: "Joan Crawford Flat Broke."

Joan wasn't proud of the story, but the publicity could only benefit her career. Pepsi executives, however, were appalled. Why did she tell the world that the chairman of the board of Pepsi was broke? Their stock could be seriously affected. Would she reissue another statement?

Joan met with the press and hoped to straighten out the misunderstanding. "I will receive an annual salary from Pepsi," she stated, "but as spokeswoman for the company, I will have enough time to make films also. When I'm offered roles that best suit my talents, I'll work in Hollywood. My penthouse apartment in New York is my official residence."

Louella Parsons was furious. "I have known Joan Crawford for more than thirty-five years. I still don't know her at all. She is the only star I know who manufactured herself. She drew up a blueprint for herself and outlined a beautiful package of skin, bones, and character and then set about to put life into the outline. She succeeded, and so Joan Crawford came into existence at the same time an overweight Charleston dancer, born Lucille LeSueur, disappeared from the world. It took me a long time to realize this. I believed, for some reason, that Lucille existed under the skin."

A source very close to Crawford remarked, "Joan hit the jackpot with Alfred Steele. He was only fifty-eight when he died. They were building the perfect life together. She wasn't as wrapped up in the star image, though it was used to very good advantage. Joan became a keen businesswoman and knew the facets of Pepsi and habits and quirks of those in power. But to obtain the ultimate dream and then find yourself back where you started—broke and desperate and alone—wasn't easy for Joan. She forged ahead and worked harder than ever before."

The Best of Everything was a film about young people struggling for power in the publishing business. Brian Aherne was the only player in Joan's age group. Hope Lange, Stephen Boyd, Suzy Parker, Martha Hyer, Diane Baker, and Robert Evans formed a very impressive youthful cast. (Joan Crawford got separate billing.) The picture was done in soft color and the theme song, "The Best of Everything," had a mellow flavor. Critics handed the film to Joan even though her best scenes were cut out. She said, "I had a small, but very strong part and made the most of it. God knows, I was more experienced than the others and, by God, I took advantage of it!" When she was on-screen all eyes were on her. The *New York Herald Tribune* ended its review as follows: "Miss Crawford comes near making the rest of the picture look like a distraction."

10

NO REGRETS

Christina settled in New York and pursued an acting career. Christopher moved in with her before going to Vietnam.

Joan opened almost thirty bottling plants a year and represented Pepsi around the world—a Heart Ball in Charlotte, North Carolina, the United Jewish Appeal in Las Vegas, as grand marshal and judge of the Miss America contest in Atlantic City, the Strategic Air Command in Omaha, Nebraska, to name a few. Her trips, like everything else in her life, were very well organized and Pepsi's publicity team was told to check her list very carefully. The following items were to be in her suite of rooms before her arrival:

Cracked ice in several buckets
Lunch and dinner menus
Paper, pens, and pencils
Professional hair dryer
Steam iron and board
Carton of Alpine cigarettes
One bowl of peppermint Life Savers
Red and yellow roses
Case of Pepsi-Cola, soda, and ginger ale

There was to be a maid waiting for Miss Crawford, and she was not to leave until dismissed by Miss Crawford. Also, the following supply of liquor was to be in the suite of rooms before her arrival:

One fifth Old Forester bourbon
One fifth Beefeater gin
Two fifths 100-proof Smirnoff vodka
One fifth Chivas Regal Scotch
Two bottles Moet & Chandon champagne (Dom Perignon)

Miss Crawford was to be met at the airport in an air-conditioned limousine with a nonsmoking chauffeur who must not exceed forty miles an hour. Miss Crawford's plane was to be met with a closed van for her luggage. A careful and accurate inventory of luggage was to be taken. Estimated pieces were fifteen.

The same instructions were given to those in charge of her accommodations when she was making a film, with the following added note:

> Miss Crawford is a star in every sense of the word, and everyone knows she is a star. As a partner in this film, Miss Crawford will not appreciate your throwing away money on empty gestures. You do not have to make empty gestures to prove to Miss Crawford or anyone else that she is a star of the first magnitude.

Clark Gable died of a heart attack on November 16, 1960. Joan was stunned and speechless. He had called her during production of *The Misfits* a few months earlier. The title, he told her, described the cast. His death was attributed to the stunts he did in the desert heat while waiting for Marilyn Monroe to arrive for work. Joan told a friend in strict confidence that when Clark collapsed trying to change a tire on the jeep near his ranch, his wife should have rushed him to the hospital. "She claimed he refused to go," Joan said, "but I got it from a reliable source—someone who was there—that she didn't realize Clark's serious condition. My source found him gasping for breath and called an ambulance. Burns my ass because people like to gossip about my drinking. They should know the truth! Maybe I use a flask, but I'm not a closet drinker."

Robert Aldrich, who had directed Joan in *Autumn Leaves*, wanted her to co-star with Bette Davis in *What Ever Happened to Baby Jane?*, a story about two sisters, former child actresses, living together in Hollywood in their late middle age. Joan was eager to do it, but Bette wanted a heart-to-heart talk with Aldrich before committing herself. "Have you slept with Miss Crawford?" she asked.

Aldrich hesitated. "No," he replied, "not that I didn't have the chance."

"Good!" Bette said. "Second question. I play Jane. Correct?"

"Correct."

"We discussed money but let's confirm it once more. Joan's getting forty thousand dollars and ten percent of the net profits. Correct?"

"Correct."

"I'm getting sixty thousand dollars up front and five percent of the take. Correct?"

"Correct."

The announcement was made and Seven Arts, in conjunction with Warner Brothers, prepared for the return of the two former queens who were, at last, working together. Hollywood came alive. With these two brassy, tough dames in town, nothing else was worth writing or talking about—they were the focus of all attention.

"I understand Joan asked for Davis," a producer gabbed.

A director smiled coyly. "Don't tell Bette."

"I love them both—from a distance."

"Is there any truth about Joan's crush on Davis?"

"All I know is Crawford requested the dressing room next to Bette's and sent her gifts, flowers, notes. . . ."

"Davis won't discuss it," the director said.

"Only with friends. I've known Joan a long time, and she told me once she crushed a kitten to death because she loved it so much. Maybe she swings both ways, but since she can't dominate Davis on the screen, she'll try to do it in bed. She tried to conquer Garbo. I'm not so sure Joan's a lesbian, but I'm positive she needs loving and touching and attention and applause . . . from a man or a woman."

"The fireworks are already starting," the director said. "One columnist referred to them as those 'two fifty-four-year-old stars' and Davis flipped!"

"Why?"

"Because Crawford is fifty-eight!"

"And Davis?" the producer asked.

"Fifty-four, but what's the difference? Joan got the break, don't you see?"

"Well, it should be a grand experience. Both dames are bringing their children for protection."

Production of *What Ever Happened to Baby Jane?* began. At the end of the first day, Bette was convinced Aldrich was in love with Joan, and Joan was certain Aldrich adored Davis. Both women called him every night until he didn't bother getting undressed.

Bette's daughter, B. D. (B. D. Hyman, *My Mother's Keeper*, Morrow, 1985), said when she was introduced to Joan she pulled back as if she were afraid of getting diseased. "Hello, dear," Joan said. "One thing . . . my daughters Cindy and Cathy are going to be on the set a great deal. See them over there on the bench? I would appreciate it if you would not try to talk to them. They have been very carefully brought up and shielded from the wicked side of the world. You, obviously, have not. I don't want your influence to corrupt them. They are so sweet and innocent. You see? I know you will do as I wish. Thank you. Bless you, dear."

Joan brought along her large Pepsi cooler and always had a glass nearby—half-filled with vodka. It was no secret, and Davis was furious. She told B. D., "Christ! You never know what size boobs that broad has strapped on! She must have a different set for every day of the week. I keep running into them like the Hollywood Hills! She's supposed to be shriveling away while Baby Jane starves her to death, but her tits keep growing. Jesus!"

When the picture was finished, Bette referred to Joan and herself as "we two old broads." Joan sent Bette a note on her traditional blue stationery: "Dear Miss Davis. Please do not continue to refer to me as an old broad. Sincerely, Joan Crawford."

What Ever Happened to Baby Jane? grossed $9 million and Davis was nominated for an Oscar. Joan was livid. She had sought revenge in the past, but, to quote Al Jolson, "You ain't seen nothing yet!" Joan campaigned openly in

New York, contacting all the Oscar nominees who were in plays in New York that year. She offered to accept their Oscars if they won and were unable to attend the ceremony. She also contacted all other members, requesting that they vote for one of the nominees appearing on Broadway. Joan's attempts to prevent Bette from winning an Oscar meant lost profits for *What Ever Happened to Baby Jane?* Davis, nonetheless, thought she deserved the Academy Award.

Both women were backstage at the Santa Monica Civil Auditorium when Anne Bancroft's name was announced for her performance in *The Miracle Worker*. As Joan headed for the stage to claim the Oscar, she elbowed Bette aside. "Excuse me!" Anne Bancroft, who could not be present, had accepted Joan's offer to accept for her.

The battle still raged. Both women agreed to promote the picture at carefully selected theaters. Joan claimed Bette was given first choice and "I'm left with the dumps." Bette shrugged and agreed to make the tour by herself. Joan changed her mind too late and fumed.

Although *What Ever Happened to Baby Jane?* put Joan back on her feet financially, she preferred not to admit it. "I needed the money," she said. "Then the studio tried to invent a feud between Bette and me. Half-true. She called me a movie star and referred to herself as an actress. Tough to swallow. I gave Bette the best scenes and allowed her top billing."

The crew enjoyed the contrast off camera—Davis wearing her floppy slippers and old stained robe, and Joan arriving and departing as if she were going for lunch at the White House.

Joan penned *A Portrait of Joan* in 1962. It was a "not tell all" autobiography, and her friends wondered why she wrote it. "For the money," she replied. Billy Haines said it was "an absolute bore" and ten years later she reluctantly agreed. "I told the truth but left most of it out," she told him. Joan spent many long hours signing books and advertising her beloved Pepsi, with a cooler nearby or a glass of "water" within reach. If anyone offered to refill it, she would smile and say, "How kind of you, but I think it's time to stretch my legs. I'll get it myself. Bless you." She drank only 100-proof vodka and trusted no one, particularly bartenders. More than once she made a scene if she ran out of her own supply and was forced to order a drink. She was known to wash utensils in restaurants to make sure they were thoroughly clean. In every hotel she scrubbed the bathrooms on her hands and knees. She traveled with her own cleaning supplies.

Joan rarely shook hands without wearing gloves.

Robert Aldrich was so proud of his achievement with *What Ever Happened to Baby Jane?,* he traded his sanity for money and approached the "two old broads" about *Hush, Hush, Sweet Charlotte.* Twentieth Century Fox agreed to do the film. Joan and Bette accepted $200,000 each. The script cast Bette as a suspected former murderess driven to the point of madness by her relentless relatives (played by Joan and Joseph Cotten).

The cast settled down at the Belmont Motel in Baton Rouge, Louisiana. Instead of traveling on the chartered flight with the others, Joan arrived with twenty-five pieces of luggage and had to wait for her rooms to be properly set up as dictated. She complained to Bette, who slammed the door in her face and called Aldrich. "I refuse to do one scene with her!"

"That's impossible!" he bellowed.

"Use doubles—do anything. I won't work with her!"

Aldrich stood his ground and tension mounted. When the cast and crew returned to the Fox studios, Joan and Bette were not speaking except on camera. Everyone was on edge, but Bette had an attitude of absolute confidence. She was on time and quick with her lines. Joan had a hard time pulling herself together and was a few minutes late. She was a nervous wreck and losing control. During one rehearsal, Bette put her hands on her hips, spread her legs apart, and cussed, "Jesus, is that the way she's going to play it?" When Aldrich did not intercede, Joan knew Bette had won. Who better than Joan understood the importance of having the director on her side?

Under stress, Joan became ill (just as she had when she won the Academy Award in 1945) and was admitted to Cedars of Lebanon Hospital with a high fever, low blood count, and cough. Her doctor announced she had an "upper respiratory virus infection." Joan returned to work for a few days and had a relapse.

The insurance company absorbed part of the loss but warned Aldrich he would either have to replace Joan or cancel the film. Bette wanted her dear friend Olivia De Havilland to replace Joan, but Olivia wasn't interested in the part and didn't relish the idea of being the actress to replace Joan Crawford. Aldrich went to Switzerland and convinced Olivia to fly back and take over.

Joan, meanwhile, waited for Aldrich or Bette to urge her out of bed and beg her to come back. As she luxuriated in flowers and get-well cards, Joan received a call from a reporter. "What's your opinion about Olivia De Havilland replacing you in *Hush, Hush, Sweet Charlotte*, Miss Crawford?"

"What?" Joan exclaimed.

"You'll read about it in all the newspapers. I understand production has started again."

Joan slammed down the receiver and threw a vase of flowers at the nurse.

The following day she had a press conference. "I cried for nine hours," she wept. "There should be some loyalty in this business. I'm going to make a lot of pictures, but I'm going to make them with decent, gentle people. I'm glad for Olivia. She needs a good picture!"

Bette was quick to respond. "The widow Steele has had her say, now I'll have mine. I regret her 'reported' illness but am very eager to work with Olivia." She embraced Miss De Havilland at the airport. Bette was radiant and happy—the knife couldn't go any deeper into Joan's back. As for Joan's health? No one asked.

Bette got a belly laugh watching Joan's trunks being packed. "Jesus," she screeched. "I've never seen so many damn hair pieces in my life!"

Bette came out the winner on all counts but one—her decision to take only 5 percent of the *Baby Jane* film. She cursed Joan for her 10-percent decision because the picture was grossing millions.

Joan said, "Bette likes to rant and rave. I just sit and knit. She yelled and I knitted a scarf from Hollywood to Malibu."

Joan appeared on television shows during this stage of her career—"GE Theater," "Zane Grey Theater," "Route 66," "The Man from U.N.C.L.E.," and "The Virginian." After the *Hush, Hush, Sweet Charlotte* catastrophe, she filmed *The Caretakers*, produced and directed by her "friend" Hall Bartlett. The picture dealt with mental illness. Joan played the role of a head nurse at odds with a crusading doctor (played by Robert Stack). *Variety* said, "Miss Crawford doesn't so much play her handful of scenes as she dresses for them, looking as if she were en route to a Pepsi board meeting." The *New York Times* considered *The Caretakers* shallow, showy, and cheap. "The only thing missing is a slinky exit by Miss Crawford, twirling her chiffon and muttering 'Curses!' "

Joan no longer cared about reviews. She did her best and was glad to get the money. Her social life varied. Mary Pickford invited her former "daughter-in-law" for lunch at Pickfair. Holding Hall Bartlett's arm with one hand and her 100-proof Smirnoff in the other, Joan entered the hallowed halls that had once closed in on her. The other guests present were from a Hollywood society that was almost forgotten. Joan looked at the living room where she had sat alone every Sunday afternoon with her knitting. She smiled at the staircase that brought back memories of a torn dress and a very gallant Douglas Fairbanks, Sr., scooping up the shreds without missing a step. "I was so enthralled in the past I didn't see Mary. Suddenly there she was—seventy years old and glistening in diamonds. She opened her arms to me and smiled. 'Joan, darling, welcome to Pickfair.' "

For $50,000 and a percentage of the profits, Joan played an ax murderess in William Castle's *Strait Jacket* (1964). The *New York Herald Tribune* said it was time to get Joan Crawford out of the housedresses and horror B-films and back into haute couture because ". . . Miss Crawford, you see, is high class." The review was interesting but far more intriguing was a telephone call Joan received from Franchot Tone while she was filming *Strait Jacket*.

"You're my darling," he said.

"And you'll always be mine."

"I miss you. Can we be together?"

"Perhaps when I finish this film."

"Will you marry me, Joan?"

Franchot was so terribly hurt by the silence that he hung up very, very quietly.

William Castle gave Joan top billing in *I Saw What You Did*, another suspense terror thriller. Critics liked this movie and thought Joan was still a handsome figure of a woman. John Ireland, who played the murderer, was lauded too. Joan said, "There was a rumor that Castle couldn't afford me because I was killed off near the beginning. That was part of the plot. Mr. Castle is a genius. He starred Stanwyck and Taylor in *The Night Walker* fifteen years after their divorce. She carried the whole damn film. Taylor popped in and out, you know, as her soft-spoken lawyer. Anyway, he turns out to be the killer. Maybe Castle's films weren't highly publicized, but they drew the crowds and they were fun to do."

It's been said if Joan had had better guidance in the mid-sixties, she might have found at least one good solid role, but she needed the money, not the Oscar nominations. She was still paying off Alfred's debts, maintaining the luxurious penthouse apartment, and paying tuition for Cindy and Cathy.

Christina had gotten the lead in the Chicago Company's production of *Barefoot in the Park* and was planning to marry the director, Harvey Medlinsky. While visiting his family in New York, she ventured a call to her mother.

"Bring your fiancé over for cocktails this evening," Joan exclaimed. "I'm very anxious to meet him." She was so impressed, in fact, that any thought of a quick marriage at City Hall was out of the question. Joan planned a lovely wedding at "21" on May 20, 1966. When Christina returned from her honeymoon, she saw her mother several times a week. Christopher was divorced and in Vietnam. Joan did not discuss him, although she asked if Christina knew exactly where he was. In other words, "Was he alive or dead?" That's all she cared to know.

Christina chose her words very carefully. She was smart enough to know that as a young actress even a daughter could be competition for Joan Crawford. When Christina realized her marriage was a mistake, Joan arranged a Mexican divorce calmly with no lectures. If Joan harped on any subject it was money. "The house in Brentwood was mortgaged," she explained, "and I borrowed on all my insurance policies. It will take me ten years to be in the black again." She failed to mention the $50,000 yearly salary from Pepsi and to confuse matters she added, "If it hadn't been for *Baby Jane* I'd be broke."

Christina did not question anything her mother said or did. To have such a close and warm social and personal relationship at last was worth the silence and conflicting stories. Nor did Christina tell her mother how often she found Joan passed out on the floor from too much liquor. The maid said this happened often, and it was a miracle Joan didn't suffer more than bruises.

*   *   *

Joan accepted another horror movie, *Berserk,* produced by Herman Cohen, a young producer who worked primarily in England. Joan was anxious for a change of scenery and was welcomed by the British press as "Her Serene Crawfordship."

Joan played the owner and ringmaster of a traveling English circus plagued with a series of mysterious murders. *Berserk* was a cheap picture, but Joan gave it style. With Ty Hardin, Diana Dors, and Judy Geeson as supporting players, *Berserk* (also known as *Circus of Blood*) packed theaters with moviegoers of all ages. For those who'd never heard of Joan Crawford, she looked barely forty years old.

Ramen Guy styled her hair with tape-lifts that pulled her facial skin back and up, eliminating wrinkles and sagging.

Herman Cohen knew how to handle his leading lady. He invited her for cocktails, or to the theater, and was attentive, encouraging, and patient. Cohen did not say whether Joan tried to seduce him, but she was very possessive and wanted him at her beck and call. When Joan was not able to reach him, she asked a million questions. He told her to "knock it off." She displayed her remarkable figure to him in the seclusion of her dressing room. She winked. "Not bad, huh?" Cohen was surprised and very impressed with Joan's body, but tactfully asked her to "lay off the vodka during working hours."

"Let's put it another way," she said. "Not unless I get your permission."

Berserk astounded the critics. The *New York Times* raved: "Miss Crawford is professional as usual and certainly the shapeliest ringmaster ever to handle a ring microphone." *Hollywood Screen Parade* agreed: "Crawford's figure is as trim as ever, her voice as warm and compelling, her legs rival Dietrich's, and her tigress' personality puts to shame most of the newest kittens who call themselves 1968-style screen actresses. She is all over the picture, radiant, forceful, authoritative, a genuine movie star whose appeal never diminishes." *Greater Amusements* likewise applauded her: "As always Miss Crawford is every inch the glamorous star, this time arrayed in leotard and red spangled jacket, and she consistently rises above the highly melodramatic yet exploitable story material."

Not wanting to wear the tape-lifts again, Joan had cosmetic surgery. She had had the wrinkles removed from around her eyes before, a procedure actors, as well as actresses, had to endure. Considering the average age for a movie queen's first face-lift is fifty-five, Joan was most certainly an exception. In the hospital her doctor wasn't fooled by the glass of "water" on the night table. "You'll take twice as long to heal," he predicted.

"I don't know what you're talking about," she said casually.

Herman Cohen convinced her to film *Trog,* a monster picture. "Why?" she said to a reporter when asked. "For the money. I'm an actress and it doesn't matter these days what the hell I do as long as the role has guts. Sorry to say,

TV is my only salvation now. TV is quite a contrast to doing movies. Another dimension. I was on 'The Lucy Show' but couldn't get my bearings. Shit, those people are another breed! They go on every week and work like robots. The routine was the same every week. I knew Lucille Ball was going to replace me, but I stayed, and when I walked on the stage the audience gave me a standing ovation. This was like TV, for Christ's sake! From that moment on, I was perfect, no thanks to the leading lady and her Cuban husband!"

In "Night Gallery," Joan played a blind woman whose sight is restored on the night of the 1965 New York City blackout. Twenty-one-year-old Steven Spielberg was asked to direct the pilot script. It was his first assignment. Joan was amused and delighted. They had dinner to get acquainted and to discuss the project. He had seen all her films and knew exactly how he was going to direct her.

"I'll make sure it's perfect," she said, patting his hand, "because it's your first big one. Don't let them scare you, Steven, and if they push, ignore. We'll do it right because we'll do it our way." Joan knew about the jokes circulating around Hollywood: "She'll crush Spielberg with her little finger." Instead, with the help of Barry Sullivan, they produced a classic.

Spielberg learned early in life how to comfort and pamper a talented and temperamental actress. Their only disharmony erupted over his not coddling her on the day of her most dramatic scene. Joan cried and refused to work. Spielberg closed down for twenty-four hours and was on the set when she arrived the following morning. He remained by her side and directed her with tenderness and authority. She followed his career and frequently sent him congratulatory notes on his successes.

In 1971 Joan wrote another book, *My Way of Life,* ". . . for every woman who wants to live beautifully and successfully—how to keep vital and young and how to keep a man and make the most out of the pleasures of life."

Billy Haines liked this book more than her autobiography. "At least you say something, Cranberry. It's done in good taste and down to earth. Very informative, too. Jimmy and I love it. Why didn't you write this book a long time ago?"

"I didn't need the money a long time ago."

He laughed. "Why did I ask? Something puzzles me, though."

"What's that?"

"How many women have swimming pools?"

"I haven't the vaguest idea. Why?"

"Because you suggest floating gardenias and candles in the evening."

"A charming memory I wanted to share."

"Jimmy says the bathtub would be a romantic substitute. Now, Cranberry, don't be angry. I especially like the fact that when you give a party you go to it, too."

"Are you criticizing my book, Billy?"

"No, but the part about not putting a red vegetable next to a yellow one because the colors clash is a bit much."

"Have you ever known me to serve such an unattractive platter?"

"But the mayonnaise on my face and the eggs in my hair have done wonders. Jimmy and I have dinner in the shower."

"My book is going into a second printing, so I must be doing something right."

"And how many women would skip the hairdresser a few times to afford caviar for her husband? If they did, this country would be made up of hags serving fish eggs."

"Billy, I spent many months writing that book, and my fans adore it."

"And you adore the royalties."

"Goddamn right!"

"What bothers me most is that I can't remember gardenias and candles in your swimming pool—only my Cranberry without the top of her bathing suit. You really knew how to tease."

"Knew?" she asked slyly.

"How *is* your love life, dearest?"

"There is no one," she replied with a tinge of sadness in her voice. "I'm bored with one-night stands. Alfred spoiled me terribly. I doubt that any man will take his place, and it doesn't matter. How is Jimmy?"

"Putting Vaseline on his eyebrows and lashes."

She laughed hysterically. "Put that book away, Billy!"

In 1968 Christina had become a regular on a daily soap opera, "The Secret Storm." When she was rushed to the hospital for an emergency abdominal operation, Joan volunteered to take her place temporarily. The publicity was excellent, but could a sixty-four-year-old woman play the role of a girl in her late twenties? Crawford arrived with her entourage, Pepsi coolers, and vodka. She slurred her words and appeared intoxicated. Friends thought it was her doctor's place to suggest she limit her vodka intake, but he said nothing. Joan surely would have fired him after denying that alcohol was dominating her life.

It was just a matter of time, however. What Crawford did to make a fool of herself on TV was her business, but to insult important guests at dinner parties became an embarrassing private matter that could not be overlooked. Her performance at the White House made the newspapers. Lyndon Johnson had asked her to dine with the members of the Supreme Court and their wives. Joan had been drinking steadily to brace herself for the occasion. Her target was Cathy Douglas, the lovely twenty-three-year-old wife of William O. Douglas, who was approaching seventy. Joan criticized Cathy's manners, appearance, and background. Mrs. Douglas tried to direct the conversation elsewhere, but, out of the corner of her eye, saw an arm reach across the table and plant a finger bowl directly on the doily in front of her.

"That's how it's properly done!" Joan exclaimed.

Cathy told reporters the next day, "That was the first time I'd ever been insulted in Washington. Up to now everyone has been so nice."

Joan faced the press calmly. "I've never met Mrs. Douglas. Besides, who the hell am I to criticize anyone? I was a waitress from the time I was nine. When I was first at Metro I was happy when anyone corrected me."

Cesar Romero and Billy Haines were the few male escorts Joan could rely on. There were dozens of producers and directors who were proud to be seen with her at "21" for lunch. Her old friends remained faithful for the most part. Those who turned their backs were quickly forgotten after a good bout with the bottle, a nasty telegram, or a late-night phone call: "You can rot in hell. This is Joan Crawford."

She and Franchot become closer shortly before he died in 1968. He came in his wheelchair for dinner at her apartment, and she joined him at Mustoka Lake in Canada, where they fished and read Shakespeare. Joan heard about his death when she was in Philadelphia to do "The Mike Douglas Show"; she left immediately to help with the painful arrangements and sobbed at the funeral. "Franchot was always there when I needed him," she said, "and I never let him down. He wanted to be cremated and his ashes strewn over Mustoka Lake in Canada. I made sure his last wish came true."

In 1970, she returned to Stephens College to receive the first President's Citation awarded to a former student "in recognition of her achievement in varied roles expected of the women of today and for her distinguished career as film actress, businesswoman, homemaker, mother, and philanthropist." Joan summed up her acceptance speech by emphasizing " . . . the desire to do my best in everything."

She told reporters, "All I do these days is open a Pepsi plant, go to a funeral, or accept an award."

Joan seemed to prefer the company of women or couples during this period of her life—Leo Jaffe, president of Columbia Pictures, and his wife; author Jackie Susann and her husband, Irving Mansfield; Anita Loos; and Dorothy Manners, who had replaced Louella Parsons.

A well-known actress and long-time friend of Joan's who prefers not to be identified thought there was an unusual relationship between Joan and Jackie. "It was a love-hate thing," the actress said. "They were very much alike. Jackie was publicity-mad, too, and I say that with admiration, but unlike Joan she needed pep pills to keep her going. Her only child was autistic, and Jackie had had a mastectomy in 1962; these were secrets she kept from the world. She was a gutsy lady like Joan. They spoke the same language, drank too much, and loved gossip. They were suspected of lesbianism, although Jackie's love affairs with women were fairly well known in the inner circles."

According to Barbara Seaman, who wrote Jackie's biography, *Lovely Me* (William Morrow, 1987), Susann had had a romantic relationship with actress

Carole Landis in 1945. "Carole fell in love with Jackie, sent flowers and exquisite pearl drop earrings. Jackie described to her girlfriends how sensual it had been when she and Carole stroked and kissed each other's breasts. Jackie was infatuated with Ethel Merman in 1959. They attended a party together at Lynn Loesser's and both had a lot to drink. They lay on the couch and made out in front of everyone. A few months later they quarrelled. Ethel didn't want to see her again. Jackie followed her home, banged on the door and yelled, 'Ethel, I love you! I love you!' Ethel called the police and Jackie was admitted to LeRoy Sanitarium with a nervous breakdown."

Seaman said in her book that in 1973 Jackie agreed to autograph books for a benefit (Doris Day's Actors and Others for Animals) on the Warner lot in Burbank and had persuaded her egomaniacal new "friend" Joan Crawford to donate free Pepsi. "Ethel Merman is a lady and philanthropist compared to Joan," Jackie said later. "If I had known Joan when I was writing *Valley of the Dolls*, Helen Lawson would have been a monster."

What prompted the rift between Joan and Jackie caused a bit of gossip, but aside from Susann's caustic remark, no one knows exactly why the "friendship" cooled. Jackie died in 1974.

Whether it was too much vodka or too much power, Joan was coming to a crossroads at Pepsi. She had been hardworking, loyal, dedicated, and had somehow managed to schedule any acting commitments so that they would not conflict with her carrying on Alfred's dream. He once told her, "The whole trick in hiring executives is to find a good man and turn him into a prick. A good man would be able to stand the course, but if a guy is a prick to begin with, he'd crumble along the way."

Such a man was Donald Kendall, president of Pepsi, who referred to Joan as "that goddamn actress." When Steele died, it was assumed that she would move back to Hollywood, but instead she gained more stature, attention, and prestige with Pepsi. On several goodwill tours, she and Kendall clashed openly. Reporters chose to interview and photograph Joan, not Kendall. Flashbulbs popped in her face, not his. And how could he forget the humiliation at the Stork Club when she demanded he ask Ernest Hemingway to join the Pepsi table? Hemingway had growled at Kendall, "Tell her to bring her ass over here if she wants to meet me!"

Joan referred to Donald Kendall as "Fang" behind his back. She took advantage of the spotlight as if he did not exist in the Pepsi organization. Those loyal to Joan in the company warned her to ease up.

"Bullshit!" she snapped. "Everyone knows I represent Pepsi. Joan Crawford will draw the crowds. Screw them!"

But she was needed less and less until Pepsi retired her in 1973. Joan was shocked and dismayed. She couldn't remember being hurt more deeply . . . including her farewell to M-G-M. Pepsi gave her no warning. There were no discussions or negotiations. She would receive an annual pension of $40,000, but the fringe benefits were discontinued—her limousine service, expense account, and private secretary. Business was business, but she blamed it on Kendall. Joan needed to be needed, and she'd thought Pepsi needed her. In her heart, she and Alfred had continued on together after his death. She knew what he wanted and how he would have gone about it. But "Fang" had taken Alfred's "baby" away from her, and there was nothing Joan could do about it. She was alone now. In 1972, she made her last appearance before the camera in "The Sixth Sense," a TV series at Universal. She was paid $2,500 for the hour program. Joan Crawford arrived and departed with her entourage and limousine.

After forty-seven years, it was just as well she didn't know the truth.

On March 8, 1973, she was honored as a "Legendary Lady" at Town Hall in New York. Publicist John Springer had a difficult time convincing her to attend.

"You know how terrified I am of stage appearances," she exclaimed. "Once I just stood there and was led off by Milton Berle, who said I was too excited to talk. Oh, I can't do it, John."

"Would you disappoint your fans, Joan?"

"God, no. But . . . all right. I'll do it. I'll do it for you and them."

After the clips of her films were shown, Springer led Joan to the stage. Wearing a black gown slit to the knee, and diamond earrings, with her red hair in an elegant chignon, Joan froze. There was a moment of silence before the deafening standing ovation filled the theater and Joan came alive. Fifteen hundred people were paying homage to her. Crowds ran to the front of the theater and threw flowers at her feet. She knelt humbly and picked them up. "I never knew there could be so much love," she said with tears in her eyes. Joan was strangely composed, almost hypnotized, and surely in need of some vodka.

The audience submitted written questions and she answered with clarity and bluntness.

What about Gable?

"He had 'em," she said.

Would she raise her children the same way again?

"Yes. I believe most kids are on pot and other junk because they don't have enough love or discipline at home."

What about Norma Shearer?

"She was married to the boss, and I was just an actress."

What about *Baby Jane?*

"Bette Davis was one of the greatest challenges I ever had."

In December 1973, Billy Haines died of cancer. His "wife," Jimmy Shields, killed himself a year later because, "It's no good without Billy." Joan outlived many dear friends who had shared the Golden Era with her, but Haines had been very special. It had been a dreadful year, and now she had to face another move into a smaller apartment in the Imperial House at 150 East 69th Street. It was the only sensible thing to do. She auctioned off crystal, china, and antiques rather than put them in storage. Without Billy's decorating tips, she carried out his tradition of yellow and green chairs and cushions against white walls.

Although Joan wasn't active, she received requests for interviews. "I have two secretaries who help with my correspondence," she said. "As always, each fan letter is answered personally." She never forgot birthdays and anniversaries and sent hundreds of Christmas cards with notes all over the world. After college, Cindy moved to Iowa and Cathy to Pennsylvania. They married and had babies, but Joan said, "I absolutely will not allow anyone to call me grandmother. Aunt Joan is okay . . . Dee Dee, Cho Cho, or anything else, but I hate the word *grandmother*. It puts a woman into her grave."

Christina decided to pursue acting in Los Angeles. Joan had opened some doors but reacted to her daughter's minor successes with resentment. Depending on her vodka intake, she asked herself, "Who the hell helped Lucille LeSueur?" Joan wielded power as Isis still does in Egypt—a legend, a symbol, an immortal goddess with the ability to strike like the cobra or the scorpion. Good scripts were hard to find then and Joan's reputation of having been box-office poison and a has-been and then being resurrected by winning an Oscar only intensified her authority, her name, and her drawing power. Producers and directors wore her gold cuff links proudly; some wore them with jealousy, knowing she gave away so many with her love and gratitude.

Joan was feared more than Bette Davis; their tactics and approaches were entirely different. Observers might have laughed at Joan's use of a limousine to cross the street or at her ultraglamorous appearance at coffee breaks or script meetings, but she represented Hollywood more than Gloria Swanson, Barbara Stanwyck, Loretta Young, or Katharine Hepburn. No other actress before or since had succeeded in establishing and maintaining so definite an impression as a glamorous star. She was the first unknown to be discovered and groomed into a major star. More importantly, the public still clamored for her.

Christina used the Crawford name, but it worked against her because Joan made it clear to her contacts in Los Angeles that she was proud of her daughter but wanted it known she was asking for no favors. Quite the contrary. A very strained, long-distance relationship developed again between Joan and Christina, who remarried and settled in California.

When Christopher returned home from Vietnam, he tried to see his mother. The doorman at the Imperial House said, "Miss Crawford says she's not at home to you, sir."

Joan's favorite restaurant was "21". Her table was on the second floor, facing the stairs, where she could see arrivals and departures and, of course, be seen. If she dined with friends, Joan demanded to be picked up in a limousine. If, for some reason, she was forced to take a taxi or ride in someone's automobile, Joan either refused to go out or pouted all evening. "My God, Joan," a friend said, "one would think you had to take a crosstown bus!"

"What the fuck's the difference?" she snapped. "Drop me off around the corner from the restaurant."

After dinner a shiny limousine would be waiting for Miss Crawford.

In September 1974, John Springer asked Joan to act as hostess at the Rainbow Room for a party honoring her good friend Rosalind Russell, who was suffering from arthritis. Rosalind was bloated from prescribed drugs, and her face reflected the pain, but she was still a glamorous and lovely woman. Joan, in red chiffon and diamonds, arrived early to make sure the tables were set correctly. She greeted guests, signed autographs, and remained the center of attention. At seventy, Crawford was a vision. The press and photographers were well represented. She posed politely and said it was such a joy to have pictures of her and Rosalind after so many years. The next day every paper carried a picture of "the girls." Rosalind's face was swollen from cortisone. It was a shock to people who were not aware of her illness. Joan looked bewildered, haggard, drawn, and matronly. The press deliberately, ungallantly selected the horrid pictures to sell newspapers.

"If that's how I look," Joan said, "I won't be seen anymore."

She accepted very few invitations after that episode and was seen less and less at "21". For the first time Joan began to appreciate her neighbors. Two or three of them became close friends, and she relied on them. "It's nice to know I'm not alone," she said. To avoid sympathy from Hollywood friends who called when they were in New York, Joan made her feelings clear: "I've spent fifty years trying to please M-G-M, my fans, producers, and directors. It's time I pleased myself for a change."

Joan wanted so desperately to be remembered as she was—a glamorous superstar. The party for Rosalind Russell shattered her confidence in herself and in the press.

She took a deeper interest in Christian Science and saw a regular spiritual adviser. In 1975 she gave up drinking "because it is against Christian Science teachings." On the telephone and in letters she was cheerful and optimistic. "Remember only the good times," she stressed. Looking at her precious dog, Princess, she often said, "Never love anything that can't love you back."

In pain and failing health (most likely stomach cancer), she managed to send a few 1976 Christmas cards but only to her dearest friends. Those who had always heard from Joan were concerned about her. "It's time to economize," she told them. "Besides, I have only one secretary now."

Knowing she was dying, Joan told her Christian Science practitioner she preferred to remain at home. "I won't see a doctor, and I will not go to a nursing home or a hospital," she declared. When Joan gave her dog away, friends knew it was just a matter of days. What could they do for her? She was down to eighty-five pounds but managed to answer the door frequently. Her housekeeper came every day, and a loyal fan often spent the night.

One neighbor said, "We wanted to do something, but we decided that Joan Crawford had always done everything her way and dying was no exception."

On May 10, 1977, the end came quickly. Death was attributed to acute coronary occlusion. Joan Crawford was cremated and interred next to Alfred in a cemetery in Ferncliff, New York.

At a memorial service for Joan Crawford in Hollywood, George Cukor said:

> She was the perfect image of the movie star, and, as such, largely the creation of her own, indomitable will. She had, of course, very remarkable material to work with: a quick native intelligence, tremendous animal vitality, a lovely figure, and, above all, her face, that extraordinary sculptured construction of line and planes, finely chiseled like the mask of some classical divinity from fifth-century Greece. It caught the light superbly, so that you could photograph her from any angle, and her face moved beautifully. The nearer the camera, the more tender and yielding she became—her eyes glistening, her lips avid in ecstatic acceptance. The camera saw, I suspect, a side of her that no flesh-and-blood lover ever saw.

Kathleen Nolan, president of the Screen Actors' Guild, told her friends and co-workers: "There will not be the slightest hint of sadness, for Joan Crawford would not have approved of that. She never looked back. Regret was not in her vocabulary."

"Anyone who has no regrets, Wayne, is full of shit! We shouldn't feel sorry for ourselves, that's all. We remember, admit our mistakes, stumble over them, get up, and try again."

"That's my philosophy," I said, "but it isn't easy."

"You're an Aries, right? That's how we are. Davis is an Aries, too. We're the leaders of the zodiac. Astrology is nonsense, but if you're not the lead dog then the view never changes."

"Do you grant many interviews for movie biographies?"

"I usually write a note—brief and to the point."

"Not in-depth?" I asked.

"I'll talk about Douglas and Franchot because the public has a right to know why I fell in love and why I fell out of love." She stirred her vodka with her finger and thought for a moment. "Hollywood is like the old English court. Lots of gossip within the confines but not beyond the gates. We protected each other, and the press did, too. Reporters knew about Hepburn and Tracy but never printed a word. We all needed each other to thrive and survive." Then she came out with a husky laugh. "Who do you think were the *real* ladies' men in Hollywood, Wayne?"

"Errol Flynn and Clark Gable?"

"No. Ray Milland, David Niven, and Walter Pidgeon! They possessed something that was lost on film. Personally, I was attracted to Jack Coogan when I first came to Hollywood. The father, not the kid! I know what Betty Grable saw in him. I wanted Richard Arlen and Henry Fonda, too, God, one of 'em! Eddie Fisher was something. Tony Curtis was downright sexy. I tried, but his bride, Janet Leigh, kept him busy. And, no, I wasn't attracted to Taylor," she smirked, "but I remember George Cukor saying Bob was without question the handsomest actor in Hollywood, but since George is gay, you might omit that from your book. He was stating a fact, that's all. George had class and our films had class. In *Gone With the Wind* you didn't see Rhett humping Scarlett, but you saw that satisfied grin on her face the next morning, and you knew damn well she'd gotten royally laid! Where were we?"

"Taylor."

"Bob was a gentleman. He had beautiful manners. The bigwigs like L. B. Mayer were animals at the dinner table. They should have had troughs."

"Do you think Lana Turner and Robert Taylor had an . . ."

"Sure! And poor Judy [Garland]. The studio fed her uppers, downers, and in-betweeners. I'm very surprised Mickey [Rooney] didn't get hooked. The beginning of the end, or is it the other way around? How do you like your Scotch?"

"Soda, please."

"You're taking it straight today. What else?"

"Taylor and Garbo in *Camille*."

"She was my favorite but retired, and who's left? I don't know how Davis got as far as she did. Take away the cigarette and what do you have? Bulging eyes and staccato speech."

"But she has a following," I said.

"She had a cult!" Joan snapped. "And what the hell is a cult except a gang of rebels without a cause! *I have fans.* There's a big difference. Why do you want to talk about Bette Davis, anyway? What does she have to do with Robert Taylor?"

"Norma Shearer and Loretta Young co-starred with him."

"Forget about Norma. Oh, God, how I tried to forget about Norma! As for Loretta, I don't think she and Bob were lovers. How he got away I'll never know. She got around . . . her love baby, for example. Clark was supposedly the father, but Jack Oakie—a good friend of mine—used to tell Clark it was his kid. They were all snowed-in on location doing *Call of the Wild.*"

"Are you serious?" I asked, washing down the question with straight Scotch.

"Those are the things we laugh about and keep to ourselves. Outsiders wouldn't understand. Your mouth is still open, for example. By now you should be used to these stories. Loretta would be a juicy subject for a biography." Joan poured herself another vodka. She took a deep breath and said, "I'm tired of talking."

"I'll be going."

She leaned back on the yellow and green pillows with a devilish smile on her face. "How about a book about Davis?" she suggested.

"She wrote *The Lonely Life*. It was a good autobiography."

"Why the fuck do you think I suggested her? Write the truth! *The Lonely Life* was a nothing book. Didn't you love that crap about sex is God's joke on humanity? I think the joke's on her. She said sex is a grotesque anachronism. Jesus! She makes Loretta look like the Virgin Mary!"

"I'll be going."

"Am I boring you?"

"You said you were tired."

"Do I look tired?"

"No."

"Books are like movies, Wayne. Always follow up with a better one. Bette went to bed with Howard Hughes, to name one. She said he couldn't 'get it up' with anyone else, but that's because he couldn't decide which he liked better—men or women. This is common in Hollywood, and I would say just about everyone tried it once. Maybe you'd label it bisexual, but I would not. Howard Hughes called me many times. I turned him down many times. I used to tease Clark about Carole [Lombard] and Howard. Clark didn't want to hear about her love life before she met him. He was furious that John Barrymore exposed himself to her at the studio, but he did that to all the girls. Anyway, ask Bette about her affair with William Wyler. He was the love of her life. I swear I don't know what the hell men saw in her. Jesus, maybe I'd better stop talking this way, or I'll have to order a soundproof coffin so I can't hear her dancing on my grave."

We finished our drinks and chatted about her cozy apartment compared with the penthouse and how nothing was the same anymore. "The other day I was about to enter my apartment building," she said, "and some broad on the street said, 'Oh, look. That used to be Joan Crawford.' I looked her in the face and said, 'Yes, I look like Joan Crawford, the movie star. If you want to see the girl next door, go next door!' "

Betty Barker, who had been Joan Crawford's secretary in California for thirty-five years, said, "On the morning of May 10, 1977, Joan made breakfast for the housekeeper and the girl who had spent the night. Joan slipped into bed, called out to the women to make sure they were eating . . . and died."

Christina Crawford offers a different version of Joan's last moments in *Mommie Dearest*. "The morning of May 10, 1977, only one woman was with Mother. When the end finally came the woman's prayers became audible. My mother raised her head for the last time and said, 'Damn it! . . . don't you dare ask God to help me!' "

Douglas Fairbanks, Jr., now seventy-nine years old, married the former wife of Huntington Hartford (the A & P heir), Mary Lee, in 1939. They have three daughters and eight grandchildren and have residences in Palm Beach, New York City, and London.

Franchot Tone, who died in 1968, had two sons by his second wife, Jean Wallace, currently married to actor Cornel Wilde.

Greg Bautzer died of a heart attack in 1987.

Christina Crawford suffered a minor stroke at the age of forty-two. In a 1981 television interview she discussed a blood clot that had developed over many years—"a result of a lifetime"—and indirectly blamed the illness on her mother. Christina takes credit for bringing child abuse to the forefront, but said she wrote *Mommie Dearest* for herself with no intent of having it published. Christina lives in the Los Angeles area with her second husband, David Koontz. She has no children.

Joan Crawford bequeathed $77,500 to Cathy and Cindy, her personal property to Cathy, small tokens to employees and friends. The rest went to charity.

Her estate has been estimated at $2 million.

CHRONOLOGY OF
JOAN CRAWFORD'S FILMS

PRETTY LADIES
(M-G-M, 1925)

Director: Monta Bell. *Cast:* ZaSu Pitts, Tom Moore, Conrad Nagel, Norma Shearer, Lucille LeSueur (Joan Crawford). *74 minutes.*

OLD CLOTHES
(M-G-M, 1925)

Producer: Jack Coogan, Sr. *Director:* Eddie Cline. *Cast:* Jackie Coogan, Joan Crawford, Max Davidson, James Mason. *65 minutes.*

THE ONLY THING
(M-G-M, 1925)

Director: Jack Conway. *Cast:* Eleanor Boardman, Conrad Nagel, Edward Connelly, Joan Crawford. *62 minutes.*

SALLY, IRENE, AND MARY
(M-G-M, 1925)

Director: Edmund Goulding. *Cast:* Constance Bennett, Joan Crawford, Sally O'Neil, Williams Haines, Douglas Gilmore. *58 minutes.*

THE BOOB
(M-G-M, 1926)

Director: William Wellman. *Cast:* Gertrude Olmstead, George K. Arthur, Joan Crawford, Charles Murray. *64 minutes.*

TRAMP, TRAMP, TRAMP
(First National, 1926)

Director: Harry Edwards. *Cast:* Harry Langdon, Joan Crawford, Edwards Davis, Carlton Griffith. *62 minutes.*

PARIS
(M-G-M, 1926)

Director: Edmund Goulding. *Cast:* Charles Ray, Joan Crawford, Douglas Gilmore, Michael Visaroff. *67 minutes.*

THE TAXI DANCER
(M-G-M, 1927)

Director: Harry Millarde. *Cast:* Joan Crawford, Owen Moore, Douglas Gilmore, Marc McDermott. *64 minutes.*

WINNERS OF THE WILDERNESS
(M-G-M, 1927)

Director: W. S. Van Dyke. *Cast:* Tim McCoy, Joan Crawford, Edward Connelly, Frank Currier. *68 minutes.*

THE UNDERSTANDING HEART
(M-G-M, 1927)

Director: Jack Conway. *Cast:* Joan Crawford, Francis X. Bushman, Jr., Rockcliffe Fellowes, Carmel Myers. *67 minutes.*

THE UNKNOWN
(M-G-M, 1927)

Director: Tod Browning. *Cast:* Lon Chaney, Joan Crawford, Norman Kerry, Nick de Ruiz. *65 minutes.*

TWELVE MILES OUT
(M-G-M, 1927)

Director: Jack Conway. *Cast:* John Gilbert, Joan Crawford, Ernest Torrence, Betty Compson, Bert Roach. *85 minutes.*

SPRING FEVER
(M-G-M, 1927)

Director: Edward Sedgwick. *Cast:* Williams Haines, Joan Crawford, George K. Arthur, George Fawcett. *60 minutes.*

WEST POINT
(M-G-M, 1928)

Director: Edward Sedgwick. *Cast:* William Haines, Joan Crawford, William Bakewell, Neil Neely, Ralph Emerson. *80 minutes.*

ROSE-MARIE
(M-G-M, 1928)

Director: Lucien Hubbard. *Cast:* Joan Crawford, James Murray, House Peters, Creighton Hale, Gibson Gowland. *70 minutes.*

ACROSS TO SINGAPORE
(M-G-M, 1928)

Director: William Nigh. *Cast:* Ramon Novarro, Joan Crawford, Ernest Torrence, Frank Currier. *78 minutes.*

THE LAW OF THE RANGE
(M-G-M, 1928)

Director: William Nigh. *Cast:* Tim McCoy, Joan Crawford, Rex Lease, Bodil Rosing, Tenen Holtz. *60 minutes.*

FOUR WALLS
(M-G-M, 1928)

Director: William Nigh. *Cast:* John Gilbert, Joan Crawford, Vera Gordon, Carmel Myers. *60 minutes.*

OUR DANCING DAUGHTERS
(M-G-M, 1928)

Director: Harry Beaumont. *Cast:* Joan Crawford, Johnny Mack Brown, Dorothy Sebastian, Anita Page, Nils Asther, Dorothy Cummings. *86 minutes.*

DREAM OF LOVE
(M-G-M, 1928)

Director: Fred Niblo. *Cast:* Joan Crawford, Nils Asther, Aileen Pringle, Warner Oland, Carmel Myers. *65 minutes.*

THE DUKE STEPS OUT
(M-G-M, 1929)

Director: James Cruze. *Cast:* William Haines, Joan Crawford, Karl Dane, Tenen Holtz, Eddie Nugent. *62 minutes.*

HOLLYWOOD REVUE OF 1929
(M-G-M, 1929)

Producer: Harry Rapf. *Director:* Charles F. Reisner. *Cast:* Conrad Nagel, Bessie Love, Joan Crawford, William Haines, Buster Keaton, Anita Page, Marie Dressler, Marion Davies, Jack Benny, Norma Shearer, John Gilbert, Lionel Barrymore. *82 minutes.*

OUR MODERN MAIDENS
(M-G-M, 1929)

Producer: Hunt Stromberg. *Director:* Jack Conway. *Cast:* Joan Crawford, Rod La Rocque, Douglas Fairbanks, Jr., Anita Page. *70 minutes.*

UNTAMED
(M-G-M, 1929)

Director: Jack Conway. *Cast:* Joan Crawford, Robert Montgomery, Ernest Torrence, Holmes Herbert, Edward Nugent. *65 minutes.*

MONTANA MOON
(M-G-M, 1930)

Director: Malcolm St. Clair. *Cast:* Joan Crawford, Johnny Mack Brown, Dorothy Sebastian, Ricardo Cortez, Karl Dane. *71 minutes.*

OUR BLUSHING BRIDES
(M-G-M, 1930)

Director: Harry Beaumont. *Cast:* Joan Crawford, Robert Montgomery, Anita Page, Dorothy Sebastian, Hedda Hopper. *74 minutes.*

PAID
(M-G-M, 1930)

Director: Sam Wood. *Cast:* Joan Crawford, Robert Armstrong, Marie Prevost, Kent Douglass, Hale Hamilton. *80 minutes.*

DANCE, FOOLS, DANCE
(M-G-M, 1931)

Director: Harry Beaumont. *Cast:* Joan Crawford,, Lester Vail, Cliff Edwards, William Bakewell, William Holden, Clark Gable. *82 minutes.*

LAUGHING SINNERS
(M-G-M, 1931)

Director: Harry Beaumont. *Cast:* Joan Crawford, Neil Hamilton, Clark Gable, Marjorie Rambeau, Guy Kibbee, Cliff Edwards. *71 minutes.*

THIS MODERN AGE
(M-G-M, 1931)

Director: Nicholas Grinde. *Cast:* Joan Crawford, Pauline Frederick, Neil Hamilton, Monroe Owsley, Hobart Bosworth. *68 minutes.*

POSSESSED
(M-G-M, 1931)

Director: Clarence Brown. *Cast:* Joan Crawford, Clark Gable, Wallace Ford, Skeets Gallagher, Frank Conroy. *76 minutes.*

GRAND HOTEL
(M-G-M, 1932)

Director: Edmund Goulding. *Cast:* Greta Garbo, Joan Crawford, Wallace Beery, John Barrymore, Lionel Barrymore, Lewis Stone, Jean Hersholt, Tully Marshall. *115 minutes.*

LETTY LYNTON
(M-G-M, 1932)

Director: Clarence Brown. *Cast:* Joan Crawford, Robert Montgomery, Nils Asther, Lewis Stone, May Robson. *84 minutes.*

RAIN
(United Artists, 1932)

Director: Lewis Milestone. *Cast:* Joan Crawford, Walter Huston, William Gargan, Beulah Bondi, Guy Kibbee. *92 minutes.*

TODAY WE LIVE
(M-G-M, 1933)

Director: Howard Hawks. *Cast:* Joan Crawford, Gary Cooper, Robert Young, Franchot Tone, Roscoe Karns. *115 minutes.*

DANCING LADY
(M-G-M, 1933)

Producer: David O. Selznick. *Director:* Robert Z. Leonard. *Cast:* Joan Crawford, Clark Gable, Franchot Tone, May Robson, Fred Astaire, Robert Benchley. *94 minutes.*

SADIE MCKEE
(M-G-M, 1934)

Producer: Lawrence Weingarten. *Director:* Clarence Brown. *Cast:* Joan Crawford, Gene Raymond, Franchot Tone, Edward Arnold, Esther Ralston, Jean Dixon. *88 minutes.*

CHAINED
(M-G-M, 1934)

Producer: Hunt Stromberg. *Director:* Clarence Brown. *Cast:* Joan Crawford, Clark Gable, Otto Kruger, Stuart Erwin, Una O'Connor. *74 minutes.*

FORSAKING ALL OTHERS
(M-G-M, 1934)

Producer: Bernard H. Hyman. *Director:* W. S. Van Dyke. *Cast:* Joan Crawford, Clark Gable, Robert Montgomery, Charles Butterworth, Billie Burke, Rosalind Russell. *82 minutes.*

NO MORE LADIES
(M-G-M, 1935)

Producer: Irving Thalberg. *Directors:* Edward H. Griffith and George Cukor. *Cast:* Joan Crawford, Robert Montgomery, Charlie Ruggles, Franchot Tone, Edna May Oliver, Gail Patrick, Reginald Denny. *79 minutes.*

I LIVE MY LIFE
(M-G-M, 1935)

Producer: Bernard H. Hyman. *Director:* W. S. Van Dyke. *Cast:* Joan Crawford, Brian Aherne, Frank Morgan, Aline MacMahon, Hedda Hopper, Sterling Holloway. *85 minutes.*

THE GORGEOUS HUSSY
(M-G-M, 1936)

Producer: Joseph L. Mankiewicz. *Director:* Clarence Brown. *Cast:* Joan Crawford, Robert Taylor, Lionel Barrymore, Franchot Tone, Melvyn Douglas, James Stewart, Louis Calhern. *105 minutes.*

LOVE ON THE RUN
(M-G-M, 1936)

Producer: Joseph L. Mankiewicz. *Director:* W. S. Van Dyke. *Cast:* Joan Crawford, Clark Gable, Franchot Tone, Reginald Owen, William Demarest. *81 minutes.*

THE LAST OF MRS. CHEYNEY
(M-G-M, 1937)

Producer: Lawrence Weingarten. *Director:* Richard Boleslawski. *Cast:* Joan Crawford, William Powell, Robert Montgomery, Frank Morgan, Nigel Bruce, Aileen Pringle. *98 minutes.*

THE BRIDE WORE RED
(M-G-M, 1937)

Producer: Joseph L. Mankiewicz. *Director:* Dorothy Arzner. *Cast:* Joan Crawford, Franchot Tone, Robert Young, Billie Burke, Reginald Owen, Lynne Carver. *103 minutes.*

MANNEQUIN
(M-G-M, 1938)

Producer: Joseph L. Mankiewicz. *Director:* Frank Borzage. *Cast:* Joan Crawford, Spencer Tracy, Alan Curtis, Ralph Morgan, Mary Phillips, Oscar O'Shea, Leo Gorcey. *95 minutes.*

THE SHINING HOUR
(M-G-M, 1938)

Producer: Joseph L. Mankiewicz. *Director:* Frank Borzage. *Cast:* Joan Crawford, Margaret Sullavan, Robert Young, Melvyn Douglas, Fay Bainter, Allyn Joslyn, Hattie McDaniel. *76 minutes.*

THE ICE FOLLIES OF 1939
(M-G-M, 1939)

Producer: Harry Rapf. *Director:* Reinhold Schunzel. *Cast:* Joan Crawford, James Stewart, Lew Ayres, Lewis Stone, Bess Ehrhardt, and "The International Ice Follies." *83 minutes.*

THE WOMEN
(M-G-M, 1939)

Producer: Hunt Stromberg. *Director:* George Cukor. *Cast:* Norma Shearer, Joan Crawford, Rosalind Russell, Mary Boland, Paulette Goddard, Phyllis Povah, Joan Fontaine, Lucile Watson, Hedda Hopper. *134 minutes.*

STRANGE CARGO
(M-G-M, 1940)

Producer: Joseph L. Mankiewicz. *Director:* Frank Borzage. *Cast:* Joan Crawford, Clark Gable, Ian Hunter, Peter Lorre, Paul Lukas, Albert Dekker. *113 minutes.*

SUSAN AND GOD
(M-G-M, 1940)

Producer: Hunt Stromberg. *Director:* George Cukor. *Cast:* Joan Crawford, Fredric March, Ruth Hussey, John Carroll, Rita Hayworth, Nigel Bruce, Bruce Cabot. *117 minutes.*

A WOMAN'S FACE
(M-G-M, 1941)

Producer: Victor Saville. *Director:* George Cukor. *Cast:* Joan Crawford, Melvyn Douglas, Conrad Veidt, Osa Massen, Reginald Owen, Marjorie Main, Donald Meek. *105 minutes.*

WHEN LADIES MEET
(M-G-M, 1941)

Producers: Robert Z. Leonard and Orville O. Dull. *Director:* Robert Z. Leonard. *Cast:* Joan Crawford, Robert Taylor, Greer Garson, Herbert Marshall, Spring Byington, Rafael Strom. *105 minutes.*

THEY ALL KISSED THE BRIDE
(Columbia, 1942)

Producer: Edward Kaufman. *Director:* Alexander Hall. *Cast:* Joan Crawford, Melvyn Douglas, Roland Young, Billie Burke, Andrew Tombes, Allen Jenkins. *86 minutes.* *Note:* In this film Joan Crawford replaced Carole Lombard, who was killed in a plane crash after a war bond drive. Joan donated her salary of $125,000 to the Red Cross.

REUNION IN FRANCE
(M-G-M, 1942)

Producer: Joseph L. Mankiewicz. *Director:* Jules Dassin. *Cast:* Joan Crawford, John Wayne, Philip Dorn, Reginald Owen, Albert Basserman, John Carradine, Henry Daniell. *102 minutes.*

ABOVE SUSPICION
(M-G-M, 1943)

Producer: Victor Saville. *Director:* Richard Thorpe. *Cast:* Joan Crawford, Fred Mac-Murray, Conrad Veidt, Basil Rathbone, Reginald Owen, Cecil Cunningham. *91 minutes.*

HOLLYWOOD CANTEEN
(Warner Brothers, 1944)

Producer: Alex Gottlieb. *Director:* Delmar Daves. *Cast:* Joan Leslie, Robert Hutton, Dane Clark, Janis Paige, Jack Benny, Joan Crawford, Bette Davis, John Garfield, Barbara Stanwyck, Jane Wyman, Dennis Morgan, Ida Lupino, Roy Rogers and Trigger, Peter Lorre. *123 minutes.*

MILDRED PIERCE
(Warner Brothers, 1945)

Producer: Jerry Wald. *Director:* Michael Curtiz. *Cast:* Joan Crawford, Jack Carson, Zachary Scott, Eve Arden, Ann Blyth, Bruce Bennett. *111 minutes.*

HUMORESQUE
(Warner Brothers, 1946)

Producer: Jerry Wald. *Director:* Jean Negulesco. *Cast:* Joan Crawford, John Garfield, Oscar Levant, J. Carroll Naish, Joan Chandler, Craig Stevens. *125 minutes.*

POSSESSED
(Warner Brothers, 1947)

Producer: Jerry Wald. *Director:* Curtis Bernhardt. *Cast:* Joan Crawford, Van Heflin, Raymond Massey, Geraldine Brooks, Stanley Ridges, John Ridgely. *108 minutes.*

DAISY KENYON
(20th Century Fox, 1947)

Producer and Director: Otto Preminger. *Cast:* Joan Crawford, Dana Andrews, Henry Fonda, Ruth Warrick, Martha Stewart, Peggy Ann Garner, Connie Marshall. *99 minutes.*

FLAMINGO ROAD
(Warner Brothers, 1949)

Producer: Jerry Wald. *Director:* Michael Curtiz. *Cast:* Joan Crawford, Zachary Scott, David Brian, Sydney Greenstreet, Gladys George, Virginia Huston, Fred Clark. *96 minutes.*

IT'S A GREAT FEELING
(Warner Brothers, 1949)

Producer: Alex Gottlieb. *Director:* David Butler. *Cast:* Dennis Morgan, Doris Day, Jack Carson, Bill Goodwin. *Guest appearances:* Gary Cooper, Joan Crawford, Danny Kaye, Errol Flynn, Ronald Reagan, Jane Wyman, Edward G. Robinson, Eleanor Parker, Patricia Neal. *85 minutes.*

THE DAMNED DON'T CRY
(Warner Brothers, 1950)

Producer: Jerry Wald. *Director:* Vincent Sherman. *Cast:* Joan Crawford, David Brian, Steve Cochran, Kent Smith, Hugh Sanders, Selena Royle. *103 minutes.*

HARRIET CRAIG
(Columbia, 1950)

Producer: William Dozier. *Director:* Vincent Sherman. *Cast:* Joan Crawford, Wendell Corey, Lucile Watson, Allyn Joslyn, William Bishop. *94 minutes.*

GOODBYE, MY FANCY
(Warner Brothers, 1951)

Producer: Henry Blanke. *Director:* Vincent Sherman. *Cast:* Joan Crawford, Robert Young, Frank Lovejoy, Eve Arden, Janice Rule, Lurene Tuttle. *107 minutes.*

THIS WOMAN IS DANGEROUS
(Warner Brothers, 1952)

Producer: Robert Sisk. *Director:* Felix Feist. *Cast:* Joan Crawford, Dennis Morgan, David Brian, Richard Webb, Mari Aldon, Philip Carey. *97 minutes.*

SUDDEN FEAR
(RKO Radio Pictures, 1952)

Producer: Joseph Kaufman. *Director:* David Miller. *Cast:* Joan Crawford, Jack Palance, Gloria Grahame, Bruce Bennett, Virginia Huston. *110 minutes.*

TORCH SONG
(M-G-M, 1953)

Producer: Henry Berman. *Director:* Charles Walters. *Cast:* Joan Crawford, Michael Wilding, Gig Young, Marjorie Rambeau, Henry Morgan, Dorothy Patrick. In Technicolor. *90 minutes.*

JOHNNY GUITAR
(Republic Pictures, 1954)

Producer: Herbert J. Yates. *Director:* Nicholas Ray. *Cast:* Joan Crawford, Sterling Hayden, Mercedes McCambridge, Scott Brady, Ward Bond, Ben Cooper, Ernest Borgnine, John Carradine, Royal Dano. *110 minutes.*

FEMALE ON THE BEACH
(Universal-International, 1955)

Producer: Albert Zugsmith. *Director:* Joseph Pevney. *Cast:* Joan Crawford, Jeff Chandler, Jan Sterling, Cecil Kellaway, Natalie Schafer, Charles Drake. *97 minutes.*

QUEEN BEE
(Columbia, 1955)

Producer: Jerry Wald. *Director:* Ranald MacDougall. *Cast:* Joan Crawford, Barry Sullivan, Betsy Palmer, John Ireland, Lucy Marlow, William Leslie, Fay Wray. *95 minutes.*

AUTUMN LEAVES
(Columbia, 1956)

Producer: William Goetz. *Director:* Robert Aldrich. *Cast:* Joan Crawford, Cliff Robertson, Vera Miles, Lorne Greene, Ruth Donnelly, Sheppard Strudwick. *108 minutes.*

THE STORY OF ESTHER COSTELLO
(Valiant Films for Columbia, 1957)

Producer and Director: David Miller. *Cast:* Joan Crawford, Rossano Brazzi, Heather Sears, Lee Patterson, Ron Randell, Fay Compton, John Loder. *127 minutes.*

THE BEST OF EVERYTHING
(20th Century Fox, 1959)

Producer: Jerry Wald. *Director:* Jean Negulesco. *Cast:* Joan Crawford, Louis Jourdan, Hope Lange, Stephen Boyd, Suzy Parker, Martha Hyer, Diane Baker, Brian Aherne. *121 minutes.*

WHAT EVER HAPPENED TO BABY JANE?
(Warner Brothers, 1962)

Producer: Kenneth Hyman. *Director:* Robert Aldrich. *Cast:* Bette Davis, Joan Crawford, Victor Buono. *132 minutes.*

THE CARETAKERS
(United Artists, 1963)

Producer and Director: Hall Bartlett. *Cast:* Robert Stack, Polly Bergen, Joan Crawford, Janis Paige, Herbert Marshall, Van Williams. *97 minutes.*

STRAIT JACKET
(Columbia, 1964)

Producer and Director: William Castle. *Cast:* Joan Crawford, Diane Baker, Leif Erickson. *93 minutes.*

I SAW WHAT YOU DID
(Universal, 1965)

Producer and Director: William Castle. *Cast:* Joan Crawford, John Ireland, Leif Erickson, Sara Lane. *82 minutes.*

BERSERK
(Columbia, 1968)

Producer: Herman Cohen. *Director:* Jim O'Connolly. *Cast:* Joan Crawford, Ty Hardin, Diana Dors. *96 minutes.*

TROG

(Warner Brothers, 1970)

Producer: Herman Cohen. *Director:* Freddie Francis. *Cast:* Joan Crawford, Michael Gough, Joe Cornelius. *90 minutes.*

JOAN CRAWFORD'S TELEVISION APPEARANCES

Mirror Theater, 1953 (CBS)
GE Theater, 1954 (CBS)
GE Theater, 1958 (CBS)
GE Theater, 1959 (CBS)
Zane Grey Theater, 1959 (CBS)
Zane Grey Theater, 1961 (CBS)
Route 66, 1963 (CBS)
The Man from U.N.C.L.E., 1967 (NBC)
The Lucy Show, 1968 (CBS)
The Secret Storm, 1969 (CBS)
Night Gallery, 1969 (NBC)
The Virginian, 1970 (NBC)
The Sixth Sense, 1972 (ABC)

INDEX